SEASONED BY SALT

A VOYAGE IN SEARCH OF THE CARIBBEAN

JERRY L. MASHAW
AND
ANNE U. MacCLINTOCK

S

SHERIDAN HOUSE

For Lily, who couldn't come. And for Jan   .

This edition first published 2007
in the United States of America by
Sheridan House Inc.
145 Palisade Street
Dobbs Ferry, NY 10522
www.sheridanhouse.com

Library of Congress Cataloging-in-Publication Data

Mashaw, Jerry L.
 Seasoned by Salt / Jerry L. Mashaw and Anne U. MacClintock; Illustrations by
 Anne U. MacClintock
  p. cm.
 Includes bibliographical references
 ISBN 1-57409-246-4 (alk. paper)
 1. Mashaw Jerry L.—Journeys—Caribbean Area. 2. MacClintock, Anne U.—
 Journeys—Caribbean Area. 3. Palaemon (Sailboat). 4. Seafaring life. 5.
 Caribbean Area—Description and travel. I. MacClintock, Anne U. II. Title.

 G540.M29 2003
 910'.9163'65—dc21   2003009671

Printed in the United States of America

ISBN: 1-57409-246-4
 978-1-57409-246-2

ACKNOWLEDGMENTS

No book gets written without a lot of help from your friends, and ours have been more than generous with both encouragement and advice. We are particularly indebted to those who read and critiqued the manuscript at various stages. Lincoln Caplan, Brett Dignam, Jan Marmor, Judi Miglio, Bill Storandt and Jerome Zuchosky bear special mention for the depth, comprehensiveness and candor of their responses.

As usual Jerry is grateful to the Yale Law School for its unstinting support of scholarly projects, however tangentially related to its faculty's principal responsibilities, and to Patricia Page for manuscript preparation. Patti at least found this one fun to read.

AUM
JLM

Branford, Connecticut
July, 2003

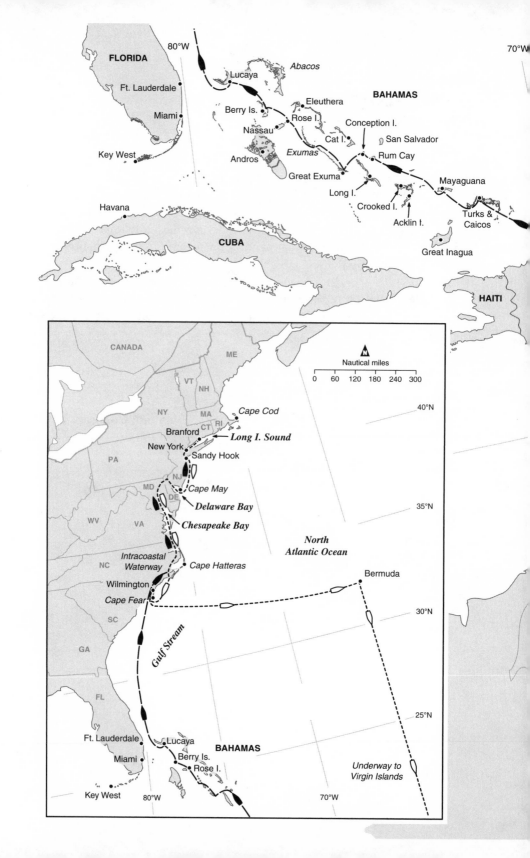

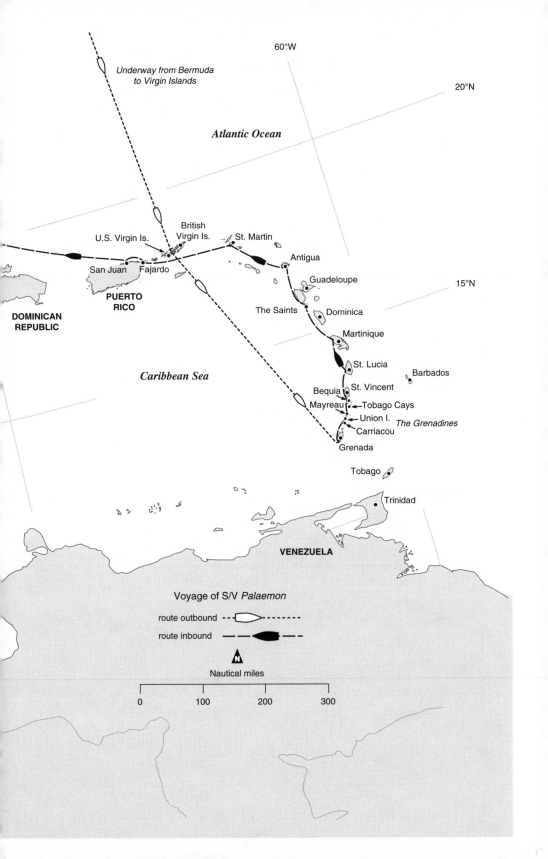

Underway from Bermuda
to Virgin Islands

60°W

20°N

Atlantic Ocean

U.S. Virgin Is.

British
Virgin Is.

St. Martin

Antigua

San Juan   Fajardo

**PUERTO
RICO**

Guadeloupe

15°N

The Saints

Dominica

**DOMINICAN
REPUBLIC**

Martinique

Caribbean Sea

St. Lucia

Barbados

Bequia

St. Vincent

Mayreau

Tobago Cays

Union I.

The Grenadines

Carriacou

Grenada

Tobago

Trinidad

VENEZUELA

Voyage of S/V *Palaemon*

route outbound

route inbound

N

Nautical miles

0   100   200   300

Lissen me some sea talk. Waves speak me true.

Philip Caputo, *Paradise,* 1997

CONTENTS

CHAPTER 1: Strangers 1
ANNE'S PASSAGE NOTES: Day One

CHAPTER 2: Sandy Hook 9
ANNE'S PASSAGE NOTES: Heading Offshore

CHAPTER 3: Offshore 19

CHAPTER 4: Dennis 25
ANNE'S PASSAGE NOTES: Beyond Cape May

CHAPTER 5: Idylling to Annapolis 33

CHAPTER 6: Floyd 42

CHAPTER 7: Leaning Against the Wind 49
ANNE'S PASSAGE NOTES: Home Waters

CHAPTER 8: ICW Blues 58

CHAPTER 9: Changing Plans 65

CHAPTER 10: Mysteries of the Bermuda Triangle 70
ANNE'S PASSAGE NOTES: Night Watches

CHAPTER 11: Have a Good Watch .78
ANNE'S PASSAGE NOTES: Radiospeak

CHAPTER 12: Bermuda: The Gem of the Ocean 89

CHAPTER 13: Bermuda Forever 92

CHAPTER 14: Fleeing St. George's 105
ANNE'S PASSAGE NOTES: Leaving Bermuda

CHAPTER 15: The Road to Foxy's .111

CHAPTER 16: Checking into Paradise 117

CHAPTER 17: Jost Time 123
ANNE'S PASSAGE NOTES: Freedom

CHAPTER 18: Sugar, Slaves, and Snorkels 132
ANNE'S PASSAGE NOTES: Watching Samantha

CHAPTER 19: Gin and the Art of Boat Maintenance 146
ANNE'S PASSAGE NOTES: Raving

CHAPTER 20: In Search of the Caribbean 156

CHAPTER 21: Imagining Grenada 164

CHAPTER 22: Reality with Nutmeg 171
ANNE'S PASSAGE NOTES: Halfway

CHAPTER 23: Charmed by Carriacou 181

CHAPTER 24: Living in the Boat-Boy Economy 191

CHAPTER 25: Bequia Sweet, Sweet 197
ANNE'S PASSAGE NOTES: Island Markets

CHAPTER 26: Skimming over the Surface 212

CHAPTER 27: Transitions 219

CHAPTER 28: Marigot to San Juan 226
ANNE'S PASSAGE NOTES: Harbors and History

CHAPTER 29: Bahamas Bound 236
ANNE'S PASSAGE NOTES: Moondancing

CHAPTER 30: Basking in Thin Water 245
ANNE'S PASSAGE NOTES: Settlements

CHAPTER 31: Closing the Circle 256

BIBLIOGRAPHY 263
INDEX 271

1

STRANGERS

The little Yamaha outboard starts on the first pull. I smile at Anne and silently bless it, stifling the "What a great engine!" that almost escaped my lips. I could hear Anne's agonized, "Will you please stop saying things like that!" It's her sailor's instinct not to change a good omen into a challenge to the gods that control engine cranking. I wish I had stifled the thought. There is absolutely no wood to touch on this dinghy.

We edge away from our dock with the last bits of fresh food and frozen meat. JEREMY BENTHAM, our utilitarian inflatable, bobs over the light chop. Later, when the Atlantic sea breeze breaks through Long Island, the Sound will fill with whitecaps and summer haze. PALAEMON waits at anchor, hardly moving in the light air.

The voyage we are beginning is nearly twenty years in the making, a flickering fire of our imagining, a dream that warmed the New England winters and turned summer cruises into research voyages, quests for skills and knowledge and gear. Would we be happier continuing to dream that dream rather than trying to live it?

A gray-shingled Victorian lies land-bound in our wake, locked, its closets emptied, refrigerator cleared, quietly awaiting the house sitters. We are leaving our comfortable, safe house to move aboard a 38-foot sailboat. PALAEMON's living space is smaller than our master bathroom. And that bathroom absolutely will not sink.

We grin at each other. Behind my grin I already miss the bathroom. Anne's grin is a mystery. We both have lockjaw.

JEREMY bumps gently against PALAEMON's hull. Her flag-blue sides sparkle in the slanting morning light, her rich teak trim glows, her metal gleams. Inside, she is crammed with supplies and spare parts. She's a good boat—nearly two decades old, but well designed, well built, well kept. We have spent hundreds of hours fitting her out, making her seaworthy and safe. She has anchors that will hold her in a blow, electric and manual bilge pumps that can dispatch a flood. Folding steps march up the side of the mast, to be broken out in case of trouble aloft. A life raft crouches on the coach roof, ready to leap overboard and provide refuge in the ghastly event of shipwreck.

For most of the last month I have lain awake in the early morning hours, my mind's eye inspecting every fitting, every mechanical or electrical connection, trying to anticipate what could fail, how to make it fail-safe. I need to trust PALAEMON to carry us safely where we want to go. I want to trust her. My left brain tells me we have prepared well, we can be confident. My right brain, or maybe my stomach, tells me that of all the mechanical and electrical gear we have been putting aboard PALAEMON, I probably only fully understand the mast steps. Ignorance seems a shaky foundation for confidence.

Anne continues her mute swan impersonation as she drags supplies below. We haul the outboard onto its mount on the stern rail. I hear the keen of the ignition alarm and the rumble of PALAEMON's diesel as I go forward to winch in the anchor. The chain comes in foot by foot while I wash off the mud before it disappears below decks. Just as the big plow anchor clears the water, Bruce and Susan Ackerman appear aboard their little daysailer. Susan is snapping pictures, maneuvering close enough for Bruce to toss us a pint of raspberries. I recollect that we have a firm date to take them cruising in the Grenadines in March. How could we possibly have had the hubris to say now, on August 28, 1999, where we would be on a date certain—seven months, one millennium shift, and thousands of miles from here? The sea gods will surely punish us for this.

So now we're all grinning and waving. The anchor is up; PALAEMON is free of the land. Anne revs up the engine. I finish washing down the deck and get ready to hoist sails. Wavelets fracture the sunlight into dizzying crystal shards as we motor past the familiar landmarks in our bay. Its glacier-carved granite ledges run parallel—sometimes defining a shore, popping up here as an island, lying in wait over there as a reef, ready to catch a prop or a hull. I know almost every crevice here, where the striped bass feed and where the tautog hide, where the blue mussels are fat and sweet, and where the quahogs are thick in the shallows. The comfort of local knowledge drains away as we pass between the Umbrellas and Kelsey Island, headed into the open Sound.

We must motorsail for an hour to recharge the batteries and freeze the holding plate that chills the icebox. I perch on the cockpit coaming; Anne is, as usual,

PALAEMON waits.

at the wheel. We share a glance, then a smile. Grins are no longer pasted on our faces. My emotions are less chaotic. The diesel started, the anchor windlass worked, the sails unfurled easily on their roller-furling drums. Little confidence-builders. Anne looks happy. Our house slips away unseen. Neither of us dares look back.

After a few minutes, I go below to check our speed and course over the ground. PALAEMON's interior is as traditional as her navigational gear is modern. The galley and navigation station face each other at the base of the companionway stairs. The stillest spot in the hull, the fulcrum about which the bow and stern rise and fall. Settees that double as sea berths lie just forward, leading to the head on the port side, the hanging lockers to starboard. The main sleeping berth lies farther forward, where the hull pinches toward the bow. A queen-size triangular playpen. Comfortable and secure at anchor, usable only as a storage bin at sea. The bow points first at the peak, then the trough of every wave—its relentless, stomach-churning rising and falling like an amusement-park ride designed by a sadist. Aft of the nav station is a quarter berth so stuffed with gear we call it the garage.

I love the harmony of PALAEMON's form and function. The warm, satin-smooth teak set off by the steel-blue fabric of the settees and berths, the crammed cabinets, the sturdy drop-leaf table between the settees, the photos of kids and grandkids on the forward bulkheads. A photo of our house, too. Lest we forget.

As I wedge myself into the nav station, I can hardly believe my eyes. Our GPS chartplotter seems to be having a nervous breakdown. We are maybe two miles from home, and the first crucial piece of gear is already broken.

Like most sailors, we have become addicted to the GPS. By triangulating on the time differences in signals from earth-orbiting satellite radio transmitters, this magic box can give us our position anywhere on earth within about 50 yards.

Our GPS is also hooked into a computer that displays electronic nautical charts on a monitor. PALAEMON appears on the chart as a blinking green circle creeping past buoys and landmarks. Her true speed over the ground, her precise direction, the distance to our next waypoint (any position on the globe we pick as a destination)—even the time it will take us to get there, given our current direction and speed—all appear brightly on the screen.

Producing all this information the old-fashioned way—taking sun, moon, or star sights and laboriously calculating a position; keeping a continuous log of speed and direction changes; estimating tide and current set and wind drift, allowing for differences between compass headings (magnetic variation) and chart data (true direction)—provided full-time employment for navigators of old. Even then, their position fixes were usually off by hundreds of yards. *My fixes the old-fashioned way are usually off by several miles.*

These little GPS boxes are a godsend to shorthanded sailors like us who need to cook, eat, sleep, keep watch, steer, trim sails, and a hundred other things just to get from here to there. The farthest "there" we plan to see is Trinidad, approximately 4,000 sailing miles (not to be confused with a straight line) south of the Branford, Connecticut, anchorage we have just left. How can our GPS already be lying to us about where we are and which direction we are headed? As with most digital electronic toys, I haven't a clue what has gone wrong when they stop working. Since it started behaving badly for no obvious reason, I guess (and hope) it might fix itself.

The GPS failure is not a good omen, but PALAEMON is sailing well, shouldering aside the chop on Long Island Sound. And we carry some luck with us. PALAEMON is named for the boy on a dolphin in Greek mythology. This Greek demigod is supposed to give aid to sailors in distress. We named our boat for him in the hope that he might follow us around. I am already looking over my shoulder.

I console myself with the recollection that this is sailing. Many wits have tried their hands at epigrammatic description of what a stupid activity sailing is. Perhaps no one did it better than Samuel Johnson, who quipped, "No man will be a sailor who has contrivance enough to get himself into a jail; for being in a ship is being in a jail with the chance of being drowned."

We have many more comforts than sailors of Johnson's day, and we haven't been brought aboard by a press gang. But he has a point. I cannot remember any sail longer than an hour when everything went as planned. Today is no different. It is late when we finally get the anchor down. We've been tacking back and forth into a headwind for hours, determined that our first day out will not be just a "motor." A three-hour sail has taken seven. Anne planned a celebratory dinner for our first night aboard but forgot to leave the steak out to thaw. I stowed a bottle of champagne but forgot to chill it. The foresail needs changing. The forecast is for dramatically heavier winds in the morning.

Taking down the big genoa and folding it on the foredeck is the usual awkward business. The sail covers the whole deck several times over, constantly threatening to spill or blow over the side. It could easily put one of us over. We skate around on the folds of slippery Dacron like incompetent roller bladers who have strayed into a logrolling contest. Finally we get the monster tamed and folded into a package small enough to fit in the sail bag.

We experienced the treachery of foresails the first time we were in the Caribbean, more than twenty years ago. Beached at a friend's house in the British Virgin Islands, we rented a 19-foot daysailer and made our way haltingly around the bay. As we were coming back to the mooring buoy, Anne went forward to gather in the foresail, stepped on it, and went flying over the side. As she swam swiftly and purposefully for a nearby swim platform, I chased her in the boat, dragging the jib in the water and trying not to let her see me laughing. I still believe that if I had been caught laughing, she would never have sailed with me again. Although she claims to be an incompetent swimmer, she looked like she was trying for Olympic gold.

It may have been on that first escape from the New England winter to Caribbean warmth, before we owned our first sailboat, that the dream of this trip began. We sat for hours watching the charter and cruising boats pick their way through the reefs into and out of Gorda Sound. From the heights of Eve and Milton's house, we could read the water perfectly—the deep ocean blue, the turquoise of the channel, the light greens and whites of the shallows, the forbidding browns of coral heads. We wondered whether we would be able to read the depths from the deck of a sailboat. We felt slightly claustrophobic on land, witnessing the freedom of the sailors, and talked of taking up sailing. I had done a little before, mostly on boats small enough to put on top of a car. Always other people's boats. That Rhodes 19 in Gorda Sound was the third sailboat Anne had ever been on.

Our talk was only that. We made no plans. Yet, even on that afternoon's sail we had felt compelled to go outside Gorda Sound for a few hundred yards, to leave the protected bay and feel the lift of the ocean swells. Within a year, we had bought our first sailboat—a beat-up 19-footer that we lovingly restored. We learned to sail by reading books and by trial and error—occasionally by trial and accidental success. We gradually became less dangerous to ourselves and to others.

Because we sail mostly as a duo, we decided early on that we both needed to be competent to handle everything—sails, navigation, engine, piloting, even routine maintenance. One accident or injury and we would find ourselves either singlehanding or needing the other to sail the boat to safety. Our confidence grew—not just in ourselves but in each other. We went from giving our lives to each other to trusting our lives to each other, the sailing partnership adding zest and depth to our emotional bond. Not only do I trust Anne at the wheel, I feel safer with her there. She has an uncanny feel for the effect of current and wind on a sailboat's trajectory; a compass seems hardwired in her brain. I could look forever at her standing there, eyes leveled at the horizon, legs braced, hands on the wheel, the glow of sunlight on her hair.

We stole as much sailing time from our jobs as we could. It was never enough: weekends, a couple of weeks each summer, a week's charter in the Caribbean in the spring. Anne was a regulatory attorney, then a vice president of Southern New England Telecommunications, handling its regulatory affairs and public policy. A challenging position, to put it mildly. She was never more than a phone call away from the crisis *du jour*. I teach law at Yale, a much more flexible job, but one for which the price of admission is a certificate from Workaholics Anonymous stamped, "Failed to complete course."

We promised ourselves that Anne would retire as soon as she was eligible; that I would take a leave; that we would go sailing. So . . . three old boats, thousands of hours of sweat equity, and twenty-two years later, here we are, only a few miles from home but pointed, vaguely, in the direction of Gorda Sound.

Sitting in the cockpit after dinner, I feel we're pointed somewhere else as well. The "boat cards" in the chart table below, the sailor's substitute for a business card, don't say, "Sterling Professor of Law and Management" or "Vice President, Public Policy and Regulatory Affairs." They have only our names, a line drawing of PALAEMON, our cell-phone number, and our e-mail address. We are headed into a world where titles and professions are irrelevant, where our

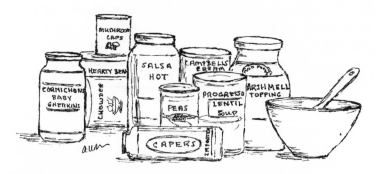

What's for dinner?

schedules are found in tide tables and weather forecasts, where time is told in degrees of arc and sea miles under the keel.

Geographically and historically, this is hardly unknown territory. We have guides and histories covering most of the West Indies islands. The courses we plot, dictated by the ancient patterns of wind and sea, will carry us along routes sailed by countless mariners before us—some for good purposes, some for ill—in the long history that bound together the developing "New World." One of our aspirations for this voyage is to begin to understand this *Continent of Islands*—as Mark Kurlansky calls the Caribbean in the title of his splendid book—a culture, like ours, born of European conquest, bearing the enduring burdens of slavery and racial division, simultaneously familiar and mysterious.

PALAEMON's bookcases are choked with manuals and reference books; the nav station is stuffed with charts for the seas we will sail and the harbors where we will take refuge from the sea. Knowing something about where we are should not be a problem. But the meaning of the names on those boat cards has become *terra incognita*. We must explore that world and map it for ourselves. None of the materials in the chart table or on the bookshelves seem designed for the task.

ANNE'S PASSAGE NOTES: DAY ONE

The trip has begun and I feel numb, nothing like I thought I would feel or like I think I should. PALAEMON does not seem like home. Her gear is poorly stowed, the food lockers are a mess, and I can't bear to think about the ice chest. When I open the first food bin to start making dinner, I see cornichons, salsa, green peas, mushrooms, capers, hot soups, and marshmallow topping. For what dishes can these be the ingredients? Pickle and mushroom casserole, with a green pea and caper salad, salsa and marshmallow toppings on the side? At the last minute, overwhelmed by the vision of so many months ahead, I threw in enough stray items to ruin weeks of careful planning. Now, instead of neat lockers, I have near-chaos.

The chaos echoes in my head. My movements are all wrong. I miss the bottom companionway step and skin my shin. I forget the low threshold between the main cabin and our forward cabin, stub my toe, and hurl myself and an armload of gear into the V-berth. Once, in a similar state of conflict and confusion, I backed out of our garage with the car door open, taking out the centerpost of the garage. Jerry spent a whole day renting construction jacks and getting the sag out of the garage roof. He becomes very anxious when he sees me this way.

Fortunately, he misses my worst antics. He is unusually quiet. I want him to talk, but he's mum. I realize I'm not saying much myself. Our plan is to spend a couple of nights moving westward in Long Island Sound, getting PALAEMON organized and ourselves oriented before heading through New York and down the New Jersey shore. This is a good idea in concept, and a practical one. Unfortunately, it does not take into account our need to get moving so that the undertaking seems real. The stop–go conflict is part of my numbness.

But only a part. I try to peel away at what's bothering me. We've dreamed about this trip for so many years. The dream has become integral to our relationship. Now that we are doing it, what will it mean for us? Our sailing has always been a partnership. But will my sailing skills be sufficient for what we're doing now? My nerve? Will I be able to hold up my end? If I prove inadequate to the task, what then?

I realize how complete my faith is in Jerry. But as I mull over things while trying to find something for us to eat, I realize that he surely has his fears too. For now they will remain unspoken. To be fearful would betray a lack of faith in the dream, a failing that neither of us can bear to inflict on the other. I feel a pang for him. He always assumes so much responsibility; his fears may actually be worse than mine. We may not be able to talk about it now, but I can support him. So when he calls me to help change down to a smaller foresail in the face of a 20-to-25-knot forecast, I do not grumble that I am in the middle of fixing dinner. We make a good job of it, and the hard physical work helps sort out my head. An edge of excitement cuts through my numbness. I stop running into things. A quick hug and I go back to the galley while Jerry stows the sail.

Dinner finally done, deckwork complete, the bunk made, we sit in the cockpit, each cradling a glass of wine. The night is mild. PALAEMON lies quietly at anchor. We feel the coming front in the air. We still say little, but the silence has a different quality. It is open, companionable. There's a touch of dream magic between us.

2

SANDY HOOK

Sandy Hook, New Jersey, points a crooked finger of sand at Coney Island and at the Manhattan skyline a few miles to the north. Facing each other across the entrance to New York Harbor, framed by the Verrazano Narrows, Sandy Hook and New York City might be alternative universes. One pulses with human energy, seemingly oblivious to a natural world rendered largely irrelevant by human ingenuity. The other is wild, tamed only by a road and a few National Park Service outposts, clutching to sands that move with the whim of the wind and the sea.

We are tucked into Horseshoe Cove off Sandy Hook's western shore. The water in the cove is calm, its banks flat, lined with marsh grass and sand. Some riprap shores up the verge near the road, delaying its inevitable slide into the sea. One other boat lies at anchor with us. A small sailboat with one person aboard—not a cruiser, more likely a refugee for a few hours from the pace and bustle of the city. We wave a greeting and leave him in peace.

Execution Rock: Hell Gate bound.

The passage from western Long Island Sound, down the East River and through New York Harbor, has been a mixture of exhilaration and high anxiety. Given PALAEMON's limited speed and power, timing was all-important. Water rushes through the East River as fast as 5 knots at the height of each flood and ebb tide. At Hell Gate, the collision point of the currents surging west from the Atlantic and east from Long Island Sound, great whirlpools form. Were PALAEMON caught in one of these, the river would be our pilot, the steering wheel and rudder useless appendages to a hull whose direction could be any point of the compass.

We left Mamaroneck early, timing our arrival at Hell Gate for dead slack tide. But outside the protected inner harbor, we were lifted on the wings of a 20-knot northeasterly that hurled us toward the Manhattan skyline. The GPS, no longer out on strike, predicted a premature arrival. Reefed down to a tiny foresail, we still surfed along at 8 knots, roaring through the narrow, rock-strewn western end of Long Island Sound, a body of water that generations of racing sailors have called "the dead sea." Perhaps nowhere in the world is the investment in high-tech racing sailboats more out of proportion to average local wind speed than in the body of water stretching from Stamford, Connecticut, to City Island, New York.

To slow our progress, we anchored for lunch just east of the Whitestone Bridge, waiting for the turn of the tide. Our braunschweiger-and-cucumber sandwiches felt like sand in our throats. I had made the trip through Hell Gate once, Anne never. We had no idea how the strong northeasterly wind would affect the East River, or how much control we would have of PALAEMON as she ran down toward the harbor in the quickening ebb tide.

Our worries were for nothing. Hell Gate was placid, a few small whirlpools and eddies, trailers for the show it would put on as the current increased. Then, gripped by the funneling wind and the ebbing tide, we flew south, beating the pace of traffic on the FDR Drive.

Why don't more Connecticut and Long Island investment bankers commute to work by boat, as the Wall Street tycoons of the 1920s did? Perhaps they soon will. The Mashantucket Pequot Tribe is now ferrying New Yorkers to their fabulously successful casino near New London, Connecticut, in 55 mph ferries built by yet another of the tribe's enterprises. Maybe after they finish saving the Connecticut economy, the Pequots will turn their fertile minds to the New York commuting problem. If every Native American tribe were as entrepreneurial as the Pequots, they could soon buy back the country from the

Miss Liberty waves goodbye.

heirs of its "discoverers." In 1650, New London was named "Pequot"; by 2050, it may be again.

Zipping down the East River on a bright fall day, dodging tugs and ferries, we felt blessed beyond belief. It was as if all these familiar sights—the United Nations, Cornell Medical Center, the Chrysler Building, South Street Seaport; the distinctive drone of the city, of New Yorkers ever on the move— were put there to remind us of what we were beginning, what we were leaving behind. The river spit us out past Coast Guard Island. We had a long, clear view of Miss Liberty—beckoning sailors home, waving us good-bye.

The temptation to keep going was strong. Just turn east out the harbor and then south-southwest down the Jersey shore. We could skip Sandy Hook and be in Cape May tomorrow morning.

Tempting, but a bad idea. The northeasterly that was giving us such a great ride had been blowing for two days at 20 to 25 knots. The waves outside would be 6 to 9 feet, maybe larger. PALAEMON was stowed for inshore sailing, not yet for offshore. We still had work to do, and Sandy Hook was a good place to do it. Besides, we wanted calmer weather. A reduction of the wind speed to 12 to 15 knots would mean wave heights of only 4 to 6 feet, perhaps only 3 to 5. This would be our first overnight passage offshore with only the two of us aboard. A comfortable sail in a 4-foot chop has much to recommend it over a roller-coaster ride in breaking 10-footers. The effects of going up or down the wind scale are dramatic. At 35 knots, gale conditions, 15-foot waves are the norm, with a few nearly twice that size thrown in at random. At 10 knots, you're talking 2-footers, a relative millpond. Of course, you don't go very fast, either.

Nautical literature constantly reminds the armchair sailor not to underestimate the difference between coastal cruising and offshore passagemaking.

We have digested thousands of pages of this stuff over the past twenty years. Sailing magazines do not pay authors to describe uneventful daysails punctuated by an occasional jellyfish sting. A popular lecturer at seminars for neophyte cruisers suggests a simple approach to stowing your boat for an offshore passage. Take a picture of the interior of your boat. Turn it upside down. Now ask yourself how to make everything in this picture stay where it is with the boat in that position.

This is not hysterical advice. The open ocean is a very uncertain place. In protected sounds and bays, waves can be nasty and uncomfortable. But their direction is generally predictable. Offshore, the situation is quite different. The Atlantic is a big, irregular bowl. Stir it over here and you get ripple effects over there. Over here may be West Africa and over there may be Cape May, New Jersey. The weather reports that we are so avidly following make clear that lots of weather systems are simultaneously occupying the Atlantic. When we round Sandy Hook into the open ocean, we could find very confused seas. If differing wave patterns are competing out there, PALAEMON may find herself being carried by waves coming from several directions at once.

If a few tons of water running west grab the bow, while a few other tons of water running south grab the stern, the result is a violent twist. PALAEMON will go lurching and rolling hard to one side as one of us wrestles the wheel, trying to get the stern to follow the bow instead of catching up with it. If her stern catches up with her bow, she will trip on her keel. A sailboat trying to move sideways through the water is like a car in a skid. The wheels don't roll to the side. The friction of their grip on the pavement slows the bottom of the car while the momentum of the top tries, sometimes successfully, to roll it over. The automotive skid is a "broach" in boatspeak. If we broach, PALAEMON could end up upside down.

Even near-broaches create awesome rolls. PALAEMON might not be upside down, but in even a 30-degree roll, books do not stay on shelves or coffee cups in their racks without some help. Cupboards spring open like magic boxes; cans jump out like kids coming off a trampoline. A saltshaker becomes a lethal object.

So in Sandy Hook we are working on getting ready for sea. Adding latches and hooks; re-stowing lockers; ensuring that the inflatable vests, sea harnesses, whistles, and strobe lights that usually live in the bottom of the least-accessible lockers are within easy reach. We re-lash the yellow jerry jugs of spare diesel on deck, and rig jacklines from the cockpit to the bow. With our sea-harness tethers attached to these lines we will be able to move the length of the boat without relying only on feet, hands, and knees to stay aboard.

This preparing-for-sea stuff is a little like waiting for your biopsy report to come back from the lab. Our every waking minute is devoted to imagining what could go wrong and what we could do about it—either now or during some unhappy event that is vividly occupying our brains. We work through one worst-case scenario after another. All of these imaginary calamities are things that we desperately do not want to happen, that probably won't happen, but that, to get prepared, we have to think might happen—and in as much detail as possible.

Perhaps the absolutely least pleasant task is packing the abandon-ship bag. We get to think about questions such as how long we should expect to drift in our life raft if we have to go over the side. This helps us to remember that we have never launched a life raft and have no idea whether ours will work as advertised. In storm conditions, could we actually launch it and get into it—much less remember to take our abandon-ship bag with us? While we are at it, we might as well try to think through what we would do if one of us were injured and couldn't make his or her own way off the boat and into the raft. And what if . . . ?

By the end of this exercise, PALAEMON might be ready, but we could easily be basket cases—anchored forever in Sandy Hook, imagining the horrors that await us if we ever venture out of the harbor. This psychological trap catches a fair number of sailors. It explains why they start out for the Caribbean and end up in Deltaville, Virginia. Why they now satisfy the residency requirement to vote in Boston City Council elections, although their original destination was the Azores.

To lighten things up, we go ashore to the visitors' center for the Gateway National Recreation Area. They have some nice exhibits on the history and geography of the peninsula: relics from sunken vessels, photos of the old lifeboat station, models showing how the awesome power of the sea has reshaped the "hook" over the last century. That kind of stuff is really interesting if you're planning to drive back to Hoboken. Since we are about to board PALAEMON and head to sea, it makes our knees rubbery. We walk out to an observation platform to gaze at the Atlantic. It looks rough out there.

We amble back to the bay side and pick our way down the shore. The Sandy Hook shoreline is littered with old gun emplacements, mostly of World War II vintage. It feels odd somehow to walk around in "ruins" that are more than history for us—to remember that in our lifetimes an invasion (or at least an attack) on the East Coast by German U-boats was a real possibility. Our trip would have been unthinkable in 1944. We might instead have been signing on with the armada of small civilian vessels that patrolled the eastern seaboard on the lookout for a periscope knifing through the water.

In fact, Sandy Hook has been a jumping-off spot for boats headed to the West Indies for 300 years. Americans are now connected to the vacation islands of the Caribbean mostly by cruise ships and airlines. But in 1770, those thirteen colonies clinging to the eastern seaboard were probably as heavily dependent on the West Indian trade as America is on all its foreign trade today. If we were leaving Connecticut a few years before the Boston Tea Party, bound for the Caribbean, we would be carrying horses or cows, barrel staves, shingles, lumber, tar, barrel hoops, pigs, chickens, and sheep. Richard Pares spent twenty-five years collecting shipping records on the colonial North American–West Indies trade. He calculates that in 1771, New Haven and New London alone shipped 4,500 horses and 3,000 head of cattle to the British West Indies colonies. Boston, Providence, New York, and Philadelphia added in two million barrel staves and hoops, 20 million board feet of pine and oak lumber, and tens of thousands of barrels of salt and pickled cod.

If we were shrewd Connecticut traders, we would have diversified our portfolio of goods to avoid glutting the market with one commodity and driving down the price. We would load up like the sloop MARY ANNE, which left Providence in 1766 carrying tobacco, candles, tar, staves, hoops, axes, beef, pork, horses, onions, butter, oil, flour, and fifty kegs of oysters. The MARY ANNE was a veritable general store—which, as I look around PALAEMON, could pretty well describe us. Anne has PALAEMON better stocked than most island markets.

Once in the West Indies, we would be looking for an island that not only would take our cargo at a decent price but also would fill us up with molasses and rum for the return trip. Sugar had become king in the British Caribbean by the late seventeenth century. On many islands, it drove out virtually all other crops. This monoculture explains why West Indian planters were desperate for North American products. The North Americans reciprocated with an almost-insatiable demand for molasses and rum. Salem and Boston alone imported 1.7 million gallons of molasses in 1771; little Rhode Island took 500,000 gallons. Some was used for sweetening. Most was distilled into rum. Returning to Connecticut, we might have had to smuggle in our West Indian rum. The Connecticut colonies experimented off and on with prohibition. But economics set harsh tests for Puritan morality. No one in the English colonies had much coin of the realm. If you were in the West Indian trade, as most merchants were, you traded for and with goods, meaning molasses or rum. Connecticut could be soberly poor or rummy rich. In the end, it always chose the latter.

A day and a half of Sandy Hook is enough to stow our cargo and more than enough for our nerves. Anne claims to be a wreck. I am calmer because I have a much less vivid imagination than she has. I habitually agree to do all sorts of things that I don't want to do when the time comes. Anne has pretty much given up trying to teach me some sense about these things. If the date of the lecture, conference, or meeting is six months away, it just doesn't seem real to me. I can't focus on how I am going to feel then because I can't imagine it now.

One of the great things about this cruise is that it has allowed me to say "no" to everything scheduled to occur between September 1999 and July 2000. My pocket calendar has become a source of joy rather than dread. I plan to pull it off the shelf from time to time just to smile at the blank pages. Not that the life of a Yale law professor is something any sane person would complain about. My standard response to, "How do you like Yale?" is "It's the next best thing to being born rich. Maybe better." Yet my current focus on PALAEMON, on Anne, on the physical and emotional demands of sailing, is liberating. As the Robert Redford character says in *The Horse Whisperer*, "I get up every morning and I know what needs to be done." Cowboys and sailors don't need pocket calendars or Palm Pilots.

Right now, however, I do need to check the weather. It's still not cooperating. Hurricane Dennis, which formed east of the Bahamas, has moved west. Dennis is now dawdling, scouting the North Carolina coast, refusing to develop a sense of direction. Today it moved a whole 5 miles to the southwest, the wrong direction for an Atlantic hurricane. What it is going to do next is anybody's guess.

Sandy Hook egrets.

Tomorrow the wind is supposed to be 15 to 25 knots from the east or northeast. Not perfect weather for a sail down the Jersey Shore, but we've got to get out of here before our spines turn to jelly. It's only a twenty-four hour trip, so Dennis could not get near enough to cause us any real problems before we reach Cape May. We'll leave midday to catch the tide and should make landfall early the next morning.

ANNE'S PASSAGE NOTES: HEADING OFFSHORE

I am ecstatic upon our arrival at Sandy Hook. The first leg of our trip is done. A relatively small one, but it seems enormous to me. We are no longer in home waters. We have traded granite ledges and rocky out-croppings for muddy marshland and sand spits, a terrain that signals the Chesapeake ahead. The day has been splendid, the rush past Manhattan breathtaking, leaving the Statue of Liberty and the Verrazano Narrows in our wake the stuff of dreams. Now we are tired, but quiet, watching egrets feeding in the shallows.

Suddenly I come thudding down off my high. We listen to the weather. Not good. I start to make lists. With the forecast the way it is, and the amount of stowing and other preparation to be done, it is clear that we will stay here at least a day. Jerry says a day. I think maybe longer.

The forecast does not improve. As I sort through our prescriptions to include adequate quantities of everything in our abandon-ship bag, I think surely there must be an easier way. I pull out the *Mid-Atlantic Waterway Guide* and search for some safe way to break up the trip into two neat, manageable legs. But in the seas that are forecast, not one of the Jersey Shore inlets makes a bit of sense. The entrances are narrow and surrounded by shifting shoals. In any seas at all, they break danger-ously. Atlantic City is the only possibility before Cape May, but if we get that far, even I would agree that it would be silly to stop.

I don't say much. After all, we're engaged in pretty grim worst-case thinking, and somehow complaining doesn't seem helpful. I'd really like to hang out here another day. I have to admit it to myself. I am very anxious about offshore sailing, and night sailing in particular. No one ever should take the ocean lightly, although experience surely makes you better at it. My vision of the sea at night is full of ghosts, unname-able fears. Is this what we're doing this trip for, I wonder, as I search through bins for things (such as dried fruit, tea, and hot chocolate) that make good offshore fare, *this* being to test our mettle against adverse, potentially dangerous physical conditions, to press ourselves against raw edges of fear?

We have lived moderately conventional lives, observant of holidays, reasonably thoughtful about thank-you notes, supporters of various charities. And we have prepared responsibly. PALAEMON is splendidly equipped. We have gotten our Red Cross first-aid certifications, stocked needed antibiotics and vaccines, taken our shots. At fifty-eight and fifty-six, our various ailments are not of the type to cause sudden problems. We are basically healthy, eat more or less right, and exercise regularly. But what we're doing is not at all conventional except among cruising sailors. In the circles we generally inhabit, it is pretty much unimaginable.

So what *are* we doing? For me, it is a nice bridge to retirement. The trip should shatter any sense of lost influence or stature that I might otherwise have felt. By the time we return, all of that should be irrelevant. I do not imagine it to be about self-discovery, the narrative backbone of countless sailing yarns. I do imagine it to be about honing skills and seeing places—some new and some old—in a slower, richer, more intimate way than before. Above all, though, it's about adventure and freedom, and sharing them with Jerry. At least I *think* that's what it's about.

Strange how little we've talked about this. A cruise of a year or more has always just been the plan, the dream. Strange, too, how few people, family included, have asked why we're taking off like this, or indeed have commented at all. I wonder if they understand something about us that we don't—or, more likely, think we understand something about ourselves that we don't.

There have been exceptions. Bobby Reinwald, who mows our lawn: "What? Are you crazy? Just the two of you?! How big is the boat? Not big enough. Let me make a prediction right now. *No* marriage is *that* good." Jack Goldberg, Connecticut public utility commissioner and telecommunications guru for the agency, does not mince words either: "It's too confining, too dangerous, too long. We call it the trip from hell." Who is "we," I remember thinking as he and I say good-bye. How many people have been secretly shaking their heads and rolling their eyes as we have burbled on about our plans?

But I put away these thoughts for now and concentrate on the next task—finding the safety harnesses and tethers. We plan a three-hour-on, three-hour-off, round-the-clock watch system. A four-hour schedule is better for off-watch sleep, but it is too long for one person to manage the vessel safely if conditions kick up at all. With the short passage ahead and the likelihood that I will be seasick—as I usually am at the beginning of a rough sail—we will not adhere rigidly to this schedule, but the watch system will get its first test.

We do not stay the extra day. Jerry is edgy to get moving and I become edgy, too. By the time we raise anchor, my jaw is set a bit tighter than I like. Jerry says my profile reminds him of Katherine Hepburn's in one of her classic movie confrontations with Spencer Tracy. I fail to see the likeness—my sense of humor may be a bit thin. But I am ready to go.

3

OFFSHORE

The range of human reactions to motion is enormous: excitement, fear, anxiety, joy—and motion sickness. Some people claim never to be bothered by motion sickness, no matter what. Perhaps. Somehow, I don't quite believe them. As a child, I think our older son, Jay, could have gotten seasick in the bathtub. Most of us have tolerances for changes in the vertical and horizontal planes of our bodies that fall somewhere in between these extremes.

My tolerance is pretty high. Anne's is not. Her symptoms will be mild in calm conditions, not at all mild in rougher ones. And seasickness is miserable. Its insults range from mere drowsiness to clammy sweats, nausea, vomiting, and overwhelming weakness and prostration, roughly in that order. In prolonged cases, dehydration is a serious threat.

If you have never been on a boat in the ocean, you may not have much idea how you would react. I once invited a landlubber friend on a tuna fishing expedition. I did have the presence of mind to ask about motion sickness. This was not simple altruism on my part. Spending hours on a boat dodging someone else's vomit is no picnic. After claiming never to have been bothered by motion sickness in cars, airplanes, or small boats, he was violently ill from almost the time we loosed the docklines until they were retied—eight excruciating hours later. Stepping ashore, he said—a trifle churlishly, I thought—"Next time you invite me to go fishing, could I just hand over my share of the charter fee and puke in my own toilet?"

The fact that Anne time after time leaves the dock or harbor *knowing* that she will be sick is a wonder to me—a testament to her grit. She also knows that she will get better as the passage progresses. After twenty-four hours, she will feel a lot better. After thirty-six to forty-eight hours, food can be discussed in non medicinal terms, as something a person might enjoy, not just "take" to maintain strength.

Lord Horatio Nelson, the great British naval commander, apparently reacted the same way. He is reported to have been virtually incapacitated for the first two or three days of every voyage. Why didn't he pick another line of work? I guess Lord Nelson was, and Anne is, made of the same stern stuff. I myself would seek adventure in hiking, cycling, mountaineering, Chinese checkers—anything but sailing.

By the time we are 20 miles from our Sandy Hook anchorage, it is clear that Anne is unlikely to remember the trip from Sandy Hook to Cape May as her favorite segment of our journey. The 6-to-10-foot seas on the stern quarter, rolling and yawing PALAEMON every fifteen seconds, are plenty rough enough to make her feel horrible. "Gracious plenty," as my grandmother used to say. The length of this passage will not provide enough time for recovery. Through sheer willpower, Anne can keep a lookout when necessary. Her only reasonably comfortable position is lying down, either lashed to one of the cockpit seats, with her eyes closed and her head wedged into a corner of the cockpit, or strapped into our sea berth in the main cabin.

The only other time I made this trip, a hired crewman and I were delivering our previous PALAEMON (a 1960s Alden Challenger yawl) from the Chesapeake to Connecticut. We turned on the engine in Norfolk and never had a sail up, except for steadying, the whole trip. Dead-flat calm. Massive trunkback turtles basking in the sun at the surface. Commercial and sportfishing boats everywhere. Tonight I see nothing except the white tops of breaking waves and the loom of Atlantic City.

Donald Trump is, by sheer accident, a great friend of seamen. The Trump Casino is so big, so bright, so overwhelmingly overwhelming that we can see it for 50 miles. It blots out the loom of Manhattan. It creates the impression that we will never, not ever, get past Atlantic City. We cannot get lost off the Jersey Shore—at least not at night—even if we lose every navigational aid on board, including the compass. So with Anne laid up, or down, Otto and I rock and roll down the 10-fathom line off the Jersey shore.

Otto needs some introduction. He is an Autohelm 7000 autopilot—our third, and near indispensable, crewman. I find Otto an engineering marvel. His eyes are a gyrocompass. His brain is a small computer. And his body consists of just one strong arm. I tell Otto's brain what heading I want, the compass tells Otto what PALAEMON's heading is and the arm, attached to the rudderpost and guided by the computer, turns the rudder until the boat's heading and my orders to Otto's brain agree.

In this lumpy sea, the waves are forever trying to push PALAEMON in some direction other than the course we want. So Otto constantly adjusts the rudder angle. Hour after hour, Otto steers us toward Cape May. He eats only electricity; he never complains; he doesn't get tired; he needs no sleep. To be sure, his conversation is pretty limited. On a small sailboat, even that can be a virtue. We're really very fond of Otto.

With Otto steering, I can attend to all the other things that need doing. The wind's strength and direction are far from steady tonight. I keep struggling to find some sail combination that will reduce the rolling and yawing. I would love to give Anne some relief. Me too, for that matter. I am not sick, but I am very uncomfortable and getting bruised all over. I am making a lot of bad decisions about when it is safe to adjust a sail or to lurch down the companionway to check the GPS or the radar. For reasons known only to itself, the GPS continues to tell the truth.

The motion is not only hard on us—it is hard on the rig. Roll right and the jib is full and pulling like a champ. Roll left and it collapses, as its angle to the wind shifts radically. Roll right again: WHAM!—the slack sail fills all at once, creating a thunderclap as it snaps taut against the tension of the stays and sheets, straining to tear the mast out of the boat. Constant attention and adjustment reduce the frequency of these heart-stopping episodes. But it is rough, anxious work.

My anxiety is, at least in part, a function of how modern sailboat rigs are engineered. The mast is not strong enough to bear the forces exerted by the wind and sea without breaking. So it is stayed fore and aft ("stays") and sideways ("shrouds") with steel wire attached to large stainless steel "chainplates" (because, before wire, boatbuilders used chain and rope). Each attachment point is under tremendous strain. If one gives way, the resulting imbalance of forces is likely to snap others, a cascade of failures that will bring down the whole rig. As one of my sailing friends put it, "A sailboat is a collection of relatively fragile parts, many of which are busy trying to destroy each other." I have suddenly realized that it would not be crazy to imagine that one $\frac{5}{16}$-inch-diameter wire supports PALAEMON's mast. That wire, if it fails, will almost certainly do so without warning. Most of the time, I am able to avoid thinking thoughts like this. Not tonight.

There is usually a good bit of shipping to worry about along the Jersey Shore. We are hanging inside the main channel for freighters and tankers. But tugs with tows also run this inside course, and the inlets along New Jersey are home to a substantial fishing fleet that is seldom in port and often casual about running lights.

I am keeping a sharp lookout, visually and by radar. Both are crucial, because neither is foolproof. It is a fair assumption that any ships we encounter will not be keeping a regular watch. Electronic aids increasingly replace crew on commercial vessels. Giant tankers, as big as a small town, may have a crew of eight to fifteen. The radars keep watch, the autopilots steer, and the crew eats, sleeps, and tends to the boat or the nets. Even if a ship's radar alarm sounds, no one may hear it. Because of the radar return off PALAEMON, it probably won't go off. Sailboats are notoriously bad radar targets. Too few sharp angles and too little steel, the stealth bombers of the sea.

My first radio contact with another vessel confirms my worst fears. I am getting a strong radar return about two miles off our stern. I can see no lights, but something large is back there. The distance between us has shrunk by a mile in the past twenty minutes.

"This is the sailing vessel PALAEMON, Whiskey, Charlie, Zulu, 4745, calling the motor vessel at approximately 39° 30' north, 74° 14' west." (WCZ 4745 is our FCC-assigned call sign.)

No reply. I call again on VHF channel 16. Silence. Then, "This is the tug ANN MARIE. Will the vessel calling please come back."

"Roger, Captain. Switch to channel 68 please." (Channel 16 is only for calling or emergency traffic. After making contact, I must choose another working channel.)

"Roger, 68."

"PALAEMON standing by on 68."

"Roger, Captain. Go ahead."

"My position is 39° 28' north, 74° 16' west. I am proceeding at 205° magnetic, approximately 6.5 knots. What's your heading and speed, Captain?"

After a slight hesitation: "Heading 206° magnetic at roughly 14 knots. Where are you again? I don't see you on my screen."

In short, this guy is headed right at our stern, at more than twice our speed, with probably three barges in tow, and he doesn't see us at all. With his turning radius, he could alter course now and still not be sure that his tow wouldn't take us out.

"We're about 2.5 miles dead ahead of you. I will alter course to 220° magnetic, that's 220° magnetic, to allow you to leave us on your starboard side."

"Roger that, Captain."

So we alter course and watch the ANN MARIE. creep by to port, her lights becoming visible about a mile away. I call the tug captain again. He has found us on the radar now—probably only because he knows we're here and has fiddled with his controls until something showed up.

Thank God for radar.

But sometimes even that doesn't help. An hour later, I am tracking another tug and tow that pose no threat to us when the VHF springs to life. "Tug and tow at 39° 18' north, 74° 26' west, this is U.S. Warship Alpha November 405. Please respond, over."

"Yes, this is the tug CHARLIE CHAN. Where are you, Captain?"

I'm as puzzled as the tugboat skipper. I see nothing on my screen but him—two closely spaced blips, a tug and tow.

"We're right behind you, Captain. Would you please alter course 5° to the west to allow us clear passage?"

That question is framed like a request, but I think it's a command. If an invisible warship wants you to move over, you move over. The tugboat captain agrees. Meanwhile, the warship remains invisible—no lights, no radar return. A sub running at conning-tower depth? A ship equipped with some gizmo that blocks out radar returns? Some electronic anomaly? We're not even in the Bermuda Triangle yet.

It's no wonder sailors are superstitious. I seem to be spending about half my time not knowing what's going to happen next and the other half not understanding what's happening now. After this voyage, when people encounter me wearing funny-looking jewelry, rubbing talismanic stones, and hugging the sides of corridors to knock on wooden doorjambs, I hope they will be tolerant.

Around 1 A.M., we begin to get a little better ride and Anne starts to improve. She insists that she can take a watch, that I should try to sleep. I don't want to leave her alone in the cockpit feeling weak, in the dark, in seas that are still steep and uncomfortable. "Go sleep," she says. "I promise I will call you if I need to." She's right. I should rest.

But in the bunk, I lie awake, listening to all the sounds I have never heard PALAEMON make before. Some inner demon compels me to try to identify each one, to decide whether it means trouble.

I should know by now that troubleshooting by sound from inside PALAE-MON is a losing cause. Sounds travel through fiberglass and wood in mysterious ways. It's like trying to find that leak in your roof by looking above the drip that's coming down through the breakfast-room light fixture. When you finally find the problem, it will be a faulty caulking job in the third-floor tub enclosure on the other side of the house. There are more mystery noises than I have theories. I even hear a weak radio station, the announcer's voice just low enough that I can't make out what he's saying. Some guy near the nav station is shouting muted, unprintable expletives.

There's too much adrenaline running through my body. I manage to stay below for an hour before rejoining Anne in the cockpit. Out here, the roar of wind and wave drives out all other sound. I ask her if she heard the radio station and the mad curser while she was below. Thank God, she did. After days at sea, solo sailors often have phantom visitors. But this is our first night out. If we both hear these noises, there must be some physical explanation. I'm not becoming delusional after only twelve hours.

By daybreak, we are closing on Cape May. The seas are still large, making most Jersey inlets impassable. Cape May, however, has two large rock jetties pushing seaward from the shore. Once we are in the lee of the north jetty, the sea should subside quickly from crashing surf to almost dead calm. At least that's the cheerful interpretation I put on the *Reed's Nautical Almanac's* assurance that Cape May has an "all-weather" inlet.

A large porpoise rises on our bow just as we enter the jetties' outstretched arms. We can't resist ascribing significance to our chance encounter with this charming, intelligent creature. After all, PALAEMON's mythological namesake is always pictured riding dolphins. I know he is just grabbing a fish. And I read a piece recently by some killjoy marine biologist who claims that porpoises save people by accident while trying to pummel them to death so they can eat them. But our porpoise hangs around, playing in our bow wake. He seems to be saying, "Welcome, well done, come on inside." We do.

Anne has recovered further on our approach to Cape May in the foggy dawn. As she steers us to our anchorage in the calm but breezy waters of Cape May Harbor, she improves by the minute. By the time the anchor is set, she is starting a monster bacon-and-French toast breakfast. It tastes at least as good as my MaMaw's fried chicken, or my Aunt Boonie's egg custard—standards by which I have judged all food for more than fifty years. Then I do something new, at least for me. I go to sleep sitting at the saloon table, a half-filled coffee cup clutched in my hand.

Cape May porpoises.

DENNIS

When I awake two hours later, Anne has extracted the coffee cup from my fingers and put PALAEMON's house back in order. Not a small thing. Even those few hours of hard sailing produced surprising disarray below: discarded foul-weather gear, boots, harnesses, and life vests littered the main cabin; salt water was tracked everywhere. A mound of books, cans, spare engine filters, and settee cushions—salvaged from the cabin sole as they jumped off shelves and out of cabinets—decorated the forward V-berth. Our efforts at Sandy Hook to create weatherproof offshore storage were not 100 percent successful.

The weather forecast is blasting from the VHF and confirms what we can see by looking outside. The wind is increasing as Hurricane Dennis continues to hang off the coastline, dumping billions of gallons of water in the Carolina low country. Dennis still has no clear path, but NOAA (the National Oceanic and Atmospheric Administration, the federal agency that includes the National Weather Service) predicts that the East Coast as far north as Cape May will have winds increasing to gale force overnight.

Two things are clear: First, we cannot leave Cape May Harbor until Dennis makes its intentions known. Second, we need a different anchorage. We are in the only area in the harbor free of shoals, but there's a lee shore with a ¾-mile fetch to the northeast across the inlet. At 20 knots, it is a bit lumpy. If it blows 35 knots or more from the northeast, we will be uncomfortable, perhaps unsafe.

But first things first. We have time to shower, launch JEREMY BENTHAM, explore the harbor, and treat ourselves to a shoreside lunch. As we ease along downwind in JEREMY BENTHAM, we spy an ancient wooden ship tied to the dock. She looks like one of the pre-steamship thoroughbreds that were the pride of the coastal and West Indies maritime trade before the age of steam. Perhaps a Baltimore Clipper. These graceful ships combined the dreary work of hauling freight with the excitement of yacht racing. Faster boats not only evaded pirates, privateers, and blockades, they made more trips per season and more money. The first to arrive at market got the best prices in an age when no one could be sure just how much additional lumber, rice, flour, cotton, indigo, rum, or molasses would come over the horizon. Commercial fisheries operate pretty much the same way today. First boat to market sets the price. Lobstermen don't get up at 3 A.M. just for the hell of it.

On closer inspection, we see that this once-proud ship is a derelict. Her keelson (the huge timber running the length of the keel) is clearly broken. The once-graceful sheer of the deck rail sags amidships and then trails off down toward the water at the stern. She is aground, sunk, irreparable.

But this deplorable state of affairs seems to be lost on the schooner's current passengers. Her deck is covered with tables; waiters scurry from table to table bearing trays of lobster, clams, and oysters; a dinghy dock is fixed alongside. The crowd suggests that the conversion from coastal thoroughbred to grounded swayback has been a success. We decide to join them for lunch. We harbor deep suspicions of restaurants that seek to attract diners by means other than the quality of the food. But, given our appetites at this point, we are prepared to eat hardtack left over from a nineteenth-century rum run.

As we survey the harbor from our almost-floating perch, it becomes increasingly obvious that Cape May is not a sailboat Mecca. The water is shoal outside the channels, and the marinas lining the shore cater to the offshore sportfishing trade. Their slips are arranged to accommodate twin-engine motor yachts that can turn on a dime and overpower contrary wind and current while easing into tight quarters. Every slip we can see has one of these behemoths in it. Unless we somehow find and make our way into an empty slip, our only better alternative is a lake two miles to the northeast. The *Waterway Guide* says that it provides an anchorage for boats drawing less than 6 feet. PALAEMON draws only 4 feet 6 inches with the centerboard up (10 feet with it all the way down). She is a shoal-draft cruiser just made for these sorts of waters.

But these waters are not as described. Not the first or last time I've wanted to send some choice words to a cruising guide editor. There may be 6 feet of water somewhere in this lake outside the marked channel, but we can't figure out how to get there. Every time we edge toward what appears to be the described anchorage, the reading on the depthsounder plummets to 5 feet or less as Anne fights to back down before the momentum of 10-plus tons of boat takes us hard aground.

The lake is not for us. But, via VHF, the South Jersey Marina assures us that they have one sailboat slip left and they will put our name on it. We are to look for a guy in a green shirt on the fuel dock; he will direct us in.

The entrance to the South Jersey Marina leads back past the schooner restaurant into a channel about 150 feet wide. The guy in the green shirt motions to us to proceed past the dock toward a slip we cannot see. This is not too promising. The wind is directly behind us and the current in the channel is following us at nearly 3 knots. A sailboat has no directional control without water flowing past its rudder. We need to be going at least 4 knots just to maintain steerage. And putting a sailboat into a slip at 4 knots is something typically done by hot dogs to impress their girlfriends just before their insurance gets canceled.

I consider bailing out, telling Anne to slap it into reverse and pull into the fuel dock to find out what the plan is. It is my call. At the wheel, Anne can hear little above the engine's noise and the wind. I am standing on deck to take directions and relay them to her.

But, trusting Mr. Green Shirt's local knowledge, I wave Anne forward, looking for the promised slip. It is not there. Or, rather, it is there, but a boat is already in it.

Just about then, the marina's public-address system broadcasts an anguished cry: "No. No. No. Not *P* Dock, the *Pier* Dock." Mr. Green Shirt looks stunned. He turns to me and shouts, "Turn around!" Meanwhile, a sailor watching our progress from the fuel dock we're surging past says laconically, "There's a bridge down there you can't get under."

"How far?" I shout.

"About 300 yards," he replies.

Sure enough, around the outstretched bowsprit of one of the million-dollar fishing boats that line the narrowing channel, I can see it. We will be there in about ninety seconds.

I shout to Anne to back down, but she can't hear me above the engine and wind. "Where are we going?" she yells.

There are some choice answers to that question, but I don't utter any of them as I scramble back to the cockpit and explain our situation as calmly as possible. My nonchalance is probably indistinguishable from hysteria. I suggest hugging the port side. A slightly wider spot is visible about 50 yards ahead. When we get there, the idea is to back down hard and try to swing the bow to starboard, through the wind, allowing us to turn back upstream.

It almost works. But PALAEMON, like most sailboats, is higher in the bow than the stern. The greater surface area of the bow acts like a sail. With no other propulsion, she wants to head downwind. In a strong breeze, we need significant momentum to get her nose through the wind and onto a new course.

Our momentum is not enough. Anne slams it into forward and we head across the channel, now about 75 feet wide (for the mathematically challenged, that's two PALAEMON lengths), straight at the line of docked motor yachts. Meanwhile, the current and wind are sweeping us down on the bridge. I am getting a closer look at the bridge than I want. I'll say we can't get under it! The clearance is about 30 inches; our mast is 58 feet tall.

Anne hits reverse again with everything our little diesel can deliver. Forty-four horsepower turning a 20-inch propeller to drive, and stop, more than 20,000 pounds of boat. We back slowly off the motor yachts and the stern kicks somewhat downstream, the bow up. This will be our last chance. If the bow won't go around this time, we will be on top of the bridge. I will try to get an anchor down and set, but I don't think much of my chances.

I shout irrelevantly, "Full speed ahead!" Anne knows what she is doing. She almost always drives the boat while I handle sails and navigation. She knows what PALAEMON will do under power much better than I do. And she does not panic in a crisis. Before or afterwards, maybe, but not during.

Out of the corner of my eye, I can see another green-shirted guy running down the dock lined with motor yachts—our apparent destination if something doesn't change soon. He is not shouting or waving. He is trying to figure out which boat we're going to hit, climb out on it, and fend us off. I am thinking the same thing as I head for PALAEMON's bow. If it is close, if we almost make it around parallel to the docks, I might be strong enough to hold the bow off whichever of the motor yachts she decides to ram. The current should then push the stern around and we can edge back out into the channel, headed upstream.

We almost make it. I have my foot on the bowsprit of a big Hatteras motor yacht when Anne slams into reverse and Mr. Green Shirt #2 hits our bowsprit with his hands at a dead run. The bow veers off and he follows his momentum over the rail onto PALAEMON. "Hi," he says, grinning. "Welcome to South Jersey Marina."

The small matter of a near-death experience aside, we do feel welcome. The place is like a hotel. Indeed, there are even guest rooms above the marina office that are available if you have invited more weekend guests than can comfortably sleep aboard. Or you can use them yourself, if you just want to get off your boat and be taken care of until you stop shaking. The heads and showers are great, with a washer and dryer across the hallway. Every morning, a cute little green bag appears in the cockpit with fruit and a copy of *The New York Times*. The ship's store is well stocked. Almost best of all, the TV in the marina office only has one option—the Weather Channel.

We are beginning to realize that one of the nice ironies of cruising south to avoid the winter is that we have embarked on a life controlled more by the current state of the weather than any we have ever lived. Whether we will be trapped in port or free on the wind, whether we will be miserably cold and wet, hunkered under the dodger in layers of foulweather gear, or basking on the foredeck in our swimsuits—it's all a function of weather changes that the shore-bound will hardly notice.

But those on shore are noticing the weather now. The Weather Channel hurricane team is in its element. The hurricane experts confer and counsel. Producers and directors treat us to archived video footage from earlier storms. Dennis's possible tracks are plotted and re-plotted, based on the latest computer projections. That poor soul who always gets to go to the scene to be filmed with his hair flying and water running down his neck is dutifully showing us the waves coming in at the Carolina beaches, the boarded-up cottages, and the old newspapers blowing briskly across empty parking lots. As the days wear on, his smile is less and less convincing, and we are more and more anxious to get moving again.

While we wait, we explore Cape May, once an elegant seaside address for wealthy Americans. Their Victorian gingerbread mansions are now hotels and guesthouses—occasional outposts of architectural interest. The contemporary Cape May landscape generally reflects the democratization of leisure that here, as elsewhere, features bland motel chains, fast-food restaurants, and video arcades.

Still, the beach is spectacular. Cape May and Cape Henlopen are vast sand spits defining the mouth of the Delaware Bay. The sand tipping each cape runs on for miles, and the water dividing them is wild and treacherous—mined with thousands of shallows, tricky rips, and strong currents. The Cape Henlopen side is protected seashore, accessible only by boat or four-wheel-drive vehicle. Home to seabirds and surf fishermen, Cape Henlopen is as different from Cape May's video arcades as Sandy Hook is from Manhattan.

Unfortunately, we need to go back out in the Atlantic and make our way between the capes to reach the Delaware Bay—the bleak, boring 60 miles of muddy water and featureless shoreline that will take us to the Chesapeake and Delaware Canal and then to the Chesapeake Bay. If our mast height were 3 feet shorter, we could go directly to the Delaware Bay from Cape May Harbor, but a bridge blocks that path. Dennis controls the other. His outer bands of wind are heaping the Atlantic into great walls and flinging them at the East Coast. At the shallow entrance to the Delaware Bay the waves are forecast to be 9 to 12 feet and breaking.

So we wait. We chat with the few other cruisers holed up with us. Some lose their crews as delay eats away at vacation time. One solo sailor leaves for New York. At least he is headed away from the storm, but we don't envy him the trip. Indeed, we worry about him. It is our first experience with the instant camaraderie of cruisers. A few minutes' conversation is all it takes to draw us into each other's plans; to create a community of concern when anyone has a problem; to make reckless invitations to visit and promises to keep in touch; to spill out personal history known only to our closest friends and relatives ashore.

Dennis takes a week to exhaust itself and quit playing around with our schedule. But we are trying hard not to think about it in those terms. For the first time, we are sailing without having to keep a schedule. We have plans to meet family and friends along the way, but those dates are weeks, even many months, away. We are not now in our customary sailing-vacation mode, struggling to clear away the chores before leaving home, or fighting headwinds to get back to work. PALAEMON is home. We are where we are with no immediate need to be somewhere else. Managing the boat and living on her is what we do, who we are—cruisers living in a few cubic feet of space, with no fixed address. The two people named on the boat cards we distribute liberally around Cape May Harbor are beginning to take on some reality.

But old habits die hard. We resent Dennis's interference with our plans. We have told our friends back home that we are off to follow the wind, that we will not fight the sea, but take what it gives us. Can two semicompulsive achievers ever really live like that?

"Go with the flow" hardly describes the way we have lived our lives. We are now cruising, but can we become cruisers, those devil-may-care, salt-encrusted, sun-baked, ponytailed adventurers that Jimmy Buffett and *Cruising World* magazine promised us would be our fate, if we would just cast off the lines and go?

ANNE'S PASSAGE NOTES: BEYOND CAPE MAY

In Dennis's leftover slop, we make a lumpy, four-hour sail to Breakwater Harbor, behind Cape Henlopen. This short move is intended to give us an easier run up the Delaware Bay than leaving from Cape May. The quiet night at anchor turns into a dim day, with the mist stirred by only the faintest breeze.

As we motor out of the harbor and work our way into the channel northward, we are embraced by unremitting gray. It is hard to know whether the bay is pretty or not. We can see nothing of its shores. We see virtually no ships or other vessels of any sort. We try to sail. Jerry optimistically puts up the spinnaker, and for a short while it flies. We make about 5 knots through the water, but the GPS tells us we're making only a little more than 2 over the ground. Our *Reed's Almanac* had told us that the current would be against us, but not at anything like this force.

Biting flies arrive one by one, then in platoons, battalions. Bug spray and our flyswatter are insufficient armaments to keep them at bay. Slapping at our legs and flailing our arms, we crawl north through the featureless waters.

At this rate, we will not make it before dark to our planned anchorage at the mouth of the Chesapeake and Delaware Canal. Jerry tells me to stop looking like a prune. But I feel like a prune. The spinnaker starts to collapse. Finally he gives up, and the spinnaker come down. We crank up the diesel, but we keep the main unfurled just in case of a puff. We rev up the rpms. Jerry stubbornly insists that we can make it as we pass by the only anchoring opportunity in the whole middle bay. I am not sorry to miss it. It is reported to have up to 5 knots of reversing current running through it. Hardly an ideal spot for a good night's rest.

But now we are committed. We carry on, swatting and swearing. The diesel, pressed hard, drones heavily in our ears. The occasional breath of air from astern is just sufficient to keep us wreathed in diesel fumes, insufficient to keep the main from flopping about pathetically. Our conversation is scintillating:

"Damn it. I just killed twenty of them. You kill some."

"I would if you ever did any of the sailhandling."

"What do you want done? I'll do it, but let's leave the main."

"Why? It's not doing anything. Just forget it, I'll take down the sail and swat flies. I don't know why you insist on steering."

"I *like* to steer. Besides, I can swat flies and steer."

"Do you think anybody lives on this godawful piece of water?"

"Well, put on Otto. I'll get lunch if you'll kill flies."

"Put on Otto yourself. Nobody lives here. Couldn't possibly."

"I got five more. *Where* are they coming from? What do you want for lunch?"

"Just get lunch, and stop talking about it. I don't care what I eat."

"Did anybody ever tell you how rewarding you are?"

"How can there be this many flies in the world?"

Suddenly we get the tide change, then a huge boost. In the space of two hours, we go from 3 knots of current against us to 2 with us. Our spirits and our conversation improve. A gray dusk sees us at our goal, Reedy Point, at the canal's mouth. We put down the hook, alone in the anchorage. The trip has taken more than ten-and-a-half hours. Happily, flies start to abandon us for land. The holding is not good, but at least it's sufficient for the night's demands. We look out at more gray and, not surprisingly, a very reedy shore. Royal terns cry raucously all about us. But there's no time to watch their antics. Hordes of mosquitoes drive us below. Jerry does not like motoring, he does not like flies, and he does not like mosquitoes. His state of mind is unprintable, and mine is not much better. We get out screens and swat mosquitoes.

I start dinner. I think I detect the beginning of the beginning of a smile on Jerry's face. We decide a toast is in order. Tomorrow we will enter Maryland, our fifth state, and the upper Chesapeake. The forecast calls for clearing skies, and the tide is perfect to carry us through the canal easily.

We pull out *Reed's* again, puzzling over the Delaware Bay and its currents. We have a nice dinner and are comfortable, PALAEMON as homey as though we had lived aboard her forever. Jerry lights our kerosene lamp, its soft light glowing against the satin interior. I ponder, as I often do, how the small but rich pleasures of cruising can make up for so much that is anything but pleasant. I come up short again. But at this moment, I would not trade places with a soul. We both look up from our books. The sound is unmistakable. We have missed at least one mosquito.

5

IDYLLING TO ANNAPOLIS

After the dreary passage up the Delaware Bay and through the Chesapeake and Delaware Canal, we are not quite prepared for the beauty of the upper Chesapeake. Rolling hills, dotted with well-kept farms, sweep down to the gentle shores of one small river or inlet after another. Each beckons with protected and secluded anchorages. Except on Friday and Saturday nights, when the weekend warriors from Philadelphia, Washington, and Baltimore escape to their boats and take to the bay, there is seldom another boat visible from whatever cove we choose as safe haven. Turning in to the southern end of the bay in 1608, Captain John Smith described what we are seeing in the north: "Heaven and earth never agreed better to frame a place for man's habitation."

Despite its well-publicized pollution problems, the Chesapeake's waters teem with fish and crabs. The striped bass (rockfish, they call them here) are schooling in almost every cove, driving the baitfish into tight circles and picking off their prey as they try to escape. I hear bass jumping outside the hull at first light almost every morning. I desperately try to go back to sleep. The opening of Maryland's fall striper season is still days away.

Much of the farmland on the fertile, well-drained western shore seems to have been given over to "gentleman farming." The well-manicured fields, the fences and buildings sparkling white in the slanting September sun, are too pristine to be believable as working farms. But who knows? Maybe it is just the look of the prosperity that Eastern Shore watermen have envied and complained about for centuries. On the east side of the bay the land is low, marshy, unsuitable for the tobacco farming that made Virginia's planters their early fortunes. But the marshy shallows are the greatest fish and crab nursery in the Western Hemisphere.

Callinectes.

We navigate the channel. Fifteen thousand years after melting Pleistocene glaciers formed the bay, the deep water still follows the drowned bed of the Susquehanna. The air is pungent with the promise of fecundity from both sea and soil.

Crabbing remains a viable occupation on the upper bay. Indeed, our greatest navigational challenge at the moment is avoiding the crab-pot floats that sprout by the thousands from every direction. The traditional plumb-bowed crab boats that work the pots are cousins to New England lobsterboats. They are somewhat narrower of beam, with smaller cabins, and sometimes with canoe sterns rounding off the flat runs of the aft sections. The lower freeboard of the Chesapeake crab boat makes hauling the pots easier and reflects the sensible expectation that the waters of the Chesapeake generally will not be as rough as a lobsterman's territory in Penobscot Bay. These handsome workboats have supported generations of baymen willing to live the hard but independent life of a crabber.

Anne's brother Buz tried crabbing for a season while living in the Mac-Clintocks' old summer cottage on a creek just off the Rappahannock River. It was great for his physical conditioning, but it was brutal, low-paying work. As a beginner, Buz crabbed in a small skiff, hauling his pots by hand, working the shallower spots where hydraulic winches weren't needed to raise a pot. But this shortened his season. The Jimmy crabs, the adult males, go deeper and deeper into the channel as the weather gets cooler; the impregnated females head south to the saltier waters at the mouth of the bay to lay their eggs in the spring. Neither returns to the shallows of the mid-bay until the late spring, long after crabbers with mechanized pot-pullers have been hauling in the deeper cuts. The undercapitalized short-season crabber hauls when the crabs are thick and the price is low. Buz now programs computers rather than fishing crabs.

Like almost every fin or shell fishery, crabbing is imperiled by pollution and the threat of overfishing. Anne and I have just finished reading Mark Kurlansky's remarkable little book *Cod*. There is no better description anywhere of the relentless pressure of technological advance on a fishery. Improved methods yield bigger catches, driving down prices, requiring yet bigger catches to sustain the fishermen's revenue. The upward spiral of technology ultimately decimated a resource that was so plentiful its exhaustion had been unimaginable. Populations on both sides of the Atlantic had relied on salt cod as a major source of protein for hundreds of years.

Until confronted with the facts, I thought Kurlansky's subtitle, *A Biogra-*

phy of the Fish that Changed the World, was something of a stretch. But much of Europe is Catholic, and nearly half the days on a Catholic's calendar used to be meatless—fifty-two Fridays, forty days of Lent, and a host of other saints' days. Fish is not meat and salt cod is fish. These simple facts, plus the difficulty of keeping uncured or fresh fish, meant that 60 percent of all fish eaten in Europe from 1550 to 1750 was salt cod. Salt cod was so popular that fresh cod was originally sold as "fresh salt cod."

Meanwhile, on seventeenth- and eighteenth-century sugar plantations in the West Indies, almost all the protein in a slave's diet was salt cod. It even had its own name—"West India Cure" or "Jamaica Cure"—a product of sufficiently low quality that it would be rejected in the European market. For centuries, a cod fishery stretching from the Georges Bank to Iceland fueled the major institutions of the Old and the New World, Catholicism, and plantation slavery. Try to buy a cod in your local fish market today.

Threatened or not, the crabs are crawling thick in the shallow waters of the Eastern Shore, where we are puttering about. Crabbers here run trotlines—crab pots are not allowed outside the main bay. Before dawn every morning, the trotliner puts out nearly 2 miles of line with "pickled" eel tied to it about every 3 feet. He anchors his lines at each end with scrap iron marked with milk-jug floats. A crabber runs his lines maybe twenty times before lunch, adjusting boat speed and direction with his knee as the trotline runs over a spool off the side. As the spool lifts each bait to the surface, the crabber stalks his prey with a wooden pole, a wire mesh scoop attached to one end.

We are mesmerized by the rhythm of the crabber's movements, his fierce concentration. He must net the crab just before the bait clears the water, for as the crab senses the light, it begins to let go. The crabber arcs his pole to dump the crab in the stern, then swings it forward again to scoop the next surprised *Callinectes sapidus* from the water. On and on down the line, never hurrying, never missing—the practiced skill of a veteran athlete. By late morning, the crabber takes in his lines. In the light of midday, the crabs let go of the eel long before the bait reaches the surface.

It is early fall, and, as they say on the bay, the crabs are crawling. If you just want a few, they are not hard to catch. One morning a small plastic runabout busies itself near PALAEMON, its skipper putting out a dozen or so baited and buoyed traps. They look like the open, collapsible baskets sold in cooking shops for storing onions or potatoes in the pantry. When all the pots are out, the man returns to the beginning of his line of floats and starts to haul. About every third basket contains a crab. The process is repeated again and again. The pace is apparently sufficient to give the crabs time to find the bait, but not enough time to eat it and crawl off the basket to go on about their crabby business. This crabber is almost certainly an amateur, one of the thousands who have bought summer houses on the Eastern Shore where waterfront property values are still reasonable. "Chicken neckers," the local watermen call them, referring to the vacation-home crabbers' usual bait. It's "damn chicken neckers" when they foul the true waterman's trotline.

The Eastern Shore watermen we observe seem to be middle-aged or older. We wonder whether their way of life is slowly dying out. They have clustered on their hummocks of high ground for centuries—insular, independent, seldom prosperous. Most Eastern Shore colonials were loyalists during the Revolution, sending out boats to prey on western shore settlements and "rebel" shipping. "Picaroons," they were called, a West Indian word for pirate.

Our first few days drifting in the shallows of the upper bay generate a languorous sense of well-being. The water is warm. The famous Chesapeake "stinging nettles" have not arrived. We have sunned and swum, crabbed and fished. We've idled about in small towns just enough to give us the (surely false) sense that we have a feel for the local culture. We've moved short distances just for a change of scene, not because we were actually going anywhere. We have eaten crabs steamed, boiled, sautéed, fried, and baked. For Anne, the Chesapeake blue crab is the taste of summer, of freedom. She seems content down to her toes.

But friends in Annapolis, who still have workday schedules, beckon. I am secretly happy to have the excuse to move on. I am becoming restless. Our destination is the Caribbean, not the Chesapeake Bay. I try to stow my need to make southward progress with the tethers and safety harnesses, but the door to that locker keeps popping open.

So, on the wings of yet another nor'easter, we fly down the bay to "The Sailing Capital of the World." Other ports hotly contest that title, but for sheer sailboat congestion, Annapolis may have no equal. Marinas and docks crowd every square inch of shoreline. Mooring fields obscure the harbor's channels to anyone but locals. Coming in, we count six different one-design races proceeding simultaneously in the harbor's mouth. And this is a Friday afternoon. What will Saturday and Sunday be like?

Miraculously, we are able to anchor only a hundred yards off the marina where Gina and Lee Reno dock PROMISE—a Bristol 38.8, like PALAEMON. Gina and Lee were friends even before we bought nearly identical boats within the same year. Those purchases forged a bond that one has only with people whose taste and judgment are demonstrably impeccable.

If South Jersey Marina is like a hotel, Mears Marina in Annapolis is like a country club. It has tennis courts complete with professional instruction and organized tournaments. Each weekend morning, the marina provides a bountiful breakfast of fruits, breads, coffee, and tea on the covered deck. Sailing is clearly optional.

While we are assured that the boats at Mears do leave the dock, we see little evidence of that on our weekend in Annapolis. These floating weekend cottages are complete with air-conditioning and cable TV. Apparently unoccupied boats are often full to the gunwales below with owners and their guests, refrigerating themselves while tuned in to the excitement of the women's rounds of the U.S. Open tennis tournament. The steering wheels missing from a number of cockpits are not evidence of an epidemic of steering-wheel theft. Removing the wheel accommodates several more guests at cocktail time.

This attachment to dockside living hardly distinguishes Mears from marinas all over the United States. Most pleasure boats, most of the time, are tied up at the dock. Even if Thorsten Veblen hadn't coined the phrase "conspicuous consumption" more than a century ago, one walk through almost any marina would cause it to surface unbidden in your brain. There is plenty of activity on the water as well. Annapolis is home to hundreds of hardy and accomplished sailors. It is, after all, the site of the U.S. Naval Academy. Annapolis's sons and daughters take home tons of silver in sailboat races all over the world. As we discovered, you need to be pretty competent just to get in and out of the place without hitting anything or going aground.

Anne and I both hate coming into congested harbors and into docks. In our early days of sailing, we felt tense leaving land. Now we grow anxious approaching it. We wonder whether we would feel the same way 500 miles offshore with open water in every direction, utterly alone, unable to run for cover from an approaching storm. Our doubts about that have guided our choice of passages south. But as PALAEMON has become more familiar, more trusted, we are beginning to reconsider our alternatives.

Our plan was always to drift down through the Chesapeake, visiting friends and family and exploring some of the hundreds of remote anchorages that line its shores. Deciding on that part of our route was relatively easy. But, while getting PALAEMON cruise-ready, we agonized for months about what to do then. Should we go offshore, out to sea for two weeks, possibly longer? Or motor down the Intracoastal Waterway (ICW), an interconnected system of rivers, bays, and canals that hovers just inshore from Florida to Norfolk, Virginia, and feeds into protected waters all the way to Boston?

For many, the answer is easy enough. Powerboats smaller than oceangoing tugs will take the waterway. Even in expert hands, a power cruiser, with its shallow keel and high center of gravity, behaves very badly—dangerously badly—in the 30-knot winds and 12-to-15-foot seas routinely encountered in the fall off the U.S. East Coast. In 35 knots of wind and 15-foot seas, a sailboat is pretty uncomfortable—an experience we had endured only once. A typical 30- to 50-foot recreational powerboat is in something approaching survival conditions.

Most sailboats bound for Florida or the Bahamas will stay "inside" as well. Fifty to 100 miles off the southeast coast of the United States, the Gulf Stream is headed north at speeds of up to 3 knots. PALAEMON's speed, on average, is about 5.5 knots. Traveling north with the stream yields a giddy 8.5 knots over the ground—south, against it, a teeth-grinding 2.5.

We could stay out of the Gulf Stream's contrary current by hugging the shore while going outside. But because we do not enjoy being cold and wet any more than most, we would probably put into port every few days anyway, as another weather system swept off the East Coast and into our path. And then we might stay in port two, three, seven, who knows how many days, waiting for weather or looking for a window of decent air to set out again. Meanwhile, we could have been chugging down the protected waters of "the Ditch," as the ICW is not-so-fondly called, making miles to the south.

Indeed, weather aside, when headed for Florida or the western Bahamas, using the Intracoastal Waterway from Norfolk to Beaufort, North Carolina, saves miles. And since that little stretch gives both Cape Hatteras and Cape Lookout a miss, the weather can hardly ever be put aside. Localized storms form off those capes, churning their shallow seas into steep, treacherous waves when the Weather Channel guys are moping because they can find no awful weather to report anywhere in the United States. From Beaufort, we could take the ICW, or harbor-hop down the coast, to Fort Lauderdale. One overnight passage and we would be in the Bahamas. From there, we could stay in protected waters most of the way to the Virgin Islands. The longest passage would be from the Turks and Caicos down to the Dominican Republic—about three days.

There is one small problem with this route. From Florida to the Virgin Islands, we would be almost always headed east or southeast. The trade winds below 25°N latitude blow from the east. Sometimes east northeast, sometimes east southeast, but basically on the nose. Upwind sailing is slow, rough, and wet. It can be great fun on Long Island Sound on a warm Sunday afternoon, but bashing into oncoming waves for 1,100 miles is a different enterprise altogether.

This inconsiderate feature of the world's standard wind patterns long ago gave the trip south to the Caribbean through the Bahamas its common name, "The Thorny Path." It also explains why so many cruisers end up spending the entire winter in the Bahamas. They stop to pick out some thorns and adopt the Bahamas tourist board's view: "It's better in the Bahamas." (I have always wondered what they really had in mind by "it." I think I know, but I bet they would deny it.) These thorns also explain why richer yachtsmen (lots richer) have their boats delivered to the islands by paid crew.

The timeless patterns of wind and current also explain the historic trade patterns that connected the Caribbean, North America, Europe, and Africa in the early days of American colonization. The Gulf Stream and easterlies carried ships laden with rum and molasses up the eastern seaboard to New England. Westerlies off the northern East Coast then sped colonial agricultural goods across to Europe. Loaded with English manufactures, the trader might head directly back to the West Indies. Or he might go south to West Africa for a cargo of slaves, then pick up the easterly trades to the Caribbean. The so-called triangular trade was sometimes rectangular.

We agonized interminably about what to do. The inside-Bahamas route sounded slow. It also sounded like a hell of a lot of motoring. We're sailors. We hate running the engine. Besides, from years of poring over cruising books and articles we knew that scores of cruisers with our itinerary would be leaving from Norfolk or Beaufort to sail straight to the Virgin Islands. If they could do it, we could do it.

Of course, we had never actually done it. Our combined offshore experience was eleven days. So we paid a preliminary fee to join the West Marine 1500 Rally that leaves Norfolk at the end of October, headed to the British Virgins. The rally provides three days of seminars on offshore sailing for neophytes like us, daily weather reports for the fleet on its way south, and the reassurance of sailing in company (at least in radio contact) with a group of fellow sailors. Some of them actually have significant offshore experience.

Then, one Saturday morning in early spring, we bumped into Bob and Joan Handschumacher in our local West Marine store in Connecticut. Bob and Joan have sailed WILDWOOD thousands of ocean miles—across the

Atlantic, up the Amazon, throughout the Med and the Caribbean. We told them our plans. Bob said, "That's a hard trip." We felt our feet turn to ice.

Bob urged us to keep to the Ditch until Fort Lauderdale and make our way in short hops through the Bahamas. The three-day trip to the Dominican Republic from the Turks and Caicos would be enough open-water sailing for sailors of our vast experience.

I resisted Bob's advice. Cold feet or not, what about that 1,100-mile slog to windward? What about the thorny path and all that? Bob strode to the book department and returned with Bruce Van Sant's *The Gentleman's Guide to Passages South*. The title is a play on an old sailor's joke about patrician yachtsmen. When asked how well his yacht sailed to windward ("to weather"), one such yachtsman supposedly replied, "Gentlemen do not sail to weather." Van Sant explains how to go more than 1,000 miles to windward without sailing to windward at all. Well, not much, anyway. Van Sant's guide is complete with routes, anchorages, and tons of unsolicited advice on how to run your boat and some of the rest of your life.

Using the Van Sant system, we would move only in two ways. For passages of less than twenty-four hours (say, 50 to 60 miles), we would get going about 4 A.M. (is that a "gentlemanly" hour?), when the winds are usually calm. Then we would put the hook down by 2 P.M., before the stronger afternoon trades kick in. For longer passages, we would have to wait for weather systems that would briefly (one to four days) shift the winds south, then southwest, west, northwest, and north, before returning to the easterly trade-wind flow. This is the familiar pattern of a "norther" on the East Coast. These systems also affect the Bahamas, Hispaniola, even Puerto Rico and the Virgin Islands, when strong enough.

Van Sant is not only clear that this system works, he is clear that if we chose some other scheme—heading offshore, for example—we would not only be ungentlemanly, we would be lunkheads. While we were battling ocean waves and trying to keep our lunch down, Van Sant and all who followed his advice would be snorkeling the Exumas and contemplating whether to put tonic or ginger beer in their rum at sundowner time. Like how-to authors of every genre, Van Sant is exasperatingly certain about the uncertain. His prose eschews not only the passive voice and the subjunctive tense, he prefers the imperative to the declarative. But Bob assured us that he is mostly right.

So we abandoned the rally and signed on with Van Sant. But I am not absolutely sure we have made the right choice. I don't really trust people who tell me they have easy ways to do hard things. And I remember what Bob said when leaving our house two weeks later, after drawing diagrams of all of his and Joan's favorite anchorages in the southern Bahamas and in the Turks and Caicos. "When you get back from that passage, I am going to think of you as different sailors than you are now." What, *exactly*, did he mean by that?

I stow Bob's remark in the mental locker marked, "Vaguely Anxiety-Producing Unanswered Questions," and we take the shoreside opportunity to soak up a little Annapolis history. Up the hill from the restored waterfront sits the Maryland statehouse, with its impressive wooden dome. Remarkable in recent decades for the number of elected officials who have left its halls to take up residence in one or another penal facility, the Maryland statehouse has a proud history. It is the oldest still in use in the United States, it served briefly as the seat of the national government, and George Washington came here to resign his command of the Continental Army. (There are so many George-Washington-did-this-or-that historical markers in Maryland that you half-expect his sneezes to be memorialized.)

Epitomizing Maryland's border-state tradition, a statue of one of Maryland's best and brightest graces the statehouse lawn. Roger B. Taney left here to become Chief Justice of the United States Supreme Court. From that high national office, he authored the infamous *Dred Scott* decision, denying citizenship to all ex-slaves under that court's benighted interpretation of the U.S. Constitution. *Dred Scott* is on most historians' short lists of proximate causes of the Civil War.

Meanwhile, back at Mears Marina, Venus and Serena Williams are providing all the excitement for the sometime-sailors glued to the television coverage of the U.S. Open. Two black women from the projects have taken over one country-club sport; Tiger Woods owns the other. I wonder what Roger Taney would make of that.

6

FLOYD

We abandon Annapolis city life for the Eastern Shore, headed vaguely toward St. Michaels, but with hundreds of remote anchorages available nearby. Backing down to set our anchor in one of these idyllic coves, we retrieve a crabber's lost trotline with our propeller.

Watching crabbers at their work is entertaining. Winding a hundred yards of synthetic trotline around PALAEMON's prop shaft is not. Coiling unseen on the spinning shaft, the culprit reveals itself only when it binds so tight the engine stops. Heated by friction, the line melts. Cooled by the water, it re-forms as a solid nylon collar.

The collar we have accidentally fabricated for PALAEMON's shaft is a beauty. I hack at it with knives, screwdrivers, chisels, a keyhole saw—everything in my toolbox that's remotely plausible. I get much of it off, but the water is silty and the visibility poor. When I get my face close enough to the problem to see what I am doing, my snorkel is too short to reach the surface. After thirty or forty dives, I am exhausted, and uncertain how much melted nylon is left to bind and heat the prop shaft. I decide to call Boat U.S. to tow us into St. Michaels, where a diver agrees to inspect the shaft and clear away the remains of the melted line.

I am scuba-certified for open-water diving, but space limitations argued against carrying bulky diving gear and tanks. Maybe the argument should have gone the other way. There is never, ever, enough room on a sailboat anyway.

The embarrassment of being towed into harbor is almost unbearable. I can imagine the conversations on the shore: "Pays to change the oil sometimes, don't it?" "Yeah, helps to watch the depthsounder, too." "Wonder why they didn't just sail in. It *is* a 'sailboat,' ain't it?" "Maybe them's just for show." Yuk, yuk, hah, hah. Where did all these people come from? Why aren't they out picking up their old trotlines?

Embarrassing arrival aside, St. Michaels is a joy. The tiny waterfront is jammed with working crab boats. Its splendid maritime museum is devoted to the crabbing industry and the boats that have worked the bay. St. Michaels also makes a somewhat indirect attempt to atone for Annapolis's celebration of Roger Taney. Its principal historical marker commemorates the birthplace of Rosa Parks. Of course, Mrs. Parks insisted on riding in the front of that bus in Montgomery, Alabama, not St. Michaels, Maryland, but it's a nice gesture anyway.

Oddly, there's nothing that seems to celebrate St. Michaels's pivotal role in the development of the distinctive fast schooners that were the forerunners of the Baltimore Clippers. Operating between 1812 and 1815 as privateers and blockade-runners, these speedy craft tormented the British navy, captured British merchantmen, and complicated the British blockade of American ports. Privateers sailed under letters of marque, authorizing the seizure of enemy vessels and "contraband of war." Without private supplementation of our feeble navy, America's "second revolution" against Great Britain might have turned out differently. Even with them it was a near thing. When the enemy burns your capital, it's a pretty good sign that the war is not going well.

Thomas Kemp of St. Michaels built some of the most successful of the Chesapeake Bay privateers, although by then he had set up shop at Fells Point near Baltimore. His famous ship CHASSEUR, sailed by Thomas Boyle of Baltimore, was perhaps the most audacious and successful American vessel of the period. Immediately upon taking delivery of CHASSEUR from Kemp, Boyle sailed to the English Channel. He sent men ashore to tack a notice to the door of Lloyd's coffeehouse—the meeting place of the insurance underwriters who would later be known as Lloyd's of London—declaring that England was under blockade. It may have sounded like pure bravado, but within five and a half months, CHASSEUR had seized forty-five British ships. Marine insurance for British merchantmen became almost prohibitively expensive. Boyle had tacked his declaration to the right door. And, in Boyle's hands, the bay-built fast schooner was obviously the right boat.

The privateer's pride.

St. Michaels seems to have forgotten Kemp, and we try to forget our sheepish arrival under tow. One compensation was that the tow introduced us to a fellow cruiser, Adam, who runs a towboat for Boat U.S. in the summer and escapes south to the islands for the winter. We anchor just forward of his cavernous CSY 44, BEAUJOLAIS, one of the early boats built for the Caribbean charter trade. It's a great live-aboard vessel, compromising looks and speed for room and heft. I chat with Adam while he tests the pressure in his refrigeration lines. As I watch, I realize that I have never seen that sort of testing gear outside a full-service marina. This is a level of preparedness and self-sufficiency I haven't even imagined.

Adam guesses that there may be six marinas in the whole Caribbean that can actually fix a refrigeration system—out of perhaps sixty that will say they can. I silently pray to meet up with more Adams if we need help along the way. Because our vision of Caribbean sailing is tightly connected to the taste of cold beer and ice in our drinks, I also swear to do every last bit of preventive maintenance that our refrigerator's owner's manual demands.

We also spend some time gabbing with Bob Fox, whose wooden ketch is hauled up on the museum's marine railway. Bob is eighty-six, only twenty years older than his boat. She seems to be falling apart faster than Bob is putting her back together, but he confidently predicts that he will be finished by his ninetieth birthday. He claims not to care much whether he finishes or not. Says she is keeping him alive. Bob has been everywhere on 'most every kind of sailboat. But he confesses that he now understands that he really prefers to work on boats—to design them and dream about them—rather than to sail them. When he talks of his sailing years, his eyes are distant, opaque; when he looks at his current project, they shine with love and energy.

We walk away to the ring of Bob's mallet driving cotton caulking into the seams of his hull. It's no mystery why the museum lets him work on his boat there. He is a living, breathing record of boating. If he talks to everyone who wanders by for as long as he has held us in thrall, he is going to be working on that boat when he is 100. The museum should put up a sign like those on the other exhibits: "Bob Fox, rebuilding his classic ketch."

I am beginning to wonder whether I might be like Bob. Anne and I love to look at boats, shop for them, prepare them for use. Most of the time while we're doing these things, we imagine ourselves sailing fast and smooth, headed toward palm-lined anchorages that would grace the pages of any sailing magazine. Perfection hardly describes the scenes that flit happily through our heads. But perfection is not a sailor's lot, certainly not ours. Maybe what I really want is to live in perpetual anticipation of sailing without ever really going.

What a traitorous thought. But the tow has left me feeling incompetent. Adam's skills make me feel unprepared. I am accustomed to being a guy who really knows his field, the subtle dynamics of academic politics, the folkways of governmental institutions—a *consigliere* dispensing wise counsel to students and colleagues. As a voyager, I'm a neophyte. I realize that I am so accustomed to giving advice that I hardly know how to ask for it. Am I really cut out for this?

On the other hand, my eagerness to get moving is increasing. We still have several weeks before the last of our planned family visits on the Chesapeake. We would be foolish to venture south of Norfolk, or perhaps Beaufort, before the hurricane season ends. Until then, we will make only a few miles toward the Caribbean. I want to go now, to make miles toward the ultimate goal. This restlessness is stupid, but escaping my habitual goal orientation is clearly not the work of an afternoon.

We are considering moving around to Oxford, Maryland, when the morning NOAA forecast provides an outlet for my pent-up energies. Hurricane Floyd is moving our way, pounding the Bahamas en route. Floyd's projected track could bring it ashore anywhere between the South Carolina border and the Delaware Bay. That includes us.

What to do? The storm might fizzle, but that seems unlikely. Floyd is big and strong. Winds of 155 mph near the center; tropical-storm-force winds 220 miles out. Floyd's swells are already damaging beaches from Florida to New Jersey.

A hurricane combines awesome power with caprice. Floyd could still turn out to sea and never reach land. Or land right on top of us. Its true track will be predictable about twelve hours before it reaches any particular position. By then, if that position is where we are, we will be a day, perhaps two days, too late to do much to protect ourselves.

We really have little choice. We have to make preparations as if Floyd will come very close. Indeed, it is so big that "close" could be 100 miles away. We debate two sharply different courses of action. Plan A is to choose a good, protected creek with plenty of swinging room, a good mud bottom, and nothing else in it. We would put out three large anchors 120 degrees apart, lay on chafing gear to protect the lines, strip the boat of everything above decks that could come loose, and ride out the storm below. The chart reveals several promising "hurricane holes" within a few miles of St. Michaels.

Plan B is to get to a sturdy, well-protected marina. As per Plan A, we would have to strip PALAEMON and make her fast to the dock with multiple lines, protected by antichafe gear. But then we could close her up and go to a motel to wait out Floyd's passage.

Plan A has the advantage that we are more in control of PALAEMON's fate. We would not be relying on someone else's dock. Nor would we be in a congested harbor where, if one boat breaks loose, it could damage many others before going ashore or sinking.

A few years ago, our original PALAEMON rode out Hurricane Bob lashed to a stone wall and three anchors in the Mystic River. Anne and I were huddled in the basement of the Planetarium at Mystic Seaport Museum with 100 other sailors who had been "evacuated" from boats by the museum staff. Following Bob's track north through Buzzards Bay over the next several days, we witnessed the almost unbelievable domino effect of one or two boats coming loose in a crowded but otherwise safe harbor. At Padanaram, Massachusetts, one or two boats had slipped their moorings and taken nearly a hundred others ashore with them. Forty-foot sailboats were stacked in piles like so many carelessly heaped toys; individual boats sat incongruously in the streets or decorated the lawns of waterfront homes; some boats were so far back in the woods that only the tips of their masts were visible above the trees. While many of these derelicts had been at moorings, others had been at docks that failed in the contest with hurricane-driven waves. Floating docks drifted up over their pilings as the Bob-driven tide rose 10 feet above its normal high.

Visions of Padanaram haunt our search through the guidebooks for likely marinas. Do we really want to risk PALAEMON in a strange place? Plan B does not make us happy. But Plan A is no prize either. If Floyd comes close, we can expect eighteen to twenty-four hours of storm-force winds and heavy rain. Even in a protected cove, the noise and motion will be dramatic. I will have to check the anchor lines for chafe every hour in winds so strong that the risk of being blown off the decks is not trivial. I will probably have to wear a snorkel and swim mask in order to see and breathe on deck.

We opt for Plan B and head for Solomons Island. It has a tight little harbor and two marinas with motels and restaurants attached. PALAEMON, we continually assure ourselves, will be safe. If the power stays on at the motel, we could even be comfortable. If the cable hookup holds, we can watch the Weather Channel nonstop.

From 500 miles away, Floyd gives us brisk northeasterlies, pushing us down the Chesapeake toward Solomons. We are into the marina by noon and have PALAEMON lashed, stripped, and stowed by 3 P.M. After hauling several loads of valuables to the motel room, we have done about all we can do.

We go back to check the lines again. We rack our brains for any contingency we might have missed. We feel like traitors. PALAEMON has taken care of us for many miles. We are leaving her stripped bare at a strange dock. We not only feel bad, we feel stupid for feeling bad. PALAEMON is a thing, for heaven's sake—a conglomeration of plastic and wood and glass and steel.

But there is nothing rational about our attachment to this boat. It is part

Gateway to Solomons.

of our attachment to each other, the most intense and cherished bond in both our lives. The thing that matters before and beyond all else, the thing that allows anything to matter at all.

I wonder, not for the first time, how Anne and I, and our relationship to each other, have gotten so mixed up with boats. I think I understand some of it. Our early years together were incandescent, our love threatening to burn us up. It had to be managed, damped, accommodated to the intrusion of careers and others. We were not kids. I had kids in high school, an ex-wife, a demanding profession; Anne was just making her way in hers after trying a dozen other things.

We wanted to hide from the world, to be just us, together, no outside demands, no crosscurrents of other emotions, responsibilities, guilt. Our boats almost always gave us that. For a weekend, a week, sometimes two, we were focused. Sailing, managing the boat, loving each other was all there was. It was the only time we felt free to let the flame burn as bright as it would—no one to hide it from, no one to embarrass by our excess. We could hardly bear to go ashore after a weekend aboard. We often stayed on the boat at our dock on Sunday nights and rose at 5 A.M. on Monday to get home and showered and to work.

Each boat became a refuge, a trysting place. They have stayed that. The place where the flame is kept, nurtured, renewed. Not the only place, but the most reliable. That's at least part of why we are infatuated with boats, why we have dreamed so long of this trip. A year together on PALAEMON. That's the real plan. Where we go is secondary.

So, safe but bereft, we wait for Floyd. The electricity stays on, but the cable lines come down almost immediately. We are reduced to listening to NOAA forecasts on our handheld VHF radio. Floyd is headed right at us, but relatively slowly. The wind has already picked up and the rain has started, but the eye of the storm is still twenty-four hours away.

We compose e-mail messages to friends, call family to let them know we are "safe." We sit in the lounge swapping boat tales and prognostications with other cruisers beached by the approaching storm. We occasionally bundle on foulweather gear and go out to check PALAEMON's lines and the state of the tide. Floyd will probably push enough water into the bay to cover the docks. The marina has switched off all electricity to the slips. We have tied PALAEMON both to the dock and to higher posts. We wish the posts were higher still.

Floyd arrives in the night and passes just southeast of us. For us, this is a lucky path. Floyd was packing 90 mph winds and traveling at 20 to 25 mph as it passed by. If it had come directly at us, we would have had winds at 110 to 115 mph. But since the eye was actually moving away from our position, we experienced no more than 70 mph winds—a huge difference. At 70 mph, damage is minimal. Trees lose some of their leaves and small branches; dead trees are toppled and anything lying about loose is likely to be lost. At 115 mph, shallow-rooted trees (such as pines) go down in droves, windows are blown out, roofs fly off. Floyd was a nuisance on our side of it, a disaster for folks on the other side.

I have been reading Robert Fagel's splendid translation of Homer's *Odyssey*. When Zeus, angered by Ulysses's starving crew's slaughter of the Cattle of the Sun, sends the storm that crushes their boat and drowns all but the epic hero, Ulysses's description sounds like what it must be like on the wrong side of a hurricane:

> Killer-squalls attacked us, screaming out of the West, a murderous blast shearing the two forestays off so the mast toppled backward, its running tackle spilling into the bilge. The mast itself went crashing into the stern. It struck the helmsman's head and crushed it to a pulp and down from his deck the man flipped like a diver—his hardy spirit life left his bones behind. Then, in the same breath Zeus hit the craft with a lightning bolt and thunder. Round she spun. Reeling under the impact, filled with racking brimstone, shipmates pitching out of fear, bobbing round like sea hawks swept along by whitecaps past the trim black hull—and the god cut short their journey home forever.

Homer's words echo in my head as I listen to the wind in the night.

Within a few hours of Floyd's passage, we put PALAEMON back together and check out of the now-claustrophobic Comfort Inn. We cast off the lines, grateful for the miss, sobered by a vision of what we have avoided.

Thanks, Zeus. And the Cattle of the Sun are absolutely safe from us.

7

LEANING AGAINST THE WIND

We are into serious piddling now. Dennis and Floyd have reinforced our resolve. We will not exit the Chesapeake, certainly not go south of Beaufort, North Carolina, until we think the hurricane season is over. I promise myself, not for the first time, to emulate Water Rat, and enjoy boating in the way he counsels in *Wind in the Willows:*

> Nothing seems really to matter: that's the charm of it. Whether you get away, or whether you don't: whether you arrive at your destination or whether you reach somewhere else, or whether you never get anywhere at all, you're always busy, and you never do anything particular; and when you've done it there's always something else to do and you can do it if you like, but you much better not.

We have arranged to meet Jay, Lisa, and grandkids Paige and Jake, at the Tides Lodge in Carter Creek off the Rappahannock. They will luxuriate at the lodge while we dock at the marina. We are eager to spend time with them, to share what we are doing, how we are feeling. But, aside from a night aboard for Paige and Jake, the visit is not a great success.

We have begun to move to the rhythm of the sea and the sun, the simple demands of our bodies and our boat. The posh, Anglophile ambience of the Tides has its charm, but for us it is utterly alien. And the chef must be on holiday; the bland food takes hours to arrive. Jay is apoplectic. He is in the retail trade (photo finishing) himself. He spends too many days biting his tongue while coddling outrageous customers to accept bad service without complaint. Sitting for an hour waiting for food to arrive seldom brings out the best in children. Jake's answer to boredom is to torment his parents. We try not to laugh, but the kid has real talent. After two excruciating meals, we all eat aboard PALAEMON, picking up carryout for lunch and dinner from nearby Kilmarnock.

Jay's disappointment is a thundercloud on our horizon, its lightning bolts kept at bay by Lisa's sunny disposition. But we feel disjointed, disconnected anyway. We're dawdling when we want to be moving. The Tides interlude makes us realize that we have become distanced from the land and its concerns. The inn's guests seem completely outside our world. The only other boaters are part of a weekend rendezvous of motor yachts. Their owners sit at the dock in their cockpits drinking and watching football on satellite TV. They are having a great time, but it is not our party.

I long to be back in a secluded cove, or in a marina with live-aboards working on their boats, talking of cruising plans. As Jay and Lisa and Paige and Jake leave, I feel more than usually estranged. Trying to stay involved in their lives is always a challenge. We know what they do, but do we feel what they feel? Are we any less mysterious to them? I seem never to know. We will not see them again until April, when they meet us in St. Martin. I miss them already, mostly because I feel that we have somehow missed them here, too.

The kids start their drive back to Richmond too late for us to depart. Besides, we have unfinished business with MISS ANN, the inn's gleaming, 127-foot wooden motor yacht. Anne watched MISS ANN cruise the Rappahannock for decades. Her mother particularly longed to be on board. We will take a ride in memory of that gentle, bright spirit whose death has left a permanent hole in our lives.

Only three couples climb the gangplank for the "sunset cruise." After exploring the luxurious interior, we hang out in the wheelhouse with the crew. The old fittings are still there, the bell for the helmsman to signal the engine room, a gleaming brass binnacle. But the engines are now connected to a throttle on the bridge. The captain steers mostly by autopilot and he looks at the radar screen more than he looks through the windscreen. Still, putting MISS ANN softly against her dock in wind and current is an impressive bit of seamanship. How they did it when all the captain could do was signal the engine room for more or less power, forward or reverse, is beyond me.

Our spirits lift as soon as we and PALAEMON are free of the Tides dock. We anchor in the Corrotoman, an unspoiled beauty, just upriver off the Rappahannock. The wooded shores are serene, bathed in the red glow of the late afternoon sunlight. We are only a few miles, but across the Rappahannock, from the cottage where Anne spent her childhood summers. She never had the opportunity to explore much beyond their little creek. The Corrotoman had always beckoned, just outside the safe range of her family's little runabout.

We move to Urbanna for supplies and to pick up mail. Anne has been there hundreds of times, even once held an Urbanna Public Library card, but it was a town for groceries, hardware, books, not some place to see, to explore. It's worth seeing. Urbanna was chartered by Act of Parliament in 1680 for a single purpose, to ship Virginia tobacco back to England. The remains of the tobacco warehouse still stand, along with the old customs house. Seventeenth- and eighteenth-century houses grace the tree-lined streets. Urbanna has grown little since the end of British mercantilist rule. A grand tour can be accomplished in an hour.

We look for the library and find it closed. But we like it here. The post-mistress wears a badge identifying herself as Miss Agnes. She's delighted to see us. She calls out to the one guy in back, "The Mashaws are here." We've been a mystery, a packet of mail posted to General Delivery, with a name Miss Agnes couldn't identify. Apparently we are the only customers, local or transient, that Miss Agnes doesn't know. She quickly remedies that defect. She is delighted when she remembers the MacClintocks, Buz and Anne's mother, anyway, maybe Anne's father. In a minute, we are locals.

Emboldened by our encounter with Miss Agnes, we go looking for Taylor's Hardware. Anne remembers buying supplies there as a kid—tools, paint and brushes, roofing nails. She wants to see what it's like now, whether old Mr. Taylor is still there. He's not, but his son is, and the window display still features kerosene lamps and zinc tubs. The narrow-board flooring creaks as we poke around trying to find something, anything, to buy. Taylor, Jr., banters with the only other customer, an old crabber who is trying to beat down the price of some line. We settle on flashlight batteries. I studiously avoid checking the date on the battery package.

We repair to Bristow's, which has a newspaper article posted at the entrance describing it as the oldest continuously operated dry-goods store in America. We are into propping up the Urbanna economy. Anne shops hard for some trousers, but apart from jeans, Bristow's ladies' apparel runs heavily to skirts and dresses and to tweed-check, tailored, no-nonsense suits. This is not boating gear.

At lunch in a "down-home" looking café, we begin to realize something odd about Urbanna. It is an integrated town. Not "mixed race" or "non-discriminatory"—integrated. There are as many black–white groups as white–white or black–black. Our white waitress greets black regulars with a hug, asks where they've been, delivers messages to take home to a wife or a daughter. Banter runs back and forth among the tables with no racial fault lines. What's going on here? This is an imagined America, surely not color-blind but obviously people-sighted. We see more easy social contact between blacks and whites at lunch in Urbanna than we see in a year in New Haven.

I don't think we're being snowed by rural southern charm. We grew up southern, our senses remarkably attuned to the racial politics of everyday life, to the subtle nuances of southern speech and body language, to the "no's" that mean "yes" and the "yeses" that mean "no," that southern indirection that frustrates and irritates northerners unable to decipher the code. I lived for years with people who would never say "nigger" but whose self-censorship was based on linguistic, not political or moral, scruples. And with many who used it freely, who could inflect the word to carry a dozen different weights—from lack of interest ("just a nigger") to contempt ("just like a nigger") to hate ("damn nigger").

The recollection knots my stomach. Some of those remembered speakers are my family. It may have been simple youthful rebellion that caused me to cut my modest, political-action teeth on civil rights: sitting in the back of the bus until I realized that I was just frightening the black folks who *had* to sit there; marching, picketing, doing sit-ins at lunch counters, mostly with the joint chapter of the NAACP in New Orleans, formed by Tulane and Dillard students. I've never felt so energized and so helpless. We fought the good fight but seemed to get nowhere.

We could barely keep ourselves together. The disputes over tactics were endless. And the New Orleans Police Department was smart. The cops continuously threatened to drive us apart by discriminatory arrests—only blacks were collared, the white kids were left alone. They wouldn't even arrest us when we locked arms to try to make them carry us two at a time, black and white together. They just pried us apart. And we let them. To resist meant the charges went from trespass or loitering to resisting arrest, maybe even assaulting an officer. If that happened, the white kids would get bail or just be released at the station. Our black colleagues would be held, not for a night's "police time" but rather to await trial on serious charges.

I had thought back then that when integration finally came to the South, it might be real. The southern segregationists' plea—"We know these people"—was a lame defense against northern agitation for change, but it contained a twisted truth. Southern whites have always been intertwined with southern blacks in more intimate and extended relations than their northern counterparts. I don't just mean sex. White kids of my generation played with black kids until separated by school; were raised by black maids, as I was; knew whole black families over generations. If racial hatred and enforced separation could be got out of the way, we had hoped these personal histories would matter, that we would have integration, not just desegregation.

I remember my dad's late conversion to the idea that the public schools probably should be integrated. It was about 1963. I was already in law school. A black mason came to the house several Saturdays to lay some concrete. He brought along his nine-year-old grandson. Dad asked the boy what he was learning in school.

"Nuthin'."

"Well, you learned to read, didn't you?"

"Naw Suh."

"Oh, come on, let's read this book."

"I cain' read no book."

And he couldn't. Dad was furious. He went to the school and observed the boy's classes. After that, he was apoplectic. He wrote the school board a blistering letter, for all the good that did. More important for what I had thought integration might mean, he spent every Saturday morning with that child until he could read at something like the third-grade level.

Was I finally seeing real integration in Urbanna, Virginia, nearly forty years after my last sit-in? Maybe. On this one, I am not easily convinced. I have too much disappointment, too much anger. I think again, as I always do when I remember those years, about a night on Calhoun Street in New Orleans.

Ernest "Dutch" Moriale and I are standing at the curb waiting for a ride. Dutch is black, but so *café au lait* he probably could have "passed." A squad car pulls up. "Whatchew doin' heah, boy?" "He's with me," I say. The cop stares at us in silence, his eyes glowing with menace. The squad car creeps on. The incident was nothing—a common occurrence. Twenty years later, Dutch Moriale would be mayor of New Orleans. But Dutch's success can't cancel out that night. Not for me. How could it for him?

We leave Urbanna for Locklies Marina, a safe harbor near the MacClintock family's cottage. We will spend the weekend seeing Buz and Laurie and their three kids, Jeff, Andy, and Bonnie. Anne's nephews and niece are my grandchildren's contemporaries. I started my family at nineteen; Buz started his at forty-three.

For Anne, this place is childhood and summer, freedom and warmth. We explore the creek. Anne and Buz bicker companionably about where the sandbar used to be, when Hermit's Island got cut off from its neighbor, which channel is the "new" channel, how long ago the first house was built on the point. On Sunday, the boys and Buz and I swim while Anne, Laurie, and Bonnie walk the beach. Anne returns with a nasty cut from a buried beer bottle.

She is furious with herself for walking barefoot. I get to try out my Red Cross first-aid training. I manage to stop the bleeding, but I don't like the look of this cut. It's deep and near the ball of the foot. It will flex open every time she takes a step.

We leave Locklies with the help and advice of local sailors who want to be leaving with us. They're looking at the end of the sailing season; we're headed for endless summer. The MacClintocks chase us down the Rappahannock in their 16-foot runabout. Buz says he wants to collect a book that we promised. He would never admit to sentiment about his sister, to concern about her foot or about the adventure she has begun.

We duck into Deltaville for the night. The explicit reason is that it's too late to go farther, that we want to see the harbor in which we anchored nearly twenty years ago on our first charter. In fact, it was the first time either of us had ever sailed a boat larger than 19 feet. We laugh about the sailing résumé we submitted to Rappahannock Yachts to qualify to charter one of their

Rappahannock herons.

33-footers. It was not really a tissue of lies; a tissue of half-truths, perhaps. We were scared out of our wits as we left their dock. But we made it back in one piece. We only went aground twice.

We talk through all the stops we made on that trip. Tangier Island, where the kids' hair is like straw and their cheeks have the glow of the Cornish folk they are. Their speech is unique to the island, a West of England dialect that no one in Cornwall has spoken in 200 years. There is the blissful Indian Creek anchorage we entered in a vicious squall. This one in Deltaville. My nostalgia for Deltaville is a little bogus. I really want to be here to be near a medical clinic. I am almost certain Anne will need stitches in the morning.

She does, and we are treated to the kindness of strangers. The owner of a marina near our anchorage drives us to the clinic. The clinic waits on Anne as though she's the most important case they've had in months. A fellow patient drives me 10 miles to the nearest pharmacy to get antibiotics. The marina owner collects Anne from the clinic and then me from the pharmacy. He's a little grumpy about it, but he mellows on the ride back.

Anne has a lot of pain and the prospect of several weeks of recovery. She berates herself again and again for being so stupid, for burdening me, spoiling our trip, and being a horrible, useless person in general. I am thankful for the millionth time that she aims these tirades at herself, never at me. She forgives me stupidity after stupidity. I have stopped trying to understand why; I just want it to continue.

Tomorrow we will move farther south, continue our Water Rat voyage. Take it easy, drink in the Chesapeake's Indian summer. But I am worried that Anne will be anything but a good patient, will insist on "carrying her own weight" when keeping her weight off her foot is what's needed. I feel the gathering pressure of time, the looming prospect of some real movement. There's a gale of wind at my back. I have to lean against it to keep floating slowly down the bay. Water Rat and I are not yet soulmates.

ANNE'S PASSAGE NOTES: HOME WATERS

I love our time on the lower Chesapeake. I spent my summers as a child and teenager on the Rappahannock River, eight miles up from where it joins the bay. The flat marshland and low wooded bluffs, the low-tide smells, the silty colors of the bay and the river, the wading herons and soaring gulls are for me the essence of summer. The fecund smell of marsh is as heady to me as the visual elegance of a great blue heron in its slow downward glide before landing in a fluster of wings, neck and legs suddenly awry. I can still feel, but do not now need, the wonderful ooze of low-tide muck between my toes. Nor do I want to chase those beautiful gray-blue birds to see them take wing.

The river is much as I remember it, somewhat more developed than before, though not a lot. But the workboats have changed. I remember salty-looking crabbers, in open wooden skiffs, poling along the edges of the shallow creeks and marshes, graceful and quiet in the early mornings. With what ease they upended the pole that doubled as a crab net and scooped up crabs lying lightly buried in the mud. I watched them scull their skiffs from cove to cove, their strokes effortless, soundless, seemingly timeless.

Rough-talking skippers ran sweet-sheered "party boats" out for an all-day or half-day charter, bottom fishing in the summer for spot and flounder, in the fall for blues and rockfish. Many of these boats took out charter parties on weekends, and crabbed or oystered the rest of the time, depending on the season. They could not afford to be idle. I remember the "buy boats," with their ungainly aft cabinhouses presiding over the sweeping grace of their forward hulls. They worked the coast, buying oysters or crabs fresh from local fishermen and ferrying them to market processing points, perhaps Weems or Reedville.

Practical plastic has replaced these able craft. We look for, and sometimes find, one of the old beauties still plying the mild waters, looking like a thoroughbred somehow dropped among a bunch of donkeys. We wave enthusiastically. The waterman, busy making ends meet and keeping her afloat, probably thinks we have lost our minds.

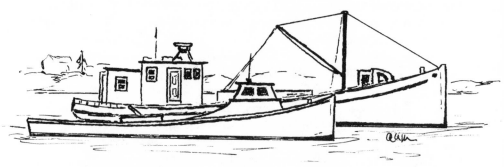

Chesapeake Boats – Crab Boat, Buy Boat
Bay boats.

Other things have changed too. The water seems cleaner, the bird life richer than I remember. Yet, we know that Chesapeake crabbing and oystering are suffering from waters that are much too nitrogen-rich.

My mind refuses to stay in the present. I remember my episodically troubled family, my father's passionate love of the water. Though he was devoted to my mother, I never saw him look at her with anything like the joy that lit his eyes when he looked at the river roiled by a fresh easterly. I wonder what he would have thought about our current endeavor, whether he would have been surprised, proud, whether he would have understood. I think he would, but he was not a sailor, and our dream encompasses so much. And it is ours, not his. He would have been uneasy. My mother is no puzzle—she would have been worried but would have tried to hide it to avoid causing us any anxiety. And she would have been perplexed, troubled that her failure to understand our dream meant that she was failing to understand us.

It is wonderful to see my brother and his wife and three young ones at the old summer cottage, now theirs and fixed up; and it is special to be here by boat, on our PALAEMON. Jeff and Andy sleep aboard. Their mother decides that Bonnie, the youngest, is best at home. Paige and Jake sleep aboard too, when we are docked at the Tides.

An adventure for both sets of children, and for us. They want to see everything and pull everything apart so they can understand what it's for and how it works. I love to see them like this aboard PALAEMON, their eyes alight with curiosity and their own visions of adventure. For me, it is a circle completed, a piece of my life brought into harmony. It is not just that I want them to love boats, indeed, that they *must* love boats. More than anything else, it is a way for them, these children who mean so much to me, to feel some part of both the magic and the reality of our dream.

Everything feeds my sense of completion—Jerry and me, PALAEMON, the smells, the colors, the memories—and mostly the family, both sides of it, blissfully unaware though they surely are, of how important these moments are to me. It's probably best that way. I stifle words and tears that would only distract the kids from their fun as they pull carefully stowed gear out of yet another locker.

8

ICW BLUES

As we make our way to the southern end of the Chesapeake, Louisiana brown pelicans, my home-state bird, line the fish traps like ungainly sentinels. Who taught these ugly birds to fish? They fall out of the sky like wounded ducks and hit the water with the concussion of a cannonball. Somehow they come up with a meal instead of a broken neck. The gulls seem to be thinning, perhaps driven north as the pelicans conquer more territory. Porpoise sightings are frequent. In the deep quiet of secluded coves, we are lulled to sleep by the clickety-click of tiny shrimp nibbling the algae clinging to PALAEMON's hull.

Fish traps are now a greater navigational hazard than crab pots. They are "pound" traps—long wire-mesh fences with a corral at the end, their irregular poles "worried" into the muddy bottom. Herring or menhaden encounter the fence and swim along it to the corral or pound. The circular enclosures confuse and trap the fish until the menhaden boats arrive to haul them aboard. The catch is prodigious. In the mid-1970s, tiny Reedville, Virginia, was the leading fishing port by tonnage in the United States—50 million pounds of fish per year.

The traps stretch out for miles from shore, forcing us into endless detours. Too much abandoned netting, too many snapped-off poles lurk beneath the surface to risk threading our way through them.

We finally make Hampton, the end of the bay. We were last here twelve years ago, taking our old PALAEMON north. We had planned to anchor out, but the piers of a new marina and mooring balls for local boats now clog the open anchorage we remember. The Hampton dockmaster provides a slip, and we are reunited with two of the boats that weathered Floyd with us at Solomons Island. We call ourselves "the Comfort Inn Six."

Hampton is a "snowbird" staging area, a gathering spot for boats fleeing the sag-

Brown pelicans.

ging jet stream, New England winters, a world plunged into the detestable early darkness of Eastern Standard Time. Snowbird boats are awash in the equipment characteristic of live-aboards—wind generators, bicycles, spare jugs of diesel and water lashed on deck, and *large* anchors. Many of the crews poised in Hampton are "early retirees," refugees from jobs ranging from plumbing to "professing." They seem like good teams. Their intense loyalties to each other and to their boats are palpable; their attention, like ours, is directed to the tasks at hand—the endless maintenance and preparation that make a boat seaworthy. Several will wait here to leave with the West Marine 1500 Rally fleet. We wonder again whether we should join them. We decide again to stick to the inshore route.

Hampton is one of the oldest English settlements in North America. Captain John Smith survived the dreadful winter of 1609 here when it was still Kecoughton, an Indian village. He wrote home, "We were never more merrie, nor fed on more plentie of good oysters, fish, flesh, wild-foule and good bread." Religious dissidents from Jamestown moved here permanently the next year. Thus began the religious splintering of the American colonies, a tradition we still relish. My stepmother has been a member of at least a dozen breakaway congregations in the past forty years. The fineness of the doctrinal disputes that motivate flight from existing Protestant congregations rivals the exquisite distinctions that Galileo deployed before the Grand Court of the Inquisition.

Born in protest, Hampton was almost comically accommodating during the American Civil War. Fort Monroe, where Lincoln planned the assault on Richmond, was occupied by an isolated garrison of Union troops throughout the war but never came under serious attack by the Confederacy. Nor did the Union forces attempt to take Hampton, which was virtually defenseless. Meanwhile, the fort served as a major refuge for runaway slaves. After years of fort-town détente, the Union troops bluffed Hampton's protectors into burning the town themselves to deny refuge to advancing Yankees, who never showed up.

Although constantly bumping into Civil War history, we are impressed again with the degree to which the tidewater "New South" through which we are edging really seems new. The official guidebook to Hampton makes as much of its African-American heritage as of its colonial beginnings and its contemporary aerospace attractions. The dockmaster is African American, his assistant white.

Anne is still hobbled by her foot, but it is improving. I run the shoreside errands alone, trying to find everything we need before entering the trackless expanse of marsh grass and scrub timber that define the Intracoastal Waterway from Norfolk to Oriental. The cuts of meat on display in the downtown super-market tell me that Hampton is not a boomtown. But there is a Rite-Aid, where I can refill prescriptions that our drug insurer's computers will only allow the pharmacy to dole out in thirty-day packages. Welcome to "managed care," surely one of the most insulting euphemisms to which American consumers are subjected. If our insurer were managing our care rather than managing its costs, it would let our physicians write prescriptions for the year's supply of drugs we need.

Shopping continues in Norfolk, where we take delivery on a sturdier dinghy. JEREMY BENTHAM has proved to be thin-skinned, springing a leak in the high-pressure inflatable floor every time it comes in contact with anything prickly—a flopping fish, for example. BENTHAM II is an RIB, a rigid inflatable boat with a plastic bottom. It should provide a sturdier platform for hauling supplies and people than our current patched wonder. Utilitarians have got to be useful or out they go.

W. T. Brownley Co., an impressive marine chart store, lies but a few blocks from our berth at Waterside Marina. We still need charts for the Florida section of the ICW and for Hispaniola. Waterway, yes, Hispaniola, no. The stretch from Cuba to Puerto Rico is not in most chart-providers' inventories. Our government's official policy is that we cannot visit Cuba without special permission. Most marine insurers, like ours, exclude coverage for visits to Haiti. Our policy even limits us to two marinas in the Dominican Republic. I'll try again at Bluewater Books in Fort Lauderdale. Their inventory is vast.

Waterside Marina holds bittersweet memories of our trek from Fort Lauderdale to Connecticut in our old PALAEMON. Battered by storms off Beaufort, we had come "inside" to slog up the Ditch. At Norfolk, our law-student crew had to leave to start summer jobs, and Anne's vacation ran out. The dockmaster hooked me up with George Coburn, a licensed captain, experienced bluewater sailor, and former U.S. Army Special Forces officer. Having sailed the Atlantic, the Med, and the Caribbean in a Cal 34, George was now "building up," as he always put it, a steel 40-footer, already named KESTREL, with his own hands.

His wife and first mate, Teresa, was working as a Legal Services lawyer while George worked on the boat and took some delivery jobs. It turned out that Teresa's boss was my first student research assistant at the University of Virginia Law School, nearly twenty years earlier, and an old friend of Anne's. Anne had bunked with John and his wife, Kay, while a consultant to Richmond Community Action, as she worked and borrowed her way through law school.

I hired George on the spot to help me pilot old PALAEMON home. He and Teresa took us in, gave us dinner, drove Anne to the airport. They are surely also somewhat to blame for this trip. Anne and I stole glances at each other across the Coburns' dinner table as they recounted their adventures and described their plans. Pieces of boat hardware—winches, cleats, blocks, a gleaming bronze windlass—littered their apartment, waiting to be installed on the new boat. George never bought retail, and he was infinitely resourceful. Not too surprising for a guy who had spent most of his army career lurking in some remote spot where being shot was probably the best he could hope for if discovered.

George had already ballasted KESTREL with lead pigs that he had molded himself on the sidewalk in front of their apartment. For days he melted used tire-balancing slugs over a single-burner propane stove and poured the molten metal into forms originally designed to make window-sash weights. Both the stove and the molds came from a junkyard for $5. The lead he scavenged for nothing from tire shops. Trained secret operative that he was, George quickly noticed the unmarked car that took up a position down his block on the third day of his tedious quest for keel ballast. Finally, after nearly a week, the stake-out approached him. Two of Norfolk's finest were convinced that he had to be cooking something illegal, but they couldn't figure it out. He had to take them inside and show them all the other gear in the apartment before they began to believe his story. But they took away a bar of lead for analysis, just in case.

We have tried to keep in touch but have lost George and Teresa's trail. I wonder whether the boat ever got built up. Where did they take her? Are they out there somewhere now? I would like to run our plans by George. He could probably draw us a map of Hispaniola from memory.

At Norfolk, we shift from sailing the Chesapeake to burrowing down the ICW, alternating between glee and gloom. Occasionally we sail on almost-blue waters under sunny skies, porpoises playing and pelicans diving; mostly we motor through narrow interior channels, their coffee-colored waters polluted by storm flooding, their banks littered with uprooted trees. Much of the pollution comes from hog farms, their sewage "lagoons" built so that they flood with surprising ease. Dennis and Floyd virtually destroyed them, releasing thousands of tons of untreated sewage into Carolina's rivers and estuaries. The hog farmers are rebuilding their lagoons—with federal loans and grants. Anti-pig feelings are strong among boating and fishing interests in eastern North Carolina. An editorial in a local weekly suggests bitterly that hurricane preparedness in North Carolina should be devoted exclusively to teaching pigs to swim.

Our pace in the ICW is glacial. We still have more than 500 nautical miles just to get to Fort Lauderdale. We are struggling to make 50 miles a day in the shrinking daylight hours of mid-October. Hard days. Underway at dawn, stopping at dusk, listening to the incessant drone of the diesel, dodging logs and shallows, swatting flies. Drawbridges stubbornly follow their half-hour opening schedules; locks will lift us up or down only on the hour. We want to explore some of the shoreside towns, but we are beginning to worry about making the Virgin Islands by Christmas. We have a date to meet Mark, Mary, and Samantha—number-two son, daughter-in-law, and oldest grandchild. From Fort Lauderdale, it's still 1,000 miles to windward through the Bahamas, the Dominican Republic, and Puerto Rico to St. Thomas. That number's not going to change because we're behind schedule.

The backwaters of the Carolina low country transport us into another world, one with the lush edginess of a Pat Conroy novel. We feel alone, slightly threatened. For a whole day, we encounter no one but deer hunters in johnboats and camouflage suits. They sit in the waterway waiting for deer to come to the water's edge for a drink. They only stare at our waves. We don't think they are really our kind of guys. Then, just south of Cape Hatteras, we burst out into the clear blue waters that lie behind the dunes of the windswept barrier islands. None too soon. We have had it with the ICW.

We sail out of Beaufort inlet to a remote anchorage behind Cape Lookout, a shallow bay framed by an elbow of sand. Its distinctive diamond-patterned lighthouse warns of the shoals that stretch east for miles offshore. This was long a harbor of refuge for merchantmen sailing north, a place to hide until the storms off Hatteras abated. When the day's crop of fishermen leave, we are alone with the sweep of the light, the five-second wink of a channel marker, and the sound of the Atlantic breaking on the shore over the dunes. In the predawn blackness,

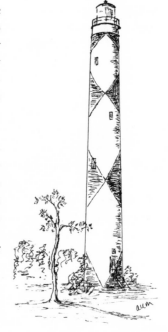

Cape Lookout Lighthouse.

we pick our way out past the shallows into the ocean. We have fled the ICW for a twelve-hour passage offshore to Wrightsville Beach.

PALAEMON feels like her shackles have been removed. After days of imprisonment, a pardon has come through and she's running, arms outspread, feeling the wind rush through her hair. The wind is east northeast again, 15 to 20 knots. The *Waterway Guide* says that Masonboro Inlet at Wrightsville Beach is another all-weather inlet. Maybe so. But as we approach the entrance, we suddenly see huge waves breaking over the entrance bar. There is no room to bail out. The breaking waves catch us from the aft quarter and fling the boat hard over. Anne and I scream as one, "Hold on!" Anne somehow steers and stays in the cockpit. Two repetitions in lesser waves and we're through. Down below, gear has been thrown all over the cabin. It's the nearest we've ever come to a knockdown.

Motoring to the anchorage, we ask ourselves what we could have done differently. We were dead center between the entrance buoys, lined up as well as we could be with the direction of the waves. We watch the sailboat behind us do the same near-death roll as she comes over the bar. This may be an "all-weather" entrance, but in 5 more knots of wind, I wouldn't try Masonboro Inlet in anything less than a Coast Guard wave-runner.

The wind seems to be piping up as we switch on NOAA for our early evening weather fix. In the twelve hours since we left Cape Lookout, a tropical depression has become Tropical Storm Irene. It is expected to gather strength over the next twenty-four hours and will be a hurricane when it comes ashore, somewhere in the Carolinas. Hurricane tag again.

We look around Wrightsville Beach, assessing the damage done by Dennis and Floyd. There is hardly a house without missing shingles. A few posts remain where docks once projected from the land. We do not want to be here for Irene. Wilmington is only 15 miles up the Cape Fear River. I call the Wilmington dockmaster. The town dock has space on a first-come, first-served basis. It's full now, and with Irene coming, no one is likely to move. I try the one marina listed in the guide. It's full too, but Terry Rose, who runs his yacht-brokerage business out of the marina, says we can dock in front of his condo. It's a new dock, not yet listed in the guides. He says a 100-footer weathered Hurricane Dennis there.

Hanging around the Carolina coast as a hurricane approaches is hardly prudent seamanship. Given the proximity of the Gulf Stream to fuel storms, and the prominent capes and shoals, these are some of the world's most dangerous temperate waters. An article published in *South Atlantic Magazine* in January 1879 described Cape Fear as

> . . . a naked, bleak elbow of sand, jutting far out into the ocean. Immediately in its front are the Frying Pan Shoals, pushing out still further, 20 miles, to sea. Together they stand for warning and for woe; and together they catch the long majestic roll of the Atlantic as it sweeps through a thousand miles of grandeur and power from the Arctic toward the Gulf. It is the playground of billows and tempests, the kingdom of silence and awe, disturbed by no sound save the sea gull's shriek and the breaker's roar. . . . And there it will stand, bleak, and threatening, and pitiless, until the earth and the sea shall give up their dead.

I tell Terry that we're on our way.

9

CHANGING PLANS

Terry's dock in Wilmington looks as though it would withstand a category 5 hurricane and berth the QE 2. Unless something big comes down the river and smashes into her, PALAEMON should be safe. Terry's condo overlooks the dock. From his balcony, he gives us restaurant recommendations. We trust his advice implicitly: His Bristol 38.8 is hull number 6; PALAEMON is hull number 8. We strip the boat again and hole up at the Wilmington Hilton, still in sight of her berth.

We do the e-mail, phone-call drill. Our family now expects a notice every other week, reporting where we are waiting out the next hurricane. Over a fabulous meal at Terry's favorite restaurant—I'm talking New York–LA– quality food here—we debate our options. The marina where Terry has his office is a first-class yard. They don't just store, service, and repair boats, they also build them. PALAEMON needs to be hauled. The trip down the Chesapeake and through the ICW has been slow enough to let some growth accumulate on her bottom. More important, her designed waterline did not account for the thousands of pounds of food and gear we have added to make this trip. She squats 4 or 5 inches lower in the water than when we bought her. Her real waterline is now above the bottom paint, up on the topsides. The topsides paint is beginning to bubble from the damp. These bubbles will soon start letting water into the fiberglass of the hull. Fiberglass will not rot, but it will blister as moisture seeks out tiny impurities in the resin and glass. Eventually, a blistered hull will delaminate.

We decide to haul out in Wilmington, repaint the bottom, and move the waterline up. Bennett Brothers says they can do this in a week, once Irene has passed. We believe they believe that estimate. But we have dealt with boatyards for more than twenty years. We double their time estimate and ignore their cost estimate. It will cost what it will cost. Living aboard is sufficiently cheap that our bank account is healthier than it has been in years.

The decision to pull PALAEMON out of the water moves our still-nagging route question from background noise to focused discussion. We interrogate

Terry about the ICW south of Wilmington, about the passage to the British Virgins from here. He has done that passage several times; he will do it again in mid-November, delivering a client's boat from Norfolk to Tortola. Terry points out the obvious. The trek from here down the ICW is really Ditch-driving. There is virtually no open water. Moreover, we will be headed almost as much west as south, away from our ultimate destination. Why not spend the time while PALAEMON is land-bound visiting Georgetown and Charleston by car, leave for the BVI from Cape Fear, and do the Bahamas on the way home?

We have no good answer to this question other than fear. We have never made a passage that long. We were preparing to do it until Bob Handschu-macher scared us silly in the Branford West Marine store. But we know PALAE-MON much better now; we have sailed her in strong winds and rough seas. We have the offshore equipment to do ocean passages. We can check out every-thing one more time while she is at Bennett Brothers, with access to their ex-pertise. Anything that needs upgrading can be done before we leave.

Irene barely brushes Wilmington. Several mobile TV news teams are at the Hilton waiting to film flying objects and a raging river. They do dreary spots in the rain instead. The look on their faces says, "This film will never be seen by anyone." It's hard to imagine a news day so slow that the news director shows footage of a hurricane that didn't happen.

We move PALAEMON to Bennett Brothers, oversee her haulout, and call Enterprise Rent-a-Car. We will first be land tourists, then bluewater sailors. Watching PALAEMON inch out of the water in the slings of the Travelift, I feel the commitment we are making to the offshore route. My guess is that she will be on the hard at Bennett's for two weeks. By the time we are ready to sail again, using the inshore route and reaching St. Thomas by Christmas will be all but impossible. Do we really want to do this? We pack our doubts and our luggage into the rental car and take off.

We are charmed by many aspects of both Georgetown and Charleston. The at-tention to history and historic preservation is admirable; the attention to food, drink, and gracious living is welcome after our relatively Spartan life. For this I am prepared to have the rhythm of our sailing life interrupted. Historic downtown Charleston retains the rich patina of its antebellum lifestyle, when it had the densest slave population of any urban area in America. We immerse ourselves in the lore of South Carolina's colonial, revolutionary, antebellum, and Civil War eras. The lecture at Fort Sumter by a National Park Service guide on the economic and social tensions giving rise to South Carolina's secession is extraordinary—broad, subtle, balanced. She turns out to be a former history professor. She has donned a Park Service uniform to get an audience that might actually be interested in what she has to say. Remarkably, the Park Service lets her say it.

But the charm begins to wear thin. Any line between history and gossip here is shadowy. The pride that drives preservation often seems prideful in a way that turns everything about the past into an occasion for some self-celebratory comment. South Carolina's present seems but an outpost from which to look back at the past. To own a house in the Charleston historic district is to achieve all of life's ambitions, perhaps a state of grace.

I am being ungenerous, generalizing on thin information, but we see little evidence in Charleston—save a long-shot mayoral candidate of African-American descent—to suggest that the integrated society we witnessed in parts of Maryland and Virginia has penetrated the South Carolina low country. Blacks seem almost universally in menial jobs, and menial jobs appear to be almost exclusively black. The local presentation of South Carolina's history glories in a life that could not have been lived without slave labor, but hardly mentions it. The video at the Rice Museum in Georgetown merely notes, without elaboration, that the techniques for successful rice cultivation came to South Carolina from West Africa. I knew we had stolen those people's lives. I didn't realize we had appropriated their agricultural technology, too.

Rather than integrating African-American history into the standard guided tours, Charleston offers visitors a separate tour exploring that heritage. "Separate but equal" still lives. Not only does the Confederate flag fly above the statehouse (soon to come down for fear of discouraging football prospects recruited by the state university), the Civil War is the "War Between the States"—a locution we have not heard uttered, save in jest, for decades.

We have arrived, unaware, in the middle of one of Charleston's biannual house tours. Tickets are being sold for nightly soirees in the opulent seventeenth- and eighteenth-century mansions of various "sea captains." As we walk the narrow cobbled streets listening to the clop, clop of carriage horses and the spiel of the tour guides, I wonder whether they ever mention that these folks were privateers, smugglers, and slavers who put the proceeds of their illegal activities into plantations as well as these town houses. Today we call it money laundering.

Actually, the privateers should be excepted from my uncharitable indictment, at least those who attacked only belligerents. When the War of 1812 began, the U.S. Navy had twenty ships to go up against the British Navy's 700. Six months later, 600 American privateers, most not nearly so successful as Thomas Boyle's CHASSEUR, had been set loose to prey on British shipping. A notice in the *Charlestown Courier* for July 7, 1812, gives a flavor of the mobilization effort. It announces the commissioning of SAUCY JACK and invites Charlestonians "to embark in an enterprise against our enemy; it is patriotic in itself, honorable to those who may engage in it, and holds out a tempting prospect of pecuniary involvement." For some, the "prospect" clearly became a reality.

Occasional attacks of social guilt and political nausea aside, we have a great time. Constant coddling forces us to admit that life afloat has its discomforts. At our Charleston hostelry, the Two Meeting Street Inn at the Battery in Charleston, "discomfort" is not a part of anyone's vocabulary. We suspect the word would be thought vulgar.

As we drive back to Wilmington, our change of plan leaps out of its hiding place and seizes control of our minds. Sometime around November 1, we will sail east from Cape Fear, following the track pioneered by Columbus for returning to Europe from "the Indies." Only by staying this far north can a sailing ship be assured of avoiding the mostly easterly trade winds that blow from West Africa to the Caribbean. Unlike the Great Navigator, we will abandon our easterly course at a point just south of Bermuda. We will then head almost directly south to the British Virgin Islands. This dogleg route is nearly 1,500 miles. It will have us at sea for ten to fourteen days. An anxious silence invades our rental car as we rack our brains for something we could have forgotten, something that might put us and PALAEMON in peril. We begin to make more lists.

As predicted, the boat is not ready when we arrive back in Wilmington. We shuttle back and forth from the Hilton to the boatyard—preparing, repairing, checking, worrying. While repainting the propane tanks, I discover that they are nearly rusted through. I order new ones and coat them with epoxy to try to prevent rust. Checking the seacocks one more time, I find that the new freshwater foot pump in the head has been located so that a seacock cannot be closed. If the rubber drain hose attached to this seacock ever let go, we would have an inch-diameter hole below the waterline. Water would come in like a geyser, with no way to shut it off. I have tied wooden plugs to each seacock to be hammered into the opening in just such an emergency. But I have no idea whether this conventional remedy actually works. Everybody recommends it; nobody ever describes having done it. I pull the seacock and reinstall it, rotated 180 degrees. How the hell did I miss this before? What else have I failed to notice?

Finally PALAEMON is back afloat and we are back aboard. Terry downloads and prints out the latest position of the Gulf Stream and wishes us well. We follow the ebbing tide back down the Cape Fear River to Bald Head Island. The marina there is as close as we can get to the Atlantic without being in it.

We hover like kids peering over the edge of a diving board at the water below, eager and anxious. We want to be off, but we are six days shy of November 1. Dodging three hurricanes in the past six weeks has made us more wary than ever of being offshore with a hurricane approaching and nowhere to escape. But in three weeks, we should be in the islands. The Holy Grail is just over the horizon.

There is not much left to do. I re-plumb sink drains that have turned balky. Anne works on easy-fix meals for offshore. We spend half of each day listening to weather forecasts, trying to choose the right window for crossing the Gulf Stream. The weather is lousy. No hurricanes, but one norther after another kicks the stream into a frenzy and sends the thermometer plunging and us into lockers for additional layers of clothing. We walk the lanes of Bald Head, live oaks giving way to marsh on the west, sand dunes and sea to the east. We trudge the soft sand of the shore, looking at the sea; rent a canoe to explore the marsh; eat the prepared sea meals; cook replacements; wait.

Yesterday was a rugged weather day even at the marina. Thirty-five knots of wind screaming out of the northwest, bringing arctic air all the way from Alberta. But a break in the frontal pattern seems to be in sight. We plug our laptop's modem into the dockmaster's credit-card verification box and send off a round of don't-worry-if-you-don't-hear-from-us-for-two-weeks e-mails. This afternoon we will ready PALAEMON for offshore duty and hope the winds subside overnight as forecast. The tide that boils past the Bald Head marina will turn out to sea at midmorning. We will go with it.

10

MYSTERIES OF THE BERMUDA TRIANGLE

It's 4:13 A.M. and I'm wedged into the windward side of the cockpit underneath the dodger. We're 480 miles east southeast of Cape Fear, headed toward a Bermuda that we do not expect to see on this trip. Around 64°30'W longitude, and 31°N latitude, we will hang a right. Somewhere between there and 25°N latitude, we will pick up the northeasterly trades and ride them to Jost Van Dyke in the British Virgin Islands. At least that's the plan.

We are, however, in the infamous Bermuda Triangle. It is an area of many mysteries—not the least of which is, "What the hell are we doing out here?"

For the last fifteen hours, it's been blowing a near-gale with sustained winds of 25 mph and gusts up to 40. Not a truly dangerous wind, but it gets our attention. In water 2,000 fathoms deep, waves can build as big as they like without tripping on the seabed. Right now they like to be very large. One of the advantages of a night watch is that I can't see these mountains bearing down on us. In the daylight, I have trouble believing that approaching waves, towering 15 feet over my head, will slide harmlessly under PALAEMON's stern. So far, they have.

Well, a little bit comes in. That's why I'm huddled under the dodger, swaddled head to toe in my foulweather suit and waterproof seaboots. I look like a yellow mummy, listening to the howling of the wind and the hissing of a thousand snakes as wave crest after wave crest collapses and slips beneath the hull.

Earlier this afternoon, in building winds and seas, we had a fit of nerves and started pulling out the sea anchor—a parachutelike device that we can deploy off the bow to stop PALAEMON and hold her bow-first into the wind and waves. If the waves get any bigger, we may use it. In that position, the strongest part of the hull will take the brunt of the wave's force and PALAEMON will ride more easily. That assumes that if conditions deteriorate further, we will be able to get the sea anchor and its 300 feet of heavy line forward, over the bow, and into the proper orientation to the boat. I'm kicking myself for not having practiced this maneuver in calmer conditions. The prospect of trying it for the first time in seas so rough that we actually need it does not fill me with joy.

Every activity is an athletic challenge. The motion below is abrupt, dramatic and unpredictable. It takes me fifteen minutes to dress to go on watch. Getting my right leg into my foulweather gear while holding onto the nav-station desk with my left leg, left arm, right elbow, and ass is treacherous and time-consuming. Then the left leg. Then try to time a still-enough moment to shift my ass and pull up the pants. Take a brief rest. Tackle the jacket. Then the boots. Then the life vest and harness.

I will not describe the contortions involved in using the head. Whether I should struggle out of my gear and back into it to take a pee, or wait another hour and a half until I go off watch and will undress anyway, is not a trivial question. Bladder pressure has to be weighed carefully against effort and risk. We both already have many bruises. We are getting better at bracing our bodies and timing our movements. Unfortunately, these skills are not easily transferable to any other line of work, at least not any that I am prepared to take up.

Cooking is not a sensible activity. We're living mostly on granola bars, fruit, trail mix, cheese, crackers, and hard-boiled eggs. We can boil water for eggs, soup, tea, or coffee. The culinary results are simple, but at sea the behavioral recipe is complex.

First I strap myself into a safety belt that prevents me from being thrown across the cabin. It is attached to a steel bar that stretches across the front of the stove. The bar also provides a solid handhold. Leaning back against the strap and clutching the bar, I can avoid pitching headfirst onto the stove. The stove is gimbaled to keep it roughly horizontal as PALAEMON yaws. Adjustable metal rods help to secure the teapot to the stove. Even so, prudence dictates that I keep one hand on the teapot to make sure it stays put, the other on the steel bar to make sure that I stay put. Pouring boiling water on myself would not be smart.

We go through the water-boiling routine as much for morale-boosting as for sustenance. Getting up after no more than two and a half hours of sleep is much more bearable if you have some tea or hot chocolate waiting for you. Our watch schedule operates twenty-four hours a day. Knowing how tired Anne is makes it almost impossible to wake her without something comforting to hand over—along with a brief summary of wind and sea state, current configuration of the rig, and any other information she may need: like whether that big blip on the radar is headed toward or away from us. She does the same for me. Thank God she is competent and tough. How do people do this singlehanded, or with a mate who is mostly along for the ride?

So what in the hell *are* we doing here? One answer is that we made an elementary mistake. Many cruising sailors live by a simple rule when arranging to meet friends and family: "I will tell you *where,* or I will tell you *when,* but I will never tell you both things at the same time unless I am already there." We failed to schedule our Christmas appointment with Mark, Mary, and Samantha in the Virgin Islands in this sensible fashion. PALAEMON might have made that date plowing down the ICW and plodding through the Bahamas. But the truth is, we were bored with the waterway. And Van Sant's laborious method of working through the Bahamas sounded less and less appealing. We headed offshore to arrive early—visions of Caribbean leisure dancing in our heads.

Unless we were very lucky, we knew the price of that choice would be some rough sailing. Not that we understood what days of rough sailing meant, either physically or emotionally. But people make this trip without getting bashed at all. As usual, that was the prospect that I considered most likely. Once again, the 10 percent of joy blocked the 90 percent of anxiety and discomfort out of my imagination. I am beginning to believe that selective myopia is the cruising sailor's most essential piece of mental equipment. I never leave port without mine.

The joy has been there, too. Thirty-six hours ago, we were coaxing a few knots of forward progress out of PALAEMON under the spinnaker in 4-to-6-knot breezes. The sun was out, the temperature a perfect 78°F. From the deep blue of the ocean, flocks of flying fish fled PALAEMON's bow, sailing on the wind, bouncing off the waves, their silver-blue bodies almost invisible against the sea and sky. We lay on the foredeck in swimsuits, wrapped in the rhythm of the waves, the hiss of the bow wake, the warmth of the sun on our skin.

The nights at sea can be at least as beautiful as the days. The surrounding darkness is alive with light, the sea luminescent with phosphorus. PALAEMON leaves a sparkling wake stretching hundreds of yards. Moonless, as it has been on this passage, and beyond the loom of the land, we can always see the Milky Way, a huge swath of white cloud that appears magically in the dark sky. Meteors, sometimes a shower, flame through the atmosphere. God's roman candles. I had no idea there were so many. At first I jumped at each one, fearing it was a distress flare from another boat. Venus rises so huge on the horizon that I mistake it for the moon. Sirius, the brightest navigational star, describes a path across the water like moonglow, lighting PALAEMON's way.

Beautiful right now it is not. And I really can't believe that we are spending days in a salt-drenched boat, wondering whether the rig will hold, or whether one of those phosphorescent cascades off a 20-foot wave is about to land in the cockpit, in order to go sunbathing or stargazing. A 747 goes great to windward.

We could have hired a boat for a family Christmas cruise in the Virgin Islands. The stars are pretty bright from a calm anchorage in the BVI, too.

There's something elusive and elemental about why we are out here. Many of our friends would think sheer perversity an adequate explanation. While perhaps necessary, that is not a sufficient answer. Compulsiveness surely plays some part. A need to go to the next level in an activity that we love. There is also that dream we have been dreaming for nearly twenty years. It is not just ours. Sailing magazines simply call it "The Dream." Half the couples piloting daysailers on Long Island Sound are dreaming about a bigger boat and going cruising. For us—for everyone, we suspect—the dream is a vision of both achievement and escape.

Escape from many things: tedium mostly, the humdrum responsibilities and frustrations of daily living. Out here, there's no commute, no work schedule, no social calendar. The phone never rings. If we missed Aunt Mabel's birthday—well, it just couldn't be helped. Because of our watch schedule, we keep a pretty good grasp on the time. But since we have moved aboard, we often have to look up the day and date. I have even managed to misplace the month—a feat that I accomplish rarely on land.

But that can't be the whole story. Not even a big part of it. Our lives on land have been blessed. No people in their right minds could be running away from them except temporarily, as we are. Nor are we so naive as to believe that the sea erases responsibilities and frustrations. Responsibility is ever-present: the necessity to keep watch, to maintain and repair the complex mechanisms that make PALAEMON function, to navigate and calculate incessantly. Frustrations abound. A lack of wind is chief among them. Right behind that is spending fifteen minutes donning your foulies because the wind is howling and the seas are mountainous.

These seagoing frustrations and seakeeping responsibilities have the virtue of being different. And they feed the achievement side of the dream. I can now read the weather pretty well, repair most things on a marine diesel engine, and interpret radar images. I do plumbing and wiring, too. But these are pretty modest achievements. My skills at any of these tasks are pale shadows of those possessed by your neighborhood garage mechanic, the toothy guy who forecasts the weather on Channel 8, or the average tugboat captain.

Some sailors claim that this combination of escape and achievement (or competence) creates a feeling of self-sufficiency, independence. That, they say, is really the joy of the cruising life. For the nonmilitant and only mildly paranoid, it's the equivalent of joining a militia and heading for a cave in Idaho.

Perhaps. But our cruising independence seems to me to be a pretty fragile construct. We are out "on our own" in part because of technological marvels that are the work of many minds and many hands.

I am in constant communion with our GPS chartplotter and our devoted third crew member, Otto. I am sitting here "independently" on my night watch in no small measure because somebody designed and built Otto and the GPS. I'm not about to throw Otto or the GPS overboard because they connect me to technological civilization and undermine my independence. Anne and I may be nutty, but not nutty enough to try to hand-steer PALAEMON 1,500 continuous miles, by ourselves, while taking inaccurate sextant sights, if there is any way to avoid it.

There is, of course, the overall plan—to use this trip just to have the luxury of time together. But we could have found a place in Florence or Provence. It's not like we couldn't "get away from it all" on land, if that just means the everyday demands of our everyday lives. Living abroad has adventures, too. If you believe Peter Mayle, every day in Provence is a new one. Not only that, our life together offshore consists mostly of incoherent, sleep-deprived mumbles as we change watches and careen around the cabin. We have had little opportunity for a sustained conversation on any topic but weather and boathandling since we left Bald Head Island. To give each other a kiss or a hug at the moment risks broken teeth or a concussion.

The truth of the matter, or some part of the truth of the matter, may be that we have partially disappeared into our roles as sailors. Or, more positively (I'm not feeling very positive right now), sailing is now part of our identity. Because we are sailors, we are doing what sailors do, making passages to get somewhere we want to be. If we don't do it, we have to give up that identity, throw those boat cards over the side, or re-imagine the identities they suggest. When we get to the BVI, we will be glad we have done it offshore. As time passes, the stories of the passage will get better and better, the bruises and the queasiness and the fright will turn into punch lines. We'll feel great about our accomplishment. Selective memory, retrospective myopia, will triumph again. We'll be ecstatic. We're idiots!

About an hour ago, a clear strong return on the radar screen interrupted my reveries. The blip was of a size and intensity that would normally indicate a small ship. The strange thing was that it showed up at only 2 miles away rather than the usual 5 or 6. This phantom craft then closed to within a few hundred yards, but there were no responses to my repeated, and increasingly frantic, radio calls. Scanning astern with the binoculars, I could see nothing, even though the sky was so bright that I should have been able to see anything larger than a petrel at 500 yards.

Still unidentified, the radar return dropped back to about a mile and a half; it closed again to within half a mile; then it disappeared from the screen as suddenly as it had appeared. Another mystery of the Bermuda Triangle.

It's true. There is joy and adventure and freedom and accomplishment in what we're doing. But rolling those all together doesn't quite tell me what we're up to, or why. If anything, I am more puzzled now than when we left—and simultaneously more committed. Anne feels the same way. Why?

On night watch, I contemplate these mysteries. Anne says she does, too. Perhaps the opportunity to contemplate mysteries is part of the key to the mystery itself. "Opportunity" is not quite right. "Necessity" is more like it. There's nothing else to do. To confront the vast emptiness of the sea is sometimes to confront myself, to ask myself questions that I can't answer. To accept that I can't, that I have limits—severe ones. I go on asking until I can't stand the sound of my voice in my head.

It's time to make Anne some hot chocolate. I want to talk to her about what I've been thinking. But not as much as I want to go to sleep. If I can get into the bunk fast enough, the scent of her body will still be there. I will go to sleep drunk on the fragrance of her skin.

ANNE'S PASSAGE NOTES: NIGHT WATCHES

We are headed for the British Virgin Islands. We are ninety minutes into my first night watch on our fourth night out from Cape Fear. Ninety minutes more and I can sleep. Then I have the midnight watch, then another blessed three hours (two and a half, at best) to sleep. I think about sleep. I long for sleep. I am huddled in my usual spot under the dodger on the port side of the cockpit, where I can keep reasonably dry and still see the navigational instruments below.

The quartering seas are ferocious, much larger and more confused than our 25-to-35-knot wind speed would suggest. Some distant force is stirring the Atlantic bowl, creating waves running at angles to those blown up by our local winds. These competing seas sometimes combine to produce enormous waves, cresting and toppling, frothing, potentially dangerous if not handled properly. These monsters jerk PALAEMON's stern and pound her bow. They send streams of water into the cockpit. Occasionally spray goes below, even with the hatch closed and the bottom weatherboard in place. I look out at the seas and wonder for the umpteenth time what we're doing out here. I know Jerry wonders, too, but it hardly helps to talk about it now. And I wonder, also for the umpteenth time, whether we should have taken on extra crew for this passage. As usual, my thoughts go in circles and I come to no conclusions.

It is increasingly squally. I stand up, beginning my every-fifteen-minute routine, hanging onto the dodger to peer over it into the night and scan the horizon for ships, before checking the instruments below deck. Damn, it looks like a ship off to starboard. I do not want to turn on the radar, now on standby, because it eats so much energy. A particularly big wave puts water in the cockpit up to my ankles, and I watch the speedo. It has been creeping up with the wind; we are now touching on 8 knots—too fast. I look for the ship again. Lights are clearly evident now. I crowbar myself below and turn the radar to transmit. The ship is crawling to the west and will pass on our starboard side. A couple of knots come out of my stomach. But not out of our speed.

I go back to the speed problem. We need to reduce sail. With his greater strength, Jerry is much better at this than I am. I do not want to call him. He has gone into a deep sleep, unusual on his early night off-watch. The mainsail is OK, but the foresail should have a deeper reef. I wait as long as I dare. Then, as we touch on 8½ knots, I wrap the furling line around the secondary winch and apply myself to the winch handle. I get in a few inches. The effort seems to take every bit of strength I have, but it is enough. The squalliness abates a bit, and we are riding more easily, although the roll remains vicious. I check the state of the batteries and our course. The changes in sail and wind speed have altered PALAEMON's course slightly. I adjust Otto a few degrees.

I settle weakly back into my port-side huddle. Soon our speed is down to 5 knots. The wind has slacked. But I do not want to unfurl what I just fought to bring in. Besides, I rationalize, the wind will probably pick up again any minute. So we lose time for a bit, as I continue my routine until the clock tells me it is the end of my watch.

I work myself below and brace into the nav station using knees, feet, and left arm. I record our position and weather data and plot our position on the universal plotting sheets. (These are empty sheets, except for latitude and longitude lines stepped off in unnamed degrees and minutes.) This effort requires bracing hard with my left hand and my legs. Otherwise, I will take frequent partial tumbles out of the nav station.

Our progress looks infinitesimal on these sheets. How can we be going so fast and not getting anywhere?

I wake Jerry. I have given him a few extra minutes. His eyes are startled pools as he remembers where he is. I would kiss him, but I am afraid that I would bash my head into his. He chooses tea over hot chocolate, and while he pulls himself together and struggles into his gear, I hand-over-hand myself into the galley and belt myself in. I hold onto the teakettle until the water is boiling, then set the mug in the sink to pour the boiling water. I struggle out of my gear, telling Jerry the state of things, admitting painfully that I have left him sailhandling to do.

My watch handoffs provide stray moments of tension. I have adrenaline flowing and want to talk. Jerry just wants quiet as he emerges from the fog of heavy sleep and the relative still of our sea berth and confronts our lurching home. Finally he tells me, in his grumpiest voice, to quit fooling around and go to bed. He clips on his safety harness and climbs into the cockpit. Gradually I unwind and fall into the bunk, still warm from his body. He is already edging sail out, his tea carefully wedged into a corner of the cockpit sole, somehow escaping salt spray.

I sleep a drugged, dreamless sleep and wake to the touch of Jerry's hand on my cheek. It is an unimaginable gentleness in the midst of the wildness around us, and I find tears in my eyes. He has already made me hot chocolate. The wind and seas are up again, sails reefed, no ships. I settle into my port huddle, trying to wake up.

I think once again about the question of extra crew. I would now have three more hours of sleep ahead, instead of three hours of struggling with sails and winds and seas. Yet, the answer to this one question at last is bell-clear. No help from added crew could possibly be worth compromising the tenderness that Jerry and I share in this small, tossing world.

HAVE A GOOD WATCH

Our communications equipment for coastal sailing has always been simple and inexpensive. Our VHF radio was long our only means for checking on the weather, and for calling marinas, other vessels, or the Coast Guard in case of emergency. Close ashore, we could call a marine operator and get patched into land-based telephone systems. But like most boats, we now have a cell phone, and VHF marine telephone operators are a disappearing breed. Both VHF and cellular work pretty reliably within 15 to 20 miles of the shore. When cruising inshore, we listen to NOAA weather first thing in the morning; it's the last thing we hear before hitting the bunk for the night.

We are currently out of range of all this familiar stuff. The loss of NOAA forecasts is not as big a blow as it once would have been. Since Congress eliminated the funding for more than half of NOAA's observation sites, their prognostications cover wider and wider areas and are less and less likely to describe what the weather will be in any one spot—that is, our spot. But the weather is not likely to be worse than NOAA predicts. A successful lawsuit by the heirs of some deceased fisherman, who relied on a balmy forecast and went down in a near-hurricane, has made NOAA's warnings positively alarmist. Every predicted rainstorm is now said to carry the possibility of "hail and damaging winds." Heat-wave forecasts are followed by advice on how to keep cool and hydrated, information that would insult the intelligence of a four-year-old. This weather-nanny boilerplate must be written by lawyers rather than meteorologists, and we never have any idea when the meteorologists might actually believe it. NOAA weather is also now read by a synthesized computer voice that sounds like a demented alien.

Out here in the middle of nowhere, access to current weather information becomes more complex. And the expense goes up exponentially. At the high end of technology and cost, we could have had our own satellite telephone for voice and data. With that and a laptop, we could have accessed the Internet and the extraordinary amount of weather info posted there by weather services all over the world. But we are not satellite-telephone equipped. We're playing the usual odds that two years from now, these things will cost a quarter of their current prices and be twice as reliable. Besides, the satellite phone was just too damned expensive.

We rely instead on single sideband radio (SSB), a variation on a ham set that gives us access to radio signals of virtually any frequency and wavelength. A few years ago, tuning one of these boxes required real skill. Today's sets allow random digital access to any frequency and have self-tuning antennas. We've had to learn something about radio-wave propagation in order to choose a frequency that will transmit or receive a readable signal, given the time of day and distance between stations. But that something is sufficiently modest that the Federal Communications Commission no longer requires any evidence of competence before issuing an SSB license.

With our SSB, we are connected. The state of the world can be determined from the BBC; the state of the United States from Armed Forces Radio's rebroadcast of National Public Radio news. More important, the SSB provides multiple paths to the weather. Coast Guard stations in Boston, Norfolk, and New Orleans provide voice and weatherfax forecasts several times a day. With an appropriate black box and a laptop, the SSB becomes a fax machine for receiving weatherfaxes. We have one of these, but I can't get it to work. An expensive add-on to the SSB will even provide Internet capability through a laptop, but the cost is high and the reliability is poor, so we gave that a pass too.

All this would seem to be enough weather access. But it's not. The Coast Guard broadcasts and weatherfaxes cover tens of thousands of square miles of ocean. Moreover, they are broadcast in a rapid-fire monotone that defies immediate understanding. I have to record them, play the tapes over and over, and plot the weather-system coordinates on a large-scale chart before finally becoming reasonably confident that I know what the guy said was happening where and when. After laboring at this for an hour, I can make my own weather predictions. That is, I can get today's wind direction right most of the time, predict wind speed within 10 knots or so, and make a reasonable guess at wave heights.

But there is a real art to forecasting two or three days out. To predict what might be in store five days hence, I would need access to information on global weather patterns, a lot of experience, and considerable chutzpah. The chutzpah is all that I currently have on board, and my supply of that is declining. Moreover, our interest is usually in a few hundred square miles of water, not the whole southwest North Atlantic. The standard reports give us too much information about where we are not, and too little about where we are. When bringing old PALAEMON up from Fort Lauderdale, we spent thirty-six hours in gale-force winds and 20-foot seas off Beaufort, North Carolina, neither of which was ever mentioned anywhere in the official weather forecasts.

Our uncertainty about the weather—constant high anxiety is perhaps more descriptive—is shared by other offshore cruisers. It has given rise to a host of professional and amateur "weather nets" that come up at designated times on various SSB frequencies. Some are commercial forecasters who, for a fee, will provide customized forecasts for your vessel's position and proposed track. Others are more like chat groups, in which each vessel reports what things are like and where they are at the moment, along with gossip, recipes, and personal opinions on the state of the world.

The Big Daddy of custom forecasts is "Herb." Herb Hilgenberg started his net as a hobby years ago, when he was living aboard SOUTHBOUND II and working in Bermuda. Herb is not a professional meteorologist, but he is a truly gifted and dedicated amateur. Over the years, his reputation and audience have grown to include virtually everyone sailing the North Atlantic and the Caribbean. We have even heard him giving advice to sailors leaving South Africa or the Galápagos. When Herb's work permit ran out in Bermuda, he moved back to Canada. He seems now to devote himself full time to weather forecasting.

While Herb has some commercial contracts with tugs, freighters, and high-stakes offshore races, he provides daily individualized forecasts for hundreds of cruisers—for free—although a thank-you note and a donation are accepted practice among Herb's groupies. And Herb's forecasts contain more than just the weather. If you ask—and sometimes if you don't—Herb will tell you what to do about it. Whether to try crossing the Gulf Stream or not, where to cross and at what angle, whether to stay north or south of your present latitude given what's going to happen three days hence. And so on. Herb estimates your average boat speed and has predicted where you are likely to be and what you will want to know before you check in and provide your position. Linus has his security blanket; offshore cruisers have Herb.

There is a small cost for all this attention. If you are in Herb's net, you must check in every day when on passage. He has prepared a report for you, and you'd damn well better be there to get it. If you slip up, he will punish you the next day by saying that because he didn't know where you were (fat chance), he couldn't prepare a report. It's like not showing up for dinner when Mom cooked your favorite potatoes. The guilt is overwhelming. Lots of cruisers listen to Herb every day but don't check in. They don't want the responsibility of living up to Herb's expectations.

But there's a big advantage to being in Herb's net. If you don't check in, Herb knows about it. If you don't check in and you're in rough conditions, Herb starts trying to find out why. And he will keep trying until he gets some sort of answer. Herb is also amazingly accurate.

We left Bald Head Island on Herb's forecast of a good window for crossing the Gulf Stream, west to southwesterlies at 15 to 20 knots. He was right on the money. We scooted across in great conditions, plotting the path of the stream by recording water-temperature changes—low 80s in the stream, mid- to high 70s outside it.

Our course hasn't changed 5 degrees since we left the Carolina coast. We're following the conventional wisdom that we need to get out to at least the longitude of Bermuda, 65°W, perhaps even farther east, before dropping south of 30°N. Somewhere between there and 25°N, the trade winds should kick in from the east. If we still needed to go east at that point, we would be in for a rough, slow ride. Rough and fast is bad enough; we sure don't want rough and slow.

Every day between 1530 and 1600 Zulu, Greenwich Mean Time, cruisers all over the Atlantic are making calls similar to ours:

"SOUTHBOUND II, SOUTHBOUND II, this is the sailing vessel PALAEMON, Whiskey, Charlie, Zulu, 4745, 35° 20' north, 67° 38' west. Standing by."

Herb does not respond during the thirty-minute check-in period. He is plotting boats' positions, grouping them in clusters for his later prognostications. At 1600 sharp, Herb comes on and announces his plan for the day. He normally starts with boats near Nova Scotia or New England, moves down the eastern seaboard, picks up vessels bound to Bermuda and the Caribbean, sweeps through Florida, Puerto Rico and the Bahamas and then out to sea, to vessels between Africa or Europe and the United States or the West Indies. After perhaps an hour of monitoring his communications with other boats, we hear the familiar:

"PALAEMON, how do you copy?"

"Good copy, Herb. The wind here is north by northwest, 20 knots, some higher gusts, seas 6 to 10 feet, broken clouds, barometer 1015 millibars and steady. How copy?"

"That's about right. Your barometer is a little high. I have 1013 at your position. You should see pretty much those same conditions into tomorrow, tomorrow night time frame. That ridge south of you is almost stationary. I would keep your present heading for another day or so, keep you in that westerly flow above the front line. That ridge has embedded squall lines, winds 35 knots, maybe higher. How copy?"

"Good copy, Herb. Thanks very much. Good to have you on board. Talk to you tomorrow. PALAEMON standing by, 12359 megahertz."

"See you tomorrow. Have a good watch! All clear with PALAEMON. WILD GOOSE, how do you copy?"

Every day we talk to Herb to find how far south we can point and still make our easting. Every day I pull out my calculator to multiply our barometer's reading in inches by 33.864 to get the millibar scale that Herb demands. Most days, he thinks the barometer is a little off. Sometimes he questions my wind and wave reports, as if he were sitting in PALAEMON's cockpit rather than in Toronto. Every day, Herb's advice is the same. We are still just on the northern edge of the front that is providing continuous northwesterlies on our side of it, but only easterlies to the south. Revising Horace Greeley's advice, Herb's is always, "Go east, young man, go east."

We are going east at a good clip in what are, for us, pretty impressive seas. But as we listen to reports on Herb's other boats scattered across the Atlantic, from Nova Scotia to Florida, from Barbados to the Azores, we decide we're having a fine time of it. Gale systems are springing up everywhere, and Herb is holding boats in harbors all up and down the East Coast. Those at sea to the north of us are really taking a beating, notwithstanding Herb's constant efforts to guide them toward the calmer edges of nasty weather systems.

We begin to crave the comfort of this radio traffic, listening to boats struggling with worse weather than we have—and surviving. The voices wafting out of the ether reflect vastly different experience and confidence levels. On being told that he is looking at three days of 45-knot-plus winds if he keeps his current heading, a gruff tugboat skipper replies, "I guess that's why they pay me to take this thing to someplace specific."

Another cruiser in similar straits says in near panic, "Herb, should we turn back?" Trying to keep the exasperation out of his voice, Herb replies, "Only if you want to spend four days in that storm instead of two, and then start your passage all over again." My sense is that this woman does not want to start this or any other passage again—ever.

After six days of following Herb's "go east" advice, we are closing on 65°W, but we haven't moved 30 miles south of our starting latitude (about 35°N) at Bald Head Island. We are feeling frustrated. We plan to tell Herb this afternoon that we're thinking about turning southeast, angling toward a position at about 25°N 64°W. When we get there, we hope to head south in earnest.

Before we reveal our intentions, Herb gives us some startling news. A major low is forming just south of Cuba. It's late in the year, but Herb doesn't like the look of it. He predicts a rapidly developing hurricane that is likely to shoot up through the Windward Passage between Cuba and Hispaniola. If it does, it will intercept us before we can reach the BVI.

We are, to put it mildly, stunned. It is mid-November. This is not supposed to happen. Yet, just last year, Hurricane Mitch did a similar number on a group of boats participating in the West Marine 1500 Rally from Norfolk to Virgin Gorda. Three boats were lost, many damaged. Mitch had been in the western Caribbean, headed at Central America and the Pacific, when the rally started. Less than a week later, he reversed direction, crossed Florida, and caught part of the rally fleet still at sea.

We do not want to mess around with a capricious November hurricane. But this one is not yet formed and has no sense of direction. Which way should we go—straight up?

Herb suggests the obvious. Go north, not south. Bermuda is only 55 miles away. Make safe harbor and wait to see what happens. Of course. How could we have thought that this passage would turn out differently from our other planned itineraries? We should have known that we are not headed at the Caribbean. We are simply wandering around the Bermuda Triangle waiting to see where we wash up.

While confident that Herb's advice is sound, I have to confess to my own imprudence. We have not planned to go to Bermuda and thus have no chart of the island or its harbors. (I am beginning to think I should have bought a chart for Greenland, too.) We can find Bermuda easily enough, but the island is surrounded by reefs. How are we going to get in?

No problem. Herb comes back in his military mode: "HERMAN MELVILLE, HERMAN MELVILLE, did you copy my conversation with PALAEMON?"

HERMAN MELVILLE: "Roger that, Herb."

Herb: "You have waypoints for approaching St. George's Harbour, don't you?"

HERMAN MELVILLE: "Roger that, Herb."

Herb: "Switch to 12365 and give them to PALAEMON."

HERMAN MELVILLE: "Roger that, Herb."

We've been listening to Jerome on HERMAN MELVILLE talk to Herb for the last several days. Herb and Jerome obviously go back awhile. I switch to

12365, confident that HERMAN MELVILLE will obey Herb's commands. It's hard not to say, "Yes, sir," rather than "Roger" when Herb tells you to do something. I find Jerome already on frequency. He gives me coordinates for approaching Bermuda well clear of the reefs and then the coordinates for the sea buoy leading to St. George's Harbour. I ask Jerome whether he is heading for Bermuda, too. He says he hasn't decided yet. He would like to press on for the BVI. He's sailing in company with some other boats. They'll have a radio conference and talk it over. When Jerome is transmitting, I can hear a female voice in the background saying, "We're going to Bermuda, Jerome."

The wind has been dropping for the past twelve hours and the seas are subsiding. This is good news. As we turn north toward Bermuda, we are punching into the seas, heading directly into the wind. We turn on the engine. It runs for about ten minutes, coughs, and dies.

I scramble down the companionway stairs, remove them, and open the doors to the engine compartment. If a diesel engine fails to run, the likely culprit is failure to get enough fuel, often caused by a clogged filter in the line between the tank and the engine. There may be a host of other reasons, but this is the one I am hoping for. It's the simplest to remedy.

I open the filter housing and remove the filter, slopping diesel all over the cabin sole, the engine compartment, and me. PALAEMON is now dead in the water, rolling with the slop. The filter is filled with black grit, the fuel in the housing looks dark. I drain off a quart of fuel and prime the engine to get the air out of the lines.

Anne cranks and the engine fires, runs ten seconds, and stops. I prime again. This time it runs—for another twenty minutes. Two filter changes later, the engine stays on. By now the fuel is looking pretty clear. For all we know, PALAEMON's fuel tank hasn't been cleaned since it left Bristol Yachts seventeen years ago. Our rough ride has probably stirred up years of sediment accumulated on the floor of the tank and mixed it with the fuel. If we're lucky, there were only three filters worth of junk in there. An hour of tossing around in the Atlantic, crouched over the engine, bathed in diesel fuel, has tested the limits of my immunity to motion sickness.

By the time I scrub myself clean of diesel, the wind has all but died. The leftover swells become gentler and gentler. The air feels soft, with a hint of land. As the sky darkens, we watch the bow rise and fall through a diaphanous mushroom on the horizon, the loom of lights on Bermuda.

I check the mileage. Bermuda is 700 miles from Bald Head Island. Jost Van Dyke in the BVI is 900 miles from Bermuda. We're not even going to make it halfway before stopping. Two days ago, heading into a safe harbor seemed like heaven. Tonight I want just as badly to keep going, complete the passage, then relax. What if we're making this detour for nothing? Herb's forecast is based as much on intuition as on fact.

I am not seasick, but I feel slightly dizzy, a sense of disorientation that I often get when caught between strongly conflicting desires. We have almost come to terms with the fatigue and fear of offshore sailing; we are in a rhythm we know we can sustain. Hurricanes aside, we are feeling confident about PALAEMON and ourselves. Making the BVI was just a matter of a week, not two. Now it's back into port, get accustomed to the land again, readapt to the sea when we leave. Will it be easier now that we know more about what to expect, how our bodies and minds and the boat will react?

Jerome calls back. They've turned north, heading for Bermuda. I tell him we'll look for them there and buy them a drink at that famous St. George's watering hole, the White Horse Inn. "Terrific," Jerome exclaims. "I'll have a 'dark and stormy.'" I figure that's a sailor's drink—I'm embarrassed to ask. My spirits lift a bit. What's wrong with some time ashore? We're no longer in a rush.

Thanks, Herb. Keep up the good watch.

ANNE'S PASSAGE NOTES: RADIOSPEAK

I am amused and amazed by the talk I hear on the VHF and the SSB. When we left Connecticut, we knew VHF radio basics, but we had never gotten the lingo, tone, and rhythm of the real stuff. We had not yet used the SSB.

Now, when at sea or traveling through busy harbors, we keep the VHF on fairly constantly. We also use the SSB regularly, picking up bits of information from the chat nets, keeping in touch with weather and news sources, and tuning in Herb. Most days provide a heavy dose of radiospeak.

I find this talk puzzling, rather like an English dialect full of familiar words but rendered almost unintelligible by peculiar word usages and strange rhythms. First, there's constant reference to "Roger," often repeated many times, like *si, si* in Italian or *oui, oui* in French. But "Roger, Roger, Roger, Roger" seems a little much. Not even the loquacious Italians string together four *si*'s. "Roger" is often followed by "that," although never "Roger, Roger that." Moreover, "Roger," although generally a noun, and a man's given name at that, has a distinctly verb-like quality in this context. It appears to mean, "I understand," or sometimes, "I agree." So, for example, I might hear Jerry saying, "If these conditions keep up, we'll be reefing down even more. Over." And the answering vessel replies, "Roger that. Roger that. I guess we ought to be thinking about that too. Over."

Certainly there are parts of the lingo that perform necessary functions. It is important to use some word (the word of choice is "over"), for example, to signal that you have completed what you have to say, and another party may now speak. The technology requires a signal of this sort, because it will not allow two people to talk at once. But why "over"? You aren't really "over" at all. When you have actually finished talking, you sign off by saying, "out," or "over and out," or "PALAEMON to 16," or "PALAEMON on the side," or "PALAEMON clear"—yet another wonderful set of phrases, each presumably with its own place and special meaning. But why "over"? Why not "pause," "stop," or "finished"? "Break" might work nicely, but it has other uses.

You often hear a "break," and sometimes a double, triple, or quadruple "break"—as in "Break, break, break, break. This is Marcie Davis with the offshore net." The person uttering the word, or words, is a "breaker," as in: first vessel, "Break, break, break"; second vessel, "I think I heard a breaker in there." ("*In* there?") "Break" clearly means that the breaker wants to get in a word. But it is not clear who gets to be a breaker and when. As I listen to breaker practice and try to understand breaker etiquette, it sometimes seems that you should not break unless you have something important to say. But sometimes not. Sometimes it seems simply a way to let others know you have joined the conversation.

Why that should be necessary, I can't imagine. Everybody eavesdrops on everybody else's conversations all the time anyway, and everybody knows that everybody else is eavesdropping. It *is* irresistible. If you hear someone you know calling someone else on a designated calling frequency, you just have to switch channels to hear what they're up to. It would be almost rude if you didn't. So if Jerry is in the midst of a conversation, and he hasn't heard some other party speak, he may say, "MIDNIGHT, MIDNIGHT, are you on frequency, do you copy?" Likely as not, MIDNIGHT will chime in with, "Roger that, PALAEMON, roger that. This is MIDNIGHT." "Breakers" are often nothing more than eavesdroppers coming out of hiding.

"Copy" is another mystery to me. At first I thought people were actually writing things down, or perhaps recording them. In my very early radio conversations with Herb (which I did not, by the way, continue), I hesitated to say the usual, "Good copy, Herb, good copy." I wasn't copying everything down. Indeed, I wasn't copying anything down. I was too busy struggling to understand Herb and his troughs and ridges. But I was wrong about "copy." It just seems to mean that the signal came through. Yet it can also mean *understanding*, as in: (Herb) "Are you with me so far? Over." (Response) "Copy that, Herb." Why didn't the speaker say, "Roger that"? Of course you wouldn't say, "Good roger, good roger," but why not just say, "I hear you," or "Good signal?"

The level of repetition suggests a community afflicted by generalized stuttering. It does kind of hit you in the face, doesn't it, doesn't it? Roger, roger, roger. Break, break, break, break. How copy? How copy? The repetition generates a surprising sense of urgency, despite a generally flat delivery. The delivery does have its proper inflections and tone, though. The last "break" usually gets more emphasis than the first, for example, and is sung in a higher key. The "that" after "roger" gets more emphasis than the "that" after "copy." Usually.

I notice that men adopt these patterns and inflections more readily and with more flair than women. This is something about which Jerry and I are not of one mind. But he has not heard himself. I am beside myself with amusement when I hear him "rogering that" in the right places and with exactly the right tone almost immediately. Here is the man with whom I have lived for years, the man I love and think I know, speaking a strange tongue in a voice that is not his. Where did he get it? I eventually adopt "roger" myself briefly. It is a mistake. I have to limit myself to "over," which is one word I have found I can handle, or I find myself "rogering" when I should be "overing." Unlike men, women generally retain most of their normal speech patterns on the radio, adopting little of the lingo and almost none of the tone. Why, I wonder.

And why is radiospeak limited to the radio? Why doesn't it spill over into cockpit conversation? How can it fail to slip into stories told over rum punches? It never does, although I did once hear Jerry "rogering that" over the phone to a directory assistance operator. He did not find this as funny as I did.

Still curious, I look up "roger" in the dictionary. Its history is varied and not traceable to its current radio usage. "Roger" is probably related to "rogue," and is Teutonic in origin. Aside from its use as a man's given name, "Roger" has been used to mean a sudden squall, a ram, a goose. It is the skull-and-crossbones pirate flag. Jolly? The word seems to engender confusion. I do ultimately find a meaning listed under "radio and signaling," a spoken version of "r" that originally stood for "received." This hardly makes things clearer for me. Why not say, "Received"? Or, at least why not use the nautical term for "r," "Romeo?" On the other hand, I guess "Romeo that" would introduce yet other forms of confusion.

So I try to avoid the radio. It makes me tongue-tied. But I enjoy Jerry's increasing skills. I appreciate them most fully when he is competently and courteously dealing with yet another freighter whose captain has headed his tons of bananas from Colombia straight at PALAEMON. Come to think of it, even all those guys with their halting English say, "Roger that." Where do *they* get it?

12

BERMUDA: THE GEM OF THE OCEAN

Heading for Jerome's waypoint, we run up the coast of Bermuda in the breaking dawn. As the sun begins to paint the hills green and the houses pink, white, green, and ochre, we enter a cut through the reefs. After seven days at sea, the smells of earth, foliage, and flowers are all distinct on the wind. A week of staring at only sea, sun, clouds, and stars seems to have impaired my brain's capacity to process multiple visual signals. The ordinary panorama of land-based shapes and colors overloads the circuits. We are nearly dancing on the decks as we pass between the limestone bluffs that guard St. George's Harbour. A friendly nod and wave from a fisherman ashore brings tears to our eyes.

The combination of sleep deprivation and hyperattentiveness to every movement and sound on PALAEMON has stretched our nerves snare-drum tight. Landfall sends our emotions into orbit. We have to work hard to keep a grip on ourselves.

I remember learning in Psychology 101 about what the behavioral psych guys call "goal gradient." The closer you are to your goal, the more pull it exerts on your emotions. As my psych professor put it, "Most bookcases are ruined while putting in the last shelf." Lots of yachts go on the rocks within hailing distance of their anchorage.

A wonderful institution called Bermuda Harbour Radio—BHR—virtually will not let you make a last-minute mistake approaching Bermuda. By international agreement, no ship carrying oil, or having a gross weight of over 100 tons, is allowed within 30 miles of the island without special clearance. *All* vessels must report to BHR when within that range of Bermuda and follow any BHR instructions concerning their approach.

While this sounds officious, in the hands of the BHR folks it is welcoming instead.

PALAEMON: "BHR, BHR this is the sailing vessel PALAEMON, Whiskey, Charlie, Zulu, 4745, approximately 30 miles south southwest of Bermuda at 31° 45' north, 64° 50' west."

BHR: "Good morning, PALAEMON. Welcome to Bermuda. I have you on radar. Can we provide any assistance with your approach?"

PALAEMON: "No, thank you—well, actually I was wondering how far off to stand as we run up the coast to the sea buoy outside St. George's."

BHR: "Roger, PALAEMON. If you stay about three miles off, you can't get into any trouble. Give us a call back when you are off Gibbs Hill Light and we will collect some information on your vessel. Have you visited Bermuda in your yacht before?"

PALAEMON: "No, we have not."

BHR: "Roger. I didn't find you in our computer. Well, I hope you've had a good passage and we will talk to you later."

This is not, in our experience, the sort of chat that one normally has with harbormasters at home or border officials anywhere in the world. Indeed, our entry into Bermuda is so civilized, so welcoming, that we fall in love with the place. Consider these items from just our first few hours.

Item: We are approaching the channel into St. George's Harbour and have decided to cut a buoy marking shallows that we believe we can safely pass over. The VHF crackles:

"PALAEMON, this is BHR. Do you see a buoy with a yellow cone off your starboard bow?"

"Roger, BHR."

"Well, you might find it more comfortable if you leave that buoy to port when entering the channel."

"Roger, BHR. Thanks very much."

What this exquisitely polite fellow meant, of course, was, "You're taking a chance of running aground and causing us no end of trouble saving you. So could you please stay in the well-marked channel, you lunkhead."

Item: At the customs dock, we are greeted by Adam, a customs official. We have arrived thirty minutes before the office opens. Do we get a surly stare and an order to come back later? Not on your life. "Welcome to Bermuda," he says, while helping with our lines. "The office will be open in just a few minutes. Meanwhile, if you'll just make yourselves comfortable, I'll zip in and get the forms so you can fill them out while you're waiting. Sorry about the delay and all these formalities."

This is a customs officer? Maybe Bermuda could set up a training school for customs officials worldwide. The formalities turn out to be minimal. Even so, Adam helps us fill out the forms because he says he finds them "a little confusing in their wording." I find it hard to keep my jaw from hanging open when people say sensible, friendly, helpful things like that. I fear that I'm staring at Adam like he's an extraterrestrial. Adam may be at the extreme end of the Bermudian customs service's friendliness scale when greeting arriving yachts. After further conversation, he admits to being the newly crowned Etchells one-design champion of Bermuda and a member of its Olympic sailing team.

Item: While we're checking in with Adam in the comfort of our cockpit, along comes Bernie Oately on his motorbike. A drinker's nose and Santa Claus eyes peek out from under Bernie's crash helmet. The nose clashes mightily with his orange windbreaker. His checked Bermuda shorts are as jarring to the eye as they are appropriate to the locale. Bernie, it seems, is the assistant harbormaster, semiofficial town greeter, and godfather to all yachties who enter St. George's Harbour.

Bernie bears a letter of welcome from the mayor of St. George's, inviting us to come by the town hall to say hello and be given a tour. He also has an invitation to a cocktail party and buffet being given two nights hence by the various yachting service establishments in St. George's, just to show their appreciation to all the visiting yachts for stopping by. Bernie explains our mooring, anchoring, and dockage options; where various services can be found; what BHR's weather forecast is for the next several days and the latest news on the developing low-pressure cell that drove us ashore. He then hands us a card with his home phone number, should we need assistance, and offers to meet us at the dock we have chosen to help with the lines.

Why in the name of Poseidon had we not planned to come to Bermuda in the first place? Should we ever leave?

13

BERMUDA FOREVER

Herb's instincts were right again. Within twenty-four hours of his warning, the low became Tropical Storm Lenny. In seventy-two hours, Lenny was a hurricane—a strong one. For the next few days, it wandered slowly the wrong way—due east rather than the Atlantic hurricanes' usual north, northwest, and then northeast track—just south of our destination in the BVI and through the northern Leeward Islands. In St. Martin, we heard, 160 boats were grounded or sunk in one harbor. Lenny's massive waves washed out roads and demolished beachfront properties as far south as Grenada. Instead of dodging a rogue hurricane, we are sitting in beautiful St. George's Harbour. Thanks, Herb, yet again.

Finding yourself in Bermuda while headed somewhere else is something of a sailing tradition. Bermuda is in the middle of nowhere and, as we have just demonstrated, on the way to everywhere. Many have washed ashore after foundering on the reefs that ring the island and sustain its very existence. Crusty coral sprouts from wrecks that bore the flags and treasure of all the great sixteenth- and seventeenth-century trading powers—Spain, Portugal, Holland, England. Sir George Somers put his flagship, DELIVERANCE, on Bermuda's reefs in 1609 while headed to Virginia to shore up the desperate Jamestown colony. Somers's wreck led directly to England's colonization of Bermuda. Both colonies ultimately prospered, but I must confess that I would trade Jamestown for Bermuda in a minute.

Bermuda's position—near the shipping lanes for the triangular or rectangular trade and its reef-encircled coastline—has permitted enterprising and seafaring Bermudians to turn a tidy profit for centuries. Given even the most charitable interpretation of international and maritime law, much of this activity hovered at the edges of legality. To be sure, Bermudian traders did a sedate but profitable business in tobacco and salt, and later in potatoes and onions. But the real money held by the contemporary heirs of Bermuda's old families came from wrecking, privateering, the slave trade, and the spectacular profits from blockade-running, particularly during the American Civil War.

Happily for Bermudian sailors and merchants, there were blockades to be run and "prizes" to capture through the legal piracy of letters of marque for almost 250 years. Virtually all private vessels could buy letters of marque from the governor to capture hostile shipping. Britain's constant conflicts with Spain, France, Holland, and its North American colonies meant that there were hostile craft within easy reach most of the time. For Bermudian wreckers, the reefs were a continuous source of treasure.

Even official, politically correct presentations of Bermuda's history fail to hide Bermudians' nostalgia for the glory days of blockade-running for the Confederacy. During those few years, virtually every seaman who survived became rich, as did the shipbuilders and merchants who made blockade-running physically and financially feasible. Bermuda's sailing ships, from the seventeenth century until the age of steam, were known for their speed. The standard fore-and-aft sail configuration of modern racing yachts is called a Bermuda rig because it was favored by the early Bermudian shipbuilders.

Guided, welcomed, and entertained by the courteous Bermudians of St. George's, we can barely credit the truth of much of Bermuda's history. Eighteenth-century Bermudian merchants seem to have been rapacious on a scale that rivals the nineteenth-century American robber barons. Their treatment of the French who fled Haiti at the height of the French-Revolution-inspired slave rebellions of the 1790s is exemplary. French planters with the right connections got their families, slaves, silver, and silks aboard Dutch or American merchantmen headed for Europe or North America. They could hardly put to sea before Bermudian privateers intercepted them. These French-Haitian refugees soon found themselves in St. George's. After hasty prize-court proceedings, their possessions, reduced nearly to the clothes on their backs, were auctioned off to local merchants for resale at a tidy profit.

The Bermuda vice-admiralty court seems somehow to have ignored the fact that many of the captured ships weren't French, and therefore could not be lawful prizes. Nor were a family's household goods the "contraband of war" that international practice allowed belligerents to seize from neutral shipping. Sometimes the court simply declared vessels to be French posturing as American or Dutch ships. After all their holds were stuffed with French nationals and French goods.

The privateering business surrounding the Haitian and French revolutions was so hot and heavy that vessels could hardly be built fast enough. Businessmen ran competing ads in the *Bermuda Gazette* seeking masters and crews. Puffery about the powers of the ships seems to have been the coin of the trade. Bridges

Goodrich, a loyalist who had made bundles seizing American ships during the American Revolution, swung into really high gear when capitalizing on the French version. The *Gazette* of April 1793 carried Goodrich's signed epistle:

> The subscribers are now fitting the remarkable fast sailing schooner LADY HAMMOND for a three months' cruise against the French. All those who are disposed to enter on board for the purpose of filling their pockets with gold are requested immediately to apply, as the privateer must sail in eight days.

By October, he had another vessel ready to go:

> In a few days will be launched from Messrs. Brown and McCallan's ship-yards, a privateer which is thought by every judge will be one of the swiftest sailing vessels ever built. She is for Bridges Goodrich, Esq., and is to carry fourteen or sixteen guns. The above builders have turned out lately some of the swiftest sailors that ever crossed the ocean and are well-known through-out the West Indies, none of them having been captured or come up in this way with any of the enemy's ships, while they, on the contrary, can run around any vessels they come in sight of.

Two more Goodrich ships followed in quick succession, but, unable to acquire enough new ships on his own account, Goodrich offered to underwrite any Bermudian vessel dedicated to plundering French refugees—with the help of Bermuda's wonderfully compliant vice-admiralty court.

Today Bermuda's economy thrives on tourism and tax evasion. Its climate, beaches and resorts attract hordes of American and European visitors and cruise ships. Its banking and insurance laws make it a major base for offshore financial intermediaries. More and more American companies are being tempted to incorporate as Bermudian companies in order to shelter foreign income from U.S. taxation. Bermuda has no corporate income tax. Then there are the yachties, like us, who show up by the hundreds each year and spend weeks or months pumping dollars, euros, and pounds into the local economy.

PALAEMON is tied stern-to, Mediterranean style, to a concrete seawall, her bow secured to a buoy. She lies next to a group of gigantic sailing yachts with professional crews. Instead of waiting for Great Britain to declare war on someone, these vessels are waiting for weather, or for the arrival of absent owners, to shove off for the Caribbean.

Mark and Andrea on BRAVEHEART, next to us, are a deep well of information on contemporary Bermuda, weather predictions, and voyaging in general. Their usual annual migration is from the Med in the summer to the Caribbean in winter. But sometimes, as this year, Maine was their owner's chosen summer cruising ground, which put Bermuda on the route south. We find the level of maintenance on BRAVEHEART breathtaking. They are stripping all the exterior teak and revarnishing it to eliminate blemishes we can't even see from our cockpit, only 10 feet away. The crews on all these boats are hard at it eight to ten hours a day. We offer them the use of our salt-encrusted PALAEMON as a work site should they run out of things to do on their boats. Guilt drives us to contemplate projects that we would otherwise defer.

About eight hours after we are secured at our bulkhead, a graceful Hans Christian 38 edges into the adjoining dock. HERMAN MELVILLE is painted on the stern. The skipper could pose as the "old salt" in a Pusser's Rum ad: bright yellow foulweather gear, piercing eyes, the line of his square jaw softened by his neatly trimmed gray beard. We shout a greeting. Jerome looks puzzled. "PALAEMON," we shout, pointing at our boat. Jerome pulls on his beard, trying hard to place us from visual cues that are useless. We have never seen each other before. And with PALAEMON tied stern-to he cannot read the name on the stern. "Oh yeah, PALAEMON. Hi!" His eyes still have a blank look that belies the verbal recognition. The "saved" remember the "savior" more readily than the other way round. We leave them alone to finish tying up.

By the next morning, Jerome has figured out why we greeted him like a long-lost friend. He ambles over, pulling on his beard. "Would you like to come over later for a 'dark and stormy'?" he asks, peering down into our cockpit from the stone bulkhead. The invitation is tentative. We aren't sure whether he doubts our interest in a meeting or his own. Perhaps both. We accept, hoping that if we don't like 'dark and stormies,' whatever they are, there is something else on HERMAN MELVILLE to drink. Anne pulls out some crackers and cheese to take along, and a bottle of scotch. Good thinking. "Dark and stormies"—dark rum and ginger beer—turn out to be an acquired taste.

Our tentativeness with Jerome and Judith soon disappears. Jerome is a retired journalist, most recently an editor at *Business Week*. He's a history buff, deeply knowledgeable about New York state and local government, a "big government" hater. We start an argument that will never be finished. Jerome is, for me, a perfect companion—similar in sensibility and relishing, as I do, the competition among ideas that are simultaneously sensible, complex, and irreconcilable.

Judith and Anne feel an instant empathy. And we have friends in common. Judith has recently retired from raising money for the NAACP Legal Defense Fund. I have known her old boss, but one, Jack Greenberg, for twenty years. Her new, old boss, Elaine Jones, was my student at the University of Virginia Law School, almost thirty years ago.

I remember Elaine and her sister Gwen with great fondness. Both bright, aggressive black women in a law-school world that was then very white and very male. A classroom exchange with Gwen has never faded. I asked a technical question. The answer, or a start toward an answer, was to be found buried in a footnote in the case under discussion. Gwen exploded, "Why do you ask us about footnotes? What does that have to do with anything?" I could see her contemplating the grand gesture, slamming her text and stalking out. "It has to do with being a professional," I replied. "It has to do with not losing when justice is on your side, but better lawyering is on the other."

I saw Gwen later that day. I offered an apology if I had been too harsh. I had responded out of instinct. On reflection, lowering the boom on a black woman in that sea of white male faces did not seem smart. "No," she said. "Not at all. I deserved it and you gave it to me. If you hadn't, you would have been saying I wasn't worth it. I didn't come here to waste my time, to graduate a mediocre lawyer. I thought you were wasting it. I was wrong." The Jones sisters are two of the students I am happiest to have taught. I am glad Elaine now runs the Legal Defense Fund. It has a proud history. She is walking in big footprints.

Being marooned in St. George's is a gift. The town sparkles with brightly painted houses and the air is fragrant with the blossoms of what we New England residents consider indoor shrubs and plants. The waters are clear, the reefs and reef fish spectacular. Good restaurants abound. Yachties are here from everywhere—all with time to socialize, swap tales, and engage in joint projects, mostly boat repair. The days are warm, the nights are mild. We are lulled to sleep by PALAEMON's gentle motion and the striking, clear notes of the Bermudian whistling tree frog. And we are surrounded by locals who seem really to like having us here. British reserve has melted in Bermuda's balmy climate.

We drink and eat and tour, often with Jerome and Judith. We worry about the weather. Plan to leave and then see the weather window shut. Meet the people and boats that sailed in company with HERMAN MELVILLE from the States. Set up radio-check routines that we hope someday to use on the way to the BVI.

Bermuda angles.

Eighty-seven foreign yachts are now sitting in St. George's Harbour waiting for weather. Bernie assures us that this is a nonrace-week record. I briefly consider trying to get some "Free the Bermuda 87" T-shirts printed, but then decide the market is too small to repay the effort. Yet while the yachting community is small, it is almost comically diverse in its approaches to the requisites for voyaging.

Representing the compulsively well-equipped end of the spectrum are Frank and Lily, who moved aboard their boat, INVINCIBLE, a year ago in Annapolis. It has taken them until now to make it to Bermuda. Virtually all of the intervening twelve months have been spent fixing the incredible array of equipment jammed into INVINCIBLE's hull.

Frank and Lily have four sources of electrical power: an engine-driven alternator, a diesel generator, two wind generators, and two large arrays of photoelectric cells. All that power may be necessary, because INVINCIBLE has every electronic convenience imaginable. A freezer and refrigerator, a water desalination machine, a washing machine, a microwave oven, a TV with videocassette player, a stereo, and a Cuisinart, just for creature comforts. Then there's the communications equipment: VHF, SSB, satellite telephone, and weatherfax machine. And, of course, the usual navigational aids: GPS, chartplotter, and radar.

INVINCIBLE is the envy of every anchorage and marina, which is where she mostly stays. Frank and Lily do not like to move unless everything on board is working. Getting all that stuff to work at the same time—on a boat—is a miracle. Well, not literally. The hand of God is not required. But the hands of an army of marine equipment specialists, not to mention Frank's and Lily's, have to be laid on this stuff constantly. Parts are always needed and have to be ordered.

So Frank and Lily work on INVINCIBLE while they wait for parts to arrive and for technicians to show up. They have supposedly embarked on a circumnavigation of the planet. INVINCIBLE traveled only 900 miles this year. Frank and Lily are in their early forties. At their current pace, they will not make it back to Annapolis by the time they are eligible for Medicare.

Bob and Gail, on IMPROBABLE, are about to begin the last leg of a four-year circumnavigation. They will sail directly from here to South Africa, with their two small kids. IMPROBABLE has 20 percent of INVINCIBLE's gear. By many cruisers' standards, IMPROBABLE should be considered a boat project, not an ocean-ready vessel.

Yet here they are, four years and 26,000 miles after leaving Durban, about to close the circle. I am standing with Bob as he clears Bermuda customs and immigration. Seeing that Bob's destination is South Africa, the chatty customs official asks how long the trip will take.

"Two months, more or less," Bob replies.

"How much water do you carry for a trip like that?"

"We have a bit over 60 gallons," says Bob.

"What?" says Mr. Conviviality, his mouth agape.

"Well," says Bob, "you only need about one liter a day per person for drinking, and you can use salt water for everything else. Besides, we'll catch some rainwater, and we might put into Brazil somewhere if it looks like we're going to run short."

I am torn between admiration for Bob's pluck and a vivid image of what IMPROBABLE's crew is going to look like by the time they arrive in Durban. I am prepared to live without a lot of INVINCIBLE 's creature comforts, but I realize that Bob is made of sterner stuff than I am. He seems to fit the description of the sailor whom Woodes Rogers, first British governor of the Bahamas, and himself a circumnavigator, had in mind when he said, "A man who would go to sea for pleasure would go to Hell for a pastime."

As the days wear on, we are torn between our joy at being in St. George's and our anxiety about picking a good time to leave. We have weather information coming in from every direction—BHR, weatherfaxes, Internet satellite photos, SSB forecasts from NMN (the U.S. Coast Guard's weather broadcasts), and Herb. With hundreds of cruisers to interpret and extrapolate from these data, there is much more weather information at the quayside in St. George's than we can intelligently process. Every third day, it looks like a window might be opening. We prepare ourselves and PALAEMON for sea. Every fourth day, the window shuts and we shift back into tourist mode.

The professional captains of the maxiyachts tied up next to us are as nervous as bananaquits. On our section of the seawall, the next smallest yacht is BRAVE-HEART, a mere 75 feet. These guys have to please owners, most of whom want their boats anywhere but Bermuda at the moment. Many are scheduled to be part of the Antigua charter-yacht show at the end of November. If they don't make it there to be inspected by the Caribbean charter brokers, they may miss out on the lucrative winter charter business that keeps some of them solvent.

Near the drop-dead date for making the charter show, four of the big boats leave. Twelve hours later, three are back in St. George's with broken gear and seasick crew. The fourth makes it to Antigua, but it is so full of salt water below it can't be shown to anybody who doesn't relish returning from a Caribbean holiday mildewed instead of suntanned. If this is what is happening to the pros, we will stay put. Maybe there is something on this 21-square-mile island we haven't seen yet.

Thanksgiving arrives. We have wondered how we would feel on major holidays cut off from home and family. Anne takes holidays seriously. We decorate and cook for days, filling the house with happy aromas—cinnamon, sage, and turkey fat. Anne says I'm a holiday Grinch, but it's a bum rap. I love it too. I just want to be one of the kids instead of one of the adults. I want to be back at my grandparents' with thirty for Thanksgiving dinner. My father had six brothers and sisters; I grew up with thirteen first cousins. We were all together for every holiday, competing to see who could eat the most and then lying on the floor all afternoon, torpid and half-sick from gluttony.

We miss our families, but the locals will not let us mope. Bernie invites us to Thanksgiving dinner at St. David's parish church. The good folks at St. David's started celebrating this most-American holiday in the 1940s as a treat for U.S. servicemen stationed in Bermuda during World War II. With the war over and the base closed, the church persevered. There were always enough Yanks around to put on a feast. By charging a little something for the dinner, the church raises some funds.

We show up to find a tiny church bursting at the seams with yachties and locals. The party spills out into the churchyard. Names are put with faces, people with boats, as introductions are made, and made, and made. My head is swimming from too many proper nouns and the smell of turkey, dressing, sweet potatoes, and ginger cake. We eat in the hall, then move back outside so more can be fed. The feel is a little more like a Salvation Army soup kitchen than a family feast, but we beam at our hosts and they beam back as they hurry from kitchen to table bearing yet more food. After thanking everyone who isn't wearing boat shoes, we stagger off to look for a ride.

The St. David's Thanksgiving feast continues the long-standing attachments between Americans and Bermudians. Bermuda was very nearly the fourteenth colony in revolt against Great Britain in 1775–83 and might have been the fourteenth state. A detailed plan to snatch Bermuda from England in the early years of the Revolutionary War was shelved only because of the American revolutionaries' almost complete lack of naval resources. Bermuda was thus only a clandestine ally, but it provided crucial support. Bermudian sympathizers with the North American rebels spirited critical supplies of gunpowder out of the governor's magazine, ferrying them under cover of night to American ships offshore at a time when Washington estimated that he had less than one-half pound of powder for each member of the Continental Army. So many Bermudians were involved in the powder theft that the royal governor had no capacity to discipline them. On the American side, the plot clearly was conceived at the highest levels:

Camp at Cambridge 3 Miles from Boston
September 6, 1775

To The Inhabitants of Bermuda

Gentlemen:

In the great conflict which agitates the continent, I cannot doubt but the asserters of freedom and the right of the Constitution are possessed of your most favorable regards and wishes for success . . . .

We are informed that there is a very large magazine in your island under a very feeble guard. We would not wish to involve you in an opposition in which, from your situation, we should be unable to support you; we know not, therefore, to what extent to solicit your assistance, in availing ourselves of this supply; but if your favour and friendship to North America and its liberties have not been misrepresented, I persuade myself you may, consistently with your own safety, promote and further this scheme, so as to give it the fairest prospect of success. Be assured that in this case the whole power and exertion of my influence will be made with the honorable Continental Congress, that your island may not only be supplied with provisions, but experience every other mark of affection and friendship which the grateful citizens of a free country can bestow on its brethren and benefactors.

George Washington

The Continental Congress reciprocated with a year's supply of food. Bermuda was desperate for it. The Royal Navy's embargo of Bermudian trade with the rebellious North American colonies was literally forcing a tenuously loyal Bermuda to the edge of starvation. The powder caper aside, Bermudians did not always seem to have the king's best interests at heart. During the course of the American Revolution, they supplied more ships and seamen/privateers to the rebel cause than to the Crown. The British government viewed the island as little more than an extension of the American rebellion.

This was a bit harsh. The ever-eager Bermudian merchants were perfectly happy to fit out privateers using the king's letters of marque and to seize American ships for prize money. Bermudian seamen much preferred to go privateering than to join the Royal Navy. As privateers, they could often work both sides. Bermudian captains sometimes carried letters from both King George and the Continental Congress. Thank God the North American colonies were too poor and disorganized in 1776 to annex Bermuda. We would have ruined it for sure.

I don't want to sound like a shill for the Bermuda Chamber of Commerce, but Bermuda is so sensibly organized it's hard to believe it is governed by humans. Vehicular traffic is minimized by high import and fuel taxes, limited automobile ownership (one car per residence), and a truly marvelous bus system. There are no suburbs, no malls, and no fast-food franchises. The schoolchildren are turned out in colorful uniforms; bankers and insurance brokers go to the office in Bermuda shorts, coats, ties, and knee socks. There are no homeless, and, judging by the fresh-scrubbed appearance of the whole place, littering must be a capital offense.

This all sounds a trifle quaint and stiff, but Bermuda has its high-tech and laid-back features as well. Bermudians convert more than 90 percent of their solid waste into electric power and the cinders into paving stones. The pubs sport dark wood-paneled interiors and tables on their lawns. The tap handles read, "Fosters" and "MacEwans Export," and no one cares how long you take to finish yours.

From necessity, Bermudians may be the most eco-conscious society in the world. Bermuda is a limestone cap atop a living reef. If the surrounding coral dies, Bermuda vanishes into the Atlantic. Coral is amazingly fragile. Jamaica, for instance, has lost 90 percent of its coral in the last decade. Pollution and overfishing have destroyed the patient work of centuries of coral polyps. For all its caution, Bermuda may not survive the twenty-first century. A one-degree-Celsius increase in ocean temperature could cause the reef's ecosystem to collapse. If so, the Atlantic rollers will eat Bermuda in less than fifty years.

The face Bermuda shows us seems too good to be true. Beneath this beautiful decorous exterior must be seething hatreds, violent passions, racial and ethnic animosities. Early records of the island's history suggest it was the most strife-riven, litigious, rebellious, and ungovernable outpost of the British Empire. Royal governors begged to be recalled home to escape its fractious inhabitants. They routinely complained that there were so few men "of good life, well-affected to government, of good estates and abilities; and not . . . so much in debt," that they could not put together a decent council to help them govern. The Colonial Assembly, elected by white freeholders, consistently refused to appropriate sufficient funds to keep forts, roads, and especially the governor's house, in repair.

Lawlessness was rampant. Customs records reveal that an astonishing number of ships clearing into the customs house in St. George's Harbour were "in ballast," that is, without cargo. Yet the merchants' warehouses at the other end of the island were constantly replenished from trade, both with North America and the West Indies. How did they fill their warehouses from empty ships? Nearly 20 percent of Bermuda's population in the eighteenth century worked in the salt trade, hauling mostly from Turks Island, at the southeastern edge of the Great Bahama Bank. Yet the British government's salt tax yielded virtually no revenue.

Meanwhile, these hardheaded traders squandered their profits on slaves that they didn't need as either seamen or household help. Bermuda was not a plantocracy demanding continuous importation of field laborers. Owning slaves was a status symbol, and Bermudians' status competition through slave ownership was not guided by a benign invisible hand. Underemployed West Africans fed white paranoia about a possible slave revolt. They reacted by passing some of the most repressive slave laws in the whole of the sorry history of North Atlantic slavery.

This history could not have vanished without a trace. A preliminary report by off-island consultants to the Bermudian government as recently as 1978 declared, "An underlying reality of racial resentments and latent seething unrest. . . are as much a part of the reality of Bermuda as . . . its idyllic climate . . . ." Bermudians, like Americans, have reaped the whirlwind of a longcontinued pigmentocracy.

Whatever the level of civil discontent, Bermudians keep it pretty firmly under wraps. By contrast, evidence of Bermudian civility is ubiquitous. We have stopped poring over street maps in public. We are embarrassed by the crowds that gather around us, offering to help. The officer directing traffic at the principal crossroads in downtown Hamilton, the capital, arms himself with teddy bears, to console lost children, rather than a 9mm sidearm. Observing his armaments, we conclude that the forces of darkness and disorder have a very small garrison here.

We could stay forever, but southern latitudes are calling. The problem, as usual, is the weather. Lenny made the Caribbean its playground for nearly a week. Then one front after another has charged off the east coast of the United States. Gales keep roaring out of the western Caribbean, up through the Florida Straits or the Windward Passage, across our track to the BVI. We need seven decent days to make the 900 miles from Bermuda to Jost Van Dyke. We seldom see two days with winds below 25 knots. In addition to its other features, Bermuda is beginning to look like a weather magnet.

As December looms, the weather news changes. A strong storm is headed at Bermuda. But behind it there seems to be nothing but 20-knot northeasterlies for three days. Herb says that if we can make 150 miles a day for three days, we should be far enough south that the next front will pass north of us. We can sail the trade winds for the remainder of the trip. We will have to leave in the 9-to-16-foot seas left over from the storm. But we have no assurance of a better forecast if we wait.

As we waver about whether to take this narrow weather window, we hope to get some sage advice at dinner. HERMAN MELVILLE is docked at Pete and Jean Outerbridge's house. Pete is the Bermuda equivalent of a New Englander whose ancestors arrived on the MAYFLOWER. His family settled here in 1611. Pete and Jean have invited us to dinner. Jean apologizes for not having done so sooner.

The Outerbridge Dock

The Outerbridge dock.

Good grief. They're Bermuda aristocracy and we're boat bums they've never seen before. It's an uproariously drunken evening. Jean, Judith, and Anne make vodka penne with 100-proof vodka while Pete pours glass after glass of this high-octane stuff down our gullets. I suppose we could have resisted.

Given Pete's family background and Jerome's historical interests, much of the conversation tries to make sense of Bermudian history and the Outer-bridges' relation to it. Outerbridges have done almost everything the island has offered over the past four centuries. They have been merchants, farmers, financiers, representatives on the council and in the assembly. Pete and Jean's homes in Nova Scotia and Florida do not suggest that Pete's generation has been deprived. As the evening is winding down, I ask Pete, "So what about the future?"

"It will soon be a black island," he predicts. "The black birth rate is twice the white. The kids are being raised by their grandmothers. We're headed for the third-world status of the rest of the Caribbean."

Pete's perspective may merely betray his roots. The days of "Front Street" dominance of Bermuda's political life are surely over. Universal adult suffrage finally arrived in 1968. But the numerically superior black Bermudians seem addicted to stability. For another decade, they elected majority white (indeed, conservative) governments. We have seen no evidence that Bermudian society is unraveling in some downward spiral that justifies Pete's gloomy prognosis. Whites still hold the real economic power, but the black middle class seems strong, mildly prosperous, energetic.

Should I put what I have just heard down to the usual *"après moi, le déluge"* mentality of aristocrats everywhere? Or to lingering prejudice? Why should black dominance yield third-world status? Or am I hearing the shrewd assessment of a seasoned local, confirmation of my suspicion that we are myopic visitors constructing a coherent, well-ordered social reality from happy but thin observation? I'm surely too drunk to tell the difference.

As we weave out the door, Pete says, "It's almost December. The weather will only get worse." We decide to make a break for it.

14

FLEEING ST. GEORGE'S

According to the BHR forecast, the storm will begin with southeasterly winds at 30 to 35 knots, go calm for about twelve hours, then switch abruptly to the northwest at 40 to 45 knots. We cannot stay on the seawall in 30-knot southeasterlies, so we move PALAEMON out to an anchorage with good holding and swinging room and rocky islets protecting her to the southeast. We put down two anchors and prepare to ride out the southeasterly winds. During the calm, we will move over to get northwesterly protection at the other end of the harbor.

This is a good plan, but the forecast is not. At about 4:15 A.M., Anne and I both sit bolt upright. The southeasterly winds have stopped as abruptly as if they have been turned off with a switch. This is not the usual pattern of a gradual shift in wind direction. Thirty seconds later, a 40-knot wall of wind slams us from the northwest. We jump out of the bunk and pull on whatever comes to hand. I grab sweatpants, Anne ends up with only a T-shirt.

By the time we are in the cockpit, there is a 75-foot megayacht lying against our hull. The professional crewmen on board are pretty good. They did not put out enough anchor rode, but they did keep watch. They have fenders over the side and slide off us without a scratch. As they drift away, their anchor bites into the mud and they pull up about 200 yards short of the rocks.

Our snug anchorage is now a cauldron of wave and spray. The rocks that had been giving us protection are now a menacing lee shore. The wind is clearly increasing, and raindrops are strafing PALAEMON's decks like machine-gun bullets. The seas are building fast. Our bow is already plunging into the waves; green water is sluicing down the side decks.

Anne starts the engine and I crawl forward to check the anchors. Both are still set hard, but the wind shift has wrapped one line around the other. The rope on the second anchor will now chafe on the chain of the primary hook. I have no idea how long it will last before it chafes through.

I look up into the pitch black and see what Anne has already seen—an even bigger yacht, maybe 90 feet, is drifting at us broadside, its anchor dragging. The boat has no lights. Either no one is on board or they are still asleep.

Anne slams the engine into gear and veers off to the left, trying to get out of the path of this behemoth. It is a desperate maneuver. If our anchors come out and foul our prop, we will go on the rocks. But if this guy hits us, he will probably take us onto the rocks with him anyway.

The wind is now gusting at over 50 knots, and we make painfully slow progress against it. But it is enough. The stern of the 90-footer misses us by about 10 feet. Miraculously, the anchor it is dragging does not foul ours.

I crawl back to the cockpit for a consultation. Wearing nothing but a drenched T-shirt, Anne is freezing. I am not too warm myself in just my sweatpants. I grab jackets from below and we try to assess our situation.

The Bermuda harbor pilot boat is standing by to try to assist boats in distress. Just behind us, the rocky islands that define one side of the harbor have already claimed three yachts. Two are pulled off without much damage, one sinks. We are only 500 yards off that shore, with the prospect of yet more yachts dragging down on us. Our anchor lines are wrapped and might chafe through or cause the anchors to pull against each other and lose their grip on the seabed. If they come out while still wrapped, the likelihood of getting them reset before we are on the rocks is small. We decide to see if the engine can make forward progress into the wind. If so, we will take up the anchors and move as far as possible from the shore and other boats before resetting them.

As I feel the engine take the load off the anchor lines, I creep forward to pull up the secondary anchor by hand. In the last stages of this operation, I will have to hang over the bowsprit, unwrap 50 pounds of chain from the primary anchor, and then wrestle the secondary on deck. I wedge myself between a stanchion and the forestay and start retrieving line. As PALAEMON plunges and bucks in the steepening seas, my head is under water three seconds out of every ten. An eternity later, I am on my hands and knees on the foredeck, spitting out seawater and staring at the secondary anchor, rode, and chain piled beside me. I don't remember having done this, but somebody did.

I haul the primary anchor and its 200 feet of chain with the electric windlass. We are now relying on engine power alone. Anne has the throttle full open and the engine temperature is getting uncomfortably high, but we are making some progress against the wind. I try to signal to Anne where I want to go, but she can't see me. The foredeck lights are on, illuminating the bow, but I am invisible in the rain and spray. I crawl to the cockpit again to confer.

Anne's teeth are chattering and her lips are blue. She has been too cold too long. Hypothermia is beginning to sap her strength. We can see what looks like an open spot in the middle of the harbor and decide to try anchoring there. Visibility is too poor to try to get to the northwest shore. Unfortunately, the water is 45 feet deep. We will just have to let out a lot of rode and hope the anchors hold.

Anchoring in these conditions is almost as ghastly as taking them up. Anne can barely keep the bow into the wind or maintain direction. We have to circle several times to get in the right spot. Each time we fall off downwind, we wonder whether the engine will have enough power to turn PALAEMON back up. We have to run hard at the rocky shore we are trying to avoid to get enough momentum to turn back up through the waves and wind. Anne's legs are rubbery, but her nerves are steel.

Somehow Anne gets PALAEMON to about the right location and I let go the primary anchor. It goes out only 30 feet before the chain jams in the windlass. On my knees, operating the anchor-down foot switch with my left hand, I reach over to hit the anchor-up switch with my right to clear the jam. I am thrown off balance by a wave, and my left hand comes down on the incoming chain. Instinctively, I hold on, and my fingers go through the windlass between the chain and the gipsy.

I now have three fingers with no feeling, but the jam is cleared. Meanwhile, the wind and waves have pushed us out of position. We will have to circle again. I signal to Anne, but she can't see me. Never mind; she is already turning back downwind to pick up speed.

On the next try, the primary anchor goes down and sets hard. We could hang onto that while keeping the motor in forward and be reasonably safe—we think. But if the engine quits, we will be on one anchor, in deep water, in winds now gusting at close to hurricane strength. We decide to put out the second anchor, even though we risk either pulling out the first or fouling it with the second.

This may not have been a good decision, but it works. Two hours after all hell broke loose, we have both anchors well set again, and the wind does not seem to be strengthening. In the gray dawn, we watch the clouds whipping by overhead. Given their speed, it is hard to believe that this storm will be here very long.

I pry Anne's fingers off the wheel and persuade her to go below to warm up and get some dry clothes. The only argument that works in this sort of situation is the old "If you're too weak to help when I really need you because you stayed up here now what then?" approach. Even that is a hard sell. On inspection, my fingers are all working—bruises but no breaks. I guess I was running the windlass so fast my fingers didn't stay in it long enough to cause much damage.

As visibility improves, we raise the anchors once again and move to the northwest shore, where we can moor in a 12-inch chop instead of the 4-foot waves in midharbor. At this point, we are safe—and numb. The trip from Cape Fear had taught us the need to respect the open ocean. That we might nearly lose PALAEMON in St. George's Harbour had never crossed our minds. Maybe the sea gods are giving us a sign. If we can get ourselves together by the time this storm passes through, we'd better take Herb's predicted weather window and bid Bermuda *adieu*.

Jerome and Judith may be leaving with us. But maybe not. Jerome is one of those sailors who loves to be at sea but has to be thrown off the dock to get there. He also hates to make quick decisions. He worried for a full day about which lines to let go first when leaving the Outerbridges' dock before the "harbor hurricane" arrived. Besides, he doesn't have enough water on board yet, and his dinghy isn't pumped up to go ashore to get any, and he really needs to lay in some more wine—and, and, and. Half the boats in the harbor seem to be helping Jerome do one thing or another. As we eavesdrop on his radio requests for assistance, I begin to wonder whether he will ask someone to sail HERMAN MELVILLE to the BVI for him. Somebody probably would. Jerome is so charming it's hard to deny him anything.

I end up taking him to customs to clear out. After we've cleared, Jerome asks me to wait for him while he goes to the wine shop. I remind him that his dinghy is stowed for sea, that I've got to go back to PALAEMON and stow mine before leaving, and that we're now racing against time and the closing of the weather window. I also remind him that he has a handheld VHF in his pocket and can call someone else to fetch him back to HERMAN MELVILLE. Jerome looks startled that I could deny so simple a request. "Oh," he says.

"Talk to you at six," I say. "We're going to try to clear the sea buoy in an hour. You had better get moving." Jerome ambles toward town as I scramble into JEREMY BENTHAM and head for PALAEMON. In an hour, we will be back in the open ocean. I have too much to do to worry about it.

ANNE'S PASSAGE NOTES: LEAVING BERMUDA

The day has gone by in a blur: last-minute preparations for sea, wisps of conversation with other sailors—who's going and who's not, endless discussions about last night's storm. I have listened from somewhere outside the conversation.

In our struggle to get PALAEMON to safety, I never knew what was happening beyond my limited visibility. I could not see Jerry on the bow. Had he gone over, I would not have known. All I could do was run the boat forward and try to hold her until the wind blew the bow off, run downwind until I could get enough momentum to try to get her back up. Over and over. I swore to myself that we would not leave on Monday. I swore to myself I would never sail again.

I found a warm lethargy coming over me. I realized my teeth were chattering, but I was no longer cold. I wanted to lie down and close my eyes. I felt almost peaceful. I knew the creeping warmth was deadly. I hung onto the wheel and throttled up. Into position, then swept back by the wind. But this time a difference: When I circled, I could feel the anchor bite and the bow come up more easily. I hadn't seen Jerry for what seemed an interminable time, but if an anchor had held, he was still there. He materialized in the cockpit to tell me the primary was down and set. Now for the secondary. The contact with him helped. The progress helped.

Another run forward hard to port. I could not tell whether it was enough before the wind caught the bow and swung it off again, overpowering the engine. The bow pulled up into the wind. I lowered the rpms and we held. Jerry reappeared. He was shaking badly. How had he done it? How had I? Behind the dodger's protection, we held onto each other. When I raised my hand to wipe the hair out of my eyes, I found tears streaming down my face.

We looked around. Our holding was solid. We judged it safe to go below. I could barely make it down and out of my soaked windbreaker and T-shirt without falling. A towel, blankets. Not enough strength to tell Jerry we must not leave tomorrow. Too much adrenaline to sleep. At daybreak, we moved PALAEMON to calm waters. The winds were down. My shaking subsided to trembling.

Later we reanchored close to the customs dock and went to town on last errands. We were operating mechanically, in standby mode. We held hands but barely talked. We saw the couple who had lost their boat so close to us on the rocks, walking together, holding each other, carrying their one sodden bag of salvaged gear, crying openly. I wanted to go to them and try to comfort them, but I could not. They had lost their boat. PALAEMON was safe.

Jerry is listening to Herb. It will be an ugly start in huge seas, and it will be a cat-and-mouse game, with the gale system threatening to meet us at 25°N. I feel tears bright behind my eyes, but I have no words, no protests. The person swearing "never again" into the wind last night has become a pale stranger. I am able to boil eggs. I boil a lot of them. I chop and bag more celery and carrots than we can possibly eat. I have started taking Dramamine. We agree to eat dinner in town, a last shore meal at a now-favorite restaurant. I am strangely close to happy. I am ready to go back to sea.

15

THE ROAD TO FOXY'S

Foxy and Lessa Callwood run the most famous beach bar in the world. *Time* magazine listed Foxy's Tamarind Bar as one of the three places to be on New Year's Eve 1999. Times Square and Piccadilly Circus were the other two. This wouldn't be too peculiar if Foxy's were somewhere other than where it is—our destination, Jost Van Dyke, British Virgin Islands, population 131. By various estimates, some of them surely Foxy's, there will be 5,000 to 10,000 people at Jost on New Year's Eve. Foxy is having a party—actually two. One will be whatever is happening in and around Foxy's that several thousand drunken revelers can dream up. The other is upstairs in Foxy's almost-finished new dining room. Dinner and champagne for only $999 per couple.

Downstairs flows so seamlessly onto the beach in front and the scrub forest behind that charging admission would be laughable. But upstairs has only one set of stairs and the tables have been sold out for weeks. According to published reports, reservations are essential. Last year, Walter Cronkite and Peter Jennings tried to get in late. No deal. Everybody upstairs is somebody. The megayacht crowd apparently can't stay away from where *it* is happening. Rumors of who is going to show up include Fergie, Mick Jagger—whoever. I'm not reliable on this. I shun *People* magazine in the barbershop. It might as well be printed in Chinese. I have no idea who 98 percent of the rich and famous are whose lives are chronicled there. Or why what they are doing is important. Anyway, the reservation list is highly confidential. They don't call him Foxy for nothing.

We somehow neglected to make our reservation in time. Maybe it was the $999. But we are headed for Jost just the same. It is 900 miles south southwest of Bermuda, with a wide-open entry that will allow us to approach 30 miles west of the dreaded Anegada Banks—home to centuries of wrecks—and 100 miles east of the Silver Banks, the only major obstruction between Bermuda and the BVI.

This trip is a navigational no-brainer. We will point PALAEMON south by southeast out of Bermuda, although at 32°N latitude and 65°W, we are now slightly east of our destination. The westerly currents pushing us southwest below 25° N should be just enough to put us off Great Harbour, Jost Van Dyke, 18° 26'N, 64° 45'W. Old hands say the routine on arrival never varies. Clear in at the customs outpost put there just for that purpose (a customs and immigration office on an island with 131 people!?) and walk down to Foxy's for a rum punch. Kick back. Paradise found.

Somewhere along our track, we will cross a divide between Anglo-European and Caribbean culture. A few of the posh restaurants in Bermuda still require jackets and ties after 6 P.M. At Foxy's, trousers—well, shorts anyway—are customary. Apparently late in the evening, they become optional. In his hackneyed fashion, I suppose Jimmy Buffett gets it right: "Changes in latitude, changes in attitude." Rumor has Buffett showing up at Foxy's on New Year's Eve, too.

The navigationally simple is, of course, not necessarily the operationally easy. Herb had advised us to get out of Bermuda fast. A front forming southwest of Cuba is developing and moving rapidly northeast. If we are not below 25° in seventy-two hours, we can expect gale-force winds. If we get below 25° by then, the front *should* pass north of us and we *should* pick up moderate (25 knots) northeast trades. From Bermuda to 25°N, we can expect 20-to-25-knot northeasterlies, 8-to-12-foot seas.

Pressed hard, PALAEMON will do 150 miles in twenty-four hours. If Herb is right, we can just outrun the front. We leave Bermuda in the leftover seas from the earlier storm—9 to 16 feet—and with 20 to 25 knots of wind. With any luck, the wind will hold, the seas will drop, and we will have a fast and uneventful trip. Five boats in our swelling radio net leave with us, three U.S., one British, one Scandinavian. A couple of the slower boats stay in St. George's. They will have to wait for a longer window. We will check in with each other by SSB every twelve hours. If anyone needs help, someone should be fairly close by—but only "fairly." It is remarkable how boats headed for the same destination spread out over seven days and 900 miles. Within twenty-four hours of clearing St. George's, we are unlikely to have visual contact with any of the other vessels with which we are sailing "in company."

For Anne, the first twenty-four hours are worse than usual. When we exit St. George's Harbour, we go directly off the reef into the open Atlantic. There is no gradual buildup to those 9-to-16-foot seas left over from the storm that nearly did us in. There is no way to get our sea legs before the going gets rough.

The wind is well north of east, almost directly astern. PALAEMON corkscrews through a vicious downwind roll as she is caught by waves first slightly to port, then slightly to starboard. We roll through an arc of nearly 60 degrees. Our stern wake looks like the weaving path of a blind-drunk sailor as PALAEMON's bow and stern debate the proper direction. "Uncomfortable" is a puny word to describe these conditions.

But we are flying. Under only a reefed jib, PALAEMON is averaging 7 knots. I don't think we have more than 50 square feet of sail up; PALAEMON's spinnaker spreads 1,100 square feet. The problem is to keep the speed low enough to avoid jumping off the front of one wave and into the back of the next. If we and PALAEMON hold together, and the wind continues, we will make 25°N in less than seventy-two hours. If Herb's forecast is right, we then will be in the clear.

Two days out, the wind begins to lighten up, first to 15 knots, then to 10. To keep up boat speed, we switch on the diesel and motorsail south. At least the calming conditions are bringing the seas down. We should still be at 25°N pretty close to Herb's timetable. But Herb has changed his forecast: 25°N is not going to be good enough. The low is tracking farther south than originally projected. It will intercept us at about 25°N and be with us until we reach nearly 22°N. The trough has squall lines embedded in it. Twenty-five knots of wind along the trough, 35 to 40 in the squalls. In twenty-four hours, the roller coaster starts again.

While Anne has pretty much recovered, Otto is complaining. The downwind roll has produced very heavy steering loads, and Otto is making strange groaning noises. I open the hatch and feel his steering arm housing. It is much too hot. Something is causing friction in Otto's gears. He needs a rest.

As the winds pick up again, we begin to hand-steer—thirty minutes on, thirty minutes off. That's about all we can manage in the increasing winds and seas. It has to be done sitting down; standing up, we can't keep our balance. To stave off exhaustion, we still let Otto steer half-time. He doesn't sound any happier. We are not getting any happier either. We are getting very tired.

The irony of this situation is that I took precautions in Bermuda precisely to avoid it. Realizing Otto's importance, and the fact that I hadn't a clue how he was put together, I called the local Autohelm distributor to ask what tended to fail in these units.

"The planetary gears," Steve replied.

"Do you have any?" I asked, not having a clue what "planetary gears" are or what they might have to do with the planets.

"Sure."

"Let's put them in and I'll save the old ones for spares."

"Fine."

And so Steve came down to the dock. He wanted to take Otto to his shop, but I demurred. There was a workbench next door that we could use. I wanted to watch him take Otto apart and change the gears. "This is really a good thing to do," Steve told me as we struggled with Otto at the workbench. "You can't do this at sea." Given that Steve and I were at the time employing four hands and a vise, he seemed to have a point—beyond making me feel good about paying his fee.

Impossible or not, I am increasingly convinced that I will have to try to undo Steve's repair. Hand-steering is sapping our strength. I kept falling asleep at the wheel last night in conditions so rough that I was sitting down and holding the wheel with both hands just to keep from being thrown around the cockpit.

Jim on MOONLIGHTING, one of our hardy radio net, assures me that the new gears have to be the problem. He had the same difficulty with his unit. The new gears, for some reason, did not mesh properly. They ground each other up. Jim wants to know if I will join his class-action suit against Autohelm. I agree, on condition that the remedy includes sending me an Autohelm technician right now.

If Jim is right, that would account for both Otto's groaning and his fever. But he is still working half-time. What if I take him apart and break or lose something trying to replace the gears? This is not uninformed anxiety. It was tricky for Steve to get Otto back together when held by me and a vise on a stable workbench. And Steve does that sort of thing for a living. I would have to operate on Otto alone on the saloon table, with no vise, in a boat rolling through 40 to 60 degrees.

Even if the operation is a success, I may not be able to get the patient to go back to work. Otto is hardwired into the electrical system in the back of a sail locker. When in a position that I can see the wiring, it is so close to my nose it makes me cross-eyed. There is also the small problem that there is only room enough to raise one hand at a time to the level of the wiring harness. And it is dark in there. Cutting Otto out, given these happy working conditions, will not be a big problem. Resplicing those six tiny wires in a bouncing boat, one-handed, with a flashlight in my teeth, sure as hell will.

The fourth night out is horrendous. A squall comes through every forty-five minutes, bringing the promised 35-plus gusts. Steering in the dark, eyes glued to a wildly gyrating compass card, is hypnotic. I find myself falling asleep again, coming to as my head bounces off the wheel.

In the early dawn, I heave PALAEMON to in order to get some rest. To accomplish this maneuver, I must turn up into the wind, sheet the mainsail flat amidships, and lash the wheel to windward. As the wind tries to push the bow off to leeward, the mainsail and rudder turn it back to windward. I turn PALAEMON up into the wind and seas. I'm climbing mountains. Spray flies off the tops. The sails flog limply in the calm of the hollows. It takes me three tries to get PALAEMON to settle down, the bow about 45 degrees off the wind. She begins to ride slowly up and over the waves. The motion is steady—at least compared to continuing to sail.

After breakfast and a nap, we get underway again with a contingency plan. If both the cruddy weather and Otto's ill health continue until midafternoon, I will either put the old gears back into Otto and reinstall him or we will heave-to for the night. We can't do another night of hand-steering. If necessary, we can sail during the day and heave-to at night all the way to Jost. It is just going to be a damn slow trip.

At 3 P.M., we decide to try operating on Otto. I should be able to get him out and back in before dark. If he works, great. If not, we heave-to and sail again in the morning.

I haul a couple of hundred pounds of gear out of the locker and into the cockpit to get at Otto. I have the saloon table open, covered with newspaper, the toolbox braced on the settee. I have collected several plastic leftover bins to hold parts. When I get Otto apart, I will have about three dozen pieces to hold onto. If I lose any of them, I doubt that I can improvise replacements.

I can barely bring myself to cut Otto's wires. With that done, though, I am committed. Fix Otto or hand-steer for five more days. As my economist friends would say, "The incentives are right for promoting optimum performance."

To an outside observer, the next two and one-half hours would have been a riot—a sort of Abbott-and-Costello-do-brain-surgery-with-a-chainsaw spectacle. Parts slipping everywhere. Long periods in which I do nothing but try to cradle everything on the table in my arms so nothing will get away. It's as if I've finally gone over the edge and think that if I hug Otto long enough, he will get well.

When I emerge from the sail locker after splicing Otto back into his electrical relays, I am shaking with fatigue. I have cramps in one shoulder, both legs, and my jaw. I can barely pry the latter open enough to get the flashlight out. At that, I may be better off than Anne. She has been hand-steering for three hours in increasing winds and heavy seas. Darkness has fallen while a project requiring an hour on the bench has gone on—and on. I see why Steve said it couldn't be done at sea.

We are both afraid to throw the autopilot switch. If nothing happens, I am not going to have a clue how I have screwed up either Otto's innards or his wiring. And I am sure as heck not going back in that locker tonight to give it another try.

I throw on the switch. "Bleep," says Otto. His control panel lights up and reads "Standby." The heading readout from his gyrocompass is eminently plausible. Electrically, Otto seems in the prime of good health.

Anne pushes the "Auto" button. Otto starts to steer. He does not groan. Relief breaks over us like a warm wave. Tears do not quite stream down our cheeks, but it's a close thing. Tonight we can sleep three hours at a stretch while still making time toward Foxy's. Is this Paradise, or what?

Well, not quite. Otto is not the only thing that is showing wear. The wiring inside the mast that feeds our wind instruments, masthead lighting, and deck lighting runs through an aluminum electrical conduit that is riveted to the inside of the mast. Some or all of the rivets have let go. The conduit crashes around in the mast cavity with every roll. It sounds like a 50-foot metal python thrashing around in there, trying to break its way out.

By now, there is no noise that can keep me awake for long. In my restless, off-watch dream, the banging of the conduit is from my childhood, the sound of my grandmother's screen door as it slams behind a flying kid. With every whack, MaMaw shouted, "Don't slam that door." Her shout wakes me. I am disappointed to find that she and the screen door aren't there. Delighted to find that Anne is.

It never worked for MaMaw. No matter how many times she shouted at us about the door, we always forgot. But I feel like screaming at the conduit. I don't have any better solutions. I hope it doesn't pull the wiring loose at the masthead before we make Jost. Two more days.

16

CHECKING INTO PARADISE

We are not the only ones with gear failures—hardly surprising, given the conditions. George and Betsy on ZORRA repeatedly lose their wind vane as the following seas batter the rudder. THOR's autopilot pegs out. MOONLIGHTING shreds a foresail.

We worry about Jerome and Judith on HERMAN MELVILLE. At sixty-eight, Jerome is the oldest of the lot of us, and while in great shape, he sounds very tired. He is unable to go on deck to reduce sail because of the vicious roll, and he worries that he has too much canvas up. We are all relieved when he heaves-to, sleeps for six hours, and modifies his sail plan. Suddenly we have a bouncy Jerome on the SSB again, his two favorite words, "terrific" and "fantastic," blasting out over the airwaves.

By day six of the passage, we are all either reducing sail to nearly nothing or heaving-to in order to eat up some hours. The rapid passage is putting our estimated arrival into Jost in the late evening instead of the early morning. There is no better way to lose your boat than to enter unfamiliar harbors in the dark. Unlike U.S. waters, which are filled with navigational buoys and lights that actually work, most Caribbean harbors boast little more than a stake here or there driven into a reef. The few lights listed on the charts may or may not be flashing. The probability that a navigational aid will be "on station" and working ranges from very high in the French islands to vanishingly small in the Bahamas. Cruising guides for the Bahamas give bearings for entering harbors by reference to houses, trees, even construction cranes, all of which are more likely to be where they were last seen by the author than a Bahamian navigational buoy.

As we close on Jost in the dark, the loom and then the lights of Tortola and St. Thomas become visible. The promise of a calm anchorage and some activity other than managing a boat has our whole armada hyperventilating with anticipation. As the sun comes up to light the mountains of Tortola, St. John, and St. Thomas, the views are breathtaking, volcanic peaks rising out of the dark sea, backlit by the brightening sky. Blacks and grays turn to blues and greens, the shallowing sea moves toward aquamarine as we round the western tip of Jost, motoring against the wind toward our anchorage. Paradise really is at hand.

But I manage to screw up the joyous arrival. While anchoring, I repeat my hand-through-the-windlass trick. Caught unaware by a boat wake, I drop to the deck with my knee on the anchor-up switch of the windlass and my left hand—again—on the anchor chain. This time, my fingers jam between the chain and the windlass gipsy rather than zipping through. I reach over and press the anchor-down switch. My hand runs back out the way it went in.

Now there clearly is some damage. I am bleeding pretty steadily from three or four places. I have no idea whether or not anything is broken. But we need to get the anchor down and set before further investigation will be possible. I hold my bleeding hand over the rail and give Anne the usual hand signals until we are secure. She is a little puzzled by the urgency I seem to be putting into my foredeck directions—until I walk back and reveal the result of my clumsiness.

I can move all my fingers, so there probably are no broken bones. But the fingers are swelling fast. My wedding ring has been on my finger for nineteen years. There is no way it is going to slide off. We need to get some ice on these fingers fast, but we have none. With my being one-handed, it probably will take forty-five minutes to inflate and launch JEREMY BENTHAM and get to shore for a bag of cubes.

Anne puts out a call on channel 16 for ice and a bolt cutter. Meantime, absolutely certain that the ring has to come off, I browbeat Anne into trying to remove it with a hacksaw. Good soldier that she is, she tries, then declares the task impossible. She is taking off as much flesh as ring. I can hardly argue, although my mangled digits hurt enough that I hadn't noticed the saw blade biting into my flesh. Jim and Alice from MOONLIGHTING are over in five minutes. The bolt cutter's jaws are too large to get a grip on the ring while leaving my finger on my hand. Smaller wire cutters are not strong enough to do the job. The handles distort in Jim's hands, barely denting the surface of the ring. Alice advises simply packing the fingers in ice for several hours, and intermittently thereafter, to keep the swelling under control. If my finger turns white and then blue, we will have to take further steps. For now, we can just ice, bandage, and observe. Alice is a nurse. Taking her advice seems sensible.

I am hopping mad at myself. I don't really believe in accidents, at least where I am concerned. I should have cut off the ring before we left home. How could I do the same dumb trick with the windlass twice? Why didn't I install those windlass switches in a position that would make this sort of mishap impossible?

Anne says that Mashaw men all have a perfection neurosis. We think we can do everything right all the time and believe ourselves to have been hopelessly stupid if anything goes wrong. She's probably right. My father was like that. So was his—as are his four brothers. Even our kids suffer from this bizarre malady. God knows we produce enough evidence that we don't do everything right. How can we keep on believing that we should never screw up? Is there a Perfectionists Anonymous group out there we could join? I wonder what the twelve steps to recovery might be.

I do see one bright side to the whole mess. This is surely a good excuse to lay on some extra rum punches at Foxy's.

My fingers stay pink, but two days later, the swelling returns. The ring has to come off. We enlist Jerome and Judith for an awkward four-person operation. I hold my ring with pliers and Anne secures a steel nail file between the ring and the top of my finger. That way, we can saw off the ring while leaving my finger reasonably intact. Jerome wields the hacksaw. Judith drips ice water on the ring and the saw blade to keep the heat down as the hacksaw bites slowly through the metal. This is pretty painful, and I keep losing my grip on the ring. Jerome, thank God, is a steady, careful guy. Twenty minutes of delicate sawing and the ring is off. Instant relief.

Between injury and operation, we have been exploring Jost, sleeping twelve-hour binges and eating and drinking about 10,000 calories a day. Anne and I both have lost 10 or more pounds on the way down. We are now pretty lean and hungry-looking, but we are headed back toward fat and happy, and finding Jost a real kick.

For one thing, like Bermuda, interesting cruisers wash up here from everywhere. For another, it is nothing like Bermuda.

Take customs and immigration. The building is right on the beach at the ferry landing, sandwiched between two beach bars and the garbage dump. We walk in with our boat papers and passports and stand at the counter. The guy at the desk is on the phone talking to his wife about something or other. He shows no inclination to cut short his conversation just because "customers" have arrived.

He hangs up the phone and never looks up. He begins to shuffle papers on his desk. I mean it—shuffle. He just moves them around.

"Good morning," I say.

Nothing.

"We would like to clear in," I say.

Nothing.

He looks at us for a long minute. He sighs and reaches into the desk for some forms. He brings them to the counter, puts them down, and returns to the desk. Still hasn't said a word.

I look at the forms and notice that there are two sets of identical forms.

"Do we fill out two copies of each of these?" I ask.

He nods.

"Do you have any carbon paper?"

He looks at me again. The look is somewhere between the one that you might bestow on a cockroach in your salad or the one you would give a small child who had just turned over his milk for the seventh time. He reaches into a drawer and brings out a piece of carbon paper. It looks like it is left over from typing quartermaster reports during World War II. He puts it on the counter and returns to his desk.

There are no pens on the counter. We are *not* asking this guy for pens. Anne digs in her bag and finds one that works. Two would be nice, but we'll just take the forms one at a time.

So we fill out the forms and take them back to the counter. The personality kid is still shuffling papers. He doesn't look up.

"We're finished," I say.

Nothing.

"Do we just leave them here, or do you need to review them, or what?"

He sighs deeply and gets up, his every movement seeming a struggle through some thick, invisible medium. He takes the forms off the counter with all the pleasure of a lab technician handling stool samples, then returns to his desk to study them. It takes awhile. He returns and puts down the forms. He points to two places he has put little "x's." "Dese not right," he says, and turns to leave.

We're looking at the two "x's" and wondering what the hell is wrong. One is an estimated departure day, "01/15/00." The other is a blank marked "crew." We put Anne's name there, since we had put mine in the one labeled "captain" above it.

"What's the problem?" I ask.

"Yeah, wrong," says Stoneface.

"You mean we can't stay in the BVI until January?" (It's now December 9.)

"Yeah, you can."

"So what's wrong with the year? It will be 2000 by then."

"Not 2000."

"What?"

"Write 2000. You write 00."

"Can we just change it on here?"

"You can."

It sounds like there should have been a "but" at the end of that sentence.

"What happens if we change it?"

"You initial fust, then pay fine."

"A fine?"

"Yeah."

"How much?"

"Tweny-fi' cents."

Holy shit.

"So what's wrong with the crew?"

"Not all deah."

"But there are only two of us," I say, wondering if we're about to be accused of smuggling aliens into the British Virgin Islands.

"Two not deah," he says.

Oh, I get it. "Crew" *includes* "captain." That I listed myself one-quarter inch above doesn't mean that I shouldn't list myself again. Hey, since I don't have to scratch anything out, maybe it won't even cost a quarter.

It only takes another twenty minutes to get Stoneface to retrieve the corrected forms, stamp them, take our entry fee—plus the 25-cent fine—and hand us back a copy.

"All done?" I ask hopefully.

"Yeah, you done heah."

"What now?" I ask, knowing that his "you done heah" means we're not done somewhere else. I suddenly know what this guy reminds me of, a well-coached hostile witness. He will answer direct questions but volunteer nothing.

"Immigration," he says.

"Where's that?"

"Tru' deah," he says, pointing to a closed, unmarked door 4 feet away.

Oh, yes, how could we have forgotten? We're not looking forward to immigration. According to Jim and Alice, the immigration officer makes Madame Defarge look like Whoopi Goldberg. Jim has bet me a rum punch I can't get her to smile. There's also a side bet on whether we can do her forms, with corrections, for less than the $1.35 in fines they had to fork over. They refused to give us any hints about which were the trick questions.

But Jim hadn't reckoned with my hand. We sit down across from the immigration officer—me with my injured hand in my lap, searching for inconspicuousness and failing to find it. She looks at our papers, but every few moments her eyes return to my clumsily bandaged appendage. Blood is still clearly visible through the gauze and tape. She is curious; she is not going to ask. "I ran it through the windlass," I say, sheepishly.

The smile begins in her eyes and proceeds to her lips. She manages not to laugh out loud. "Are you OK?" she asks.

"I've been better, but nothing seems to be broken."

"Good," she says, barely stifling a giggle. "Let me help you with these forms and we can get you out of here in just a few minutes."

She does, and we are—no fines. I am not even going to try to collect the rum punch. Jim will never believe it.

17

JOST TIME

The allure of Great Harbour, Jost Van Dyke, is something of a mystery. The anchorage is deep and the holding is only fair. Snorkeling is rotten by any reasonable standard. Shoreside accommodations are not the stuff of travel brochures. Cinder-block houses with rusting tin roofs, dusty lanes, scrawny chickens pecking in the dirt.

Foxy's has attracted four competing beach bars. None seem to be thriving. Provisioning is minimal. The bakery and the four grocery stores together probably have only as much stock as a gas-station food mart in the United States. Scrub and cactus provide the landscaping, and the cocoa-colored "freshwater" lagoon emptying into the harbor bubbles like a sewage-plant settling pond. Yet cruisers, us included, hang out here for days, often weeks.

Perhaps we are overwhelmed by the sheer joy of settling down in calm water after a week or more at sea. Raising anchor and charging off somewhere else has modest appeal. There's also something about the place that seems to define the Caribbean island. From the anchorage, Jost lives up to the sailing-mag image—half-moon beach, palm trees, turquoise water. A casual glance ashore suggests that there is no population, or at least none that moves. Everything appears totally laid back.

A bit of poking about reveals that there's a lot more going on than meets the casual eye. Although they may be barely scraping by (Foxy excepted), everybody on Jost seems to have two or three occupations. The beach bars double as gift shops or grocery stores. Mrs. Smallwood, who runs the ice house, also makes cunning Christmas tree ornaments—bells, angels, kewpie dolls—from shells and scraps of wood and bird feathers. Her homemade chutneys are first-rate too.

Great Harbor, Jost Van Dyke.

Mrs. Smallwood's ornaments are not just for tourists. Jostians decorate the whole island for Christmas. Christmas trees are the dried stalks of century plants—a form of aloe that puts up a 20-foot flower stalk about every twenty-five years. Most of these are erected outside, festooned with empty beer cans and bottles, aluminum pie plates, and bits of foil. In the Caribbean sunshine, the effect is festive and decadent at the same time, like a Dickens trollop decked out in cheap finery, laughing at her own appearance, ready for whatever is next.

We are informed by Foxy's son and bartender that the woman in "the blue house by the big tree" does laundry. We can sure use that, and she is not hard to find. There is only one "big tree" on this side of Jost. The house at one time may have been blue. Business must be good. She seems to be supporting her husband, her father, two daughters, a son, and three grandchildren. The women work in the plywood shack that houses the washing machines. It overflows with black plastic garbage bags of washing, each marked with the name of a visiting boat. So far as we can tell, the guys drink rum and watch TV.

Most homes or shops seem to be either falling down or under construction. It's hard to tell which, because "both" is usually the right answer. Everyone seems to be adding a room or a porch or redoing the roof. Progress on the new is slow, and the sun and salt of the Caribbean, not to mention tropical storms and hurricanes, ravage the old.

The impression that folks are letting things go is inconsistent with their constant industry. Construction is laborious. No one has a project of sufficient scale to justify purchasing building equipment heavier than a portable circular saw. Lack of financing slows progress further. Banks often require that construction projects be financed 50 percent with cash to qualify for a loan—at 20 percent interest. The banks are not particularly rapacious. Their terms reflect a realistic appraisal of the likely market for half-finished cinder-block and concrete shacks on Jost Van Dyke. No one but government officials and Foxy's relatives has secure employment. The default rate must be pretty high. The sensible islander's response to these lending terms is to tell the bank to stuff it. He builds as and when he gets enough cash to buy some more materials. The materials, brought in by boat, usually from the United States, Puerto Rico, or Venezuela, are horrendously expensive.

In short, while a lot of things look run-down, indolence of the local population is not the reason. The rum-and-ganja culture has its captives, but most Jostians are working hard. This seemingly benign environment, the vacation paradise that we pasty northerners crave, is hellishly difficult for those trying to live off the land and the sea. "Old money" of the sort that helps capitalize the Bermudian economy seems virtually nonexistent.

The British Virgin Islands, Jost included, were strangers to the economic boom that made colonial plantation owners wealthy on the British sugar islands: Barbados, Jamaica, Nevis, St. Kitts, Antigua. Settlers in the BVI were seldom the second or third sons of gentry, sent out to gather in easy fortunes on land grants from the Crown, a favored duke, or the British West Indies Company. They were mostly freed bondsmen who had worked off their indentures in the cane fields of Barbados and found all the island's arable land taken. They followed the wind and current northwest to unoccupied territory.

Unoccupied for a reason. The soil of much of the Virgins is thin, the rainfall modest and vacillating. In the whole BVI group, there is no river, hardly a stream. These debt-ridden settlers bought or brought African slaves to work the ground crops and cotton that could be cultivated in the BVI; ran a few cattle and pigs (goats seemed to fare best); took up fishing, privateering, and piracy. They produced some sugar cane, but only in a few of the better-watered locations.

Seventeenth-century governors of the Leeward Islands, whose administrative domain included the BVI, routinely suggested that all the inhabitants of the BVI be removed and resettled in some more hospitable colony. In 1709, Governor Parke complained, "They live like wild people, with no order and no government." These were tough men—desperate East Anglian, Welsh, and Irish laborers who had indentured themselves, or been tricked or dragooned ("Barbadosed" in seventeenth-century slang), into the tropical bondage of the Barbados plantations, and survived. "A sort of loose, vagrant people, vicious and destitute of means to live at home," claimed a 1693 treatise on the sugar trade. About all they could have learned from their Barbados masters was greed, gluttony, habitual drunkenness, and cruelty.

There were some good times. Privateering was exceedingly profitable for half a century—from the Seven Years' War (1756–73) through the American Revolution (1775–83) to the end of the Napoleonic Wars (1793–1815). War made even high-cost BVI sugar marketable. During this brief period, little Jost must have looked much less laid back than it does today. A census in 1756 put the population at 54 whites and 472 slaves. Learning and accomplishment followed the money. William Thornton, a Quaker planter on Jost, won the competition to design both the Philadelphia Public Library and the U.S. Capitol building. This polymath was also awarded a gold medal by the American

Philological Society in 1793 for his *Cadmus, or a Treatise on the Elements of Language.*

Had Anne and I been sitting in Great Harbour in 1789 rather than 1999, we would almost surely have been privateers. The Virgins lie athwart the north–south shipping lanes from North America to the West Indies and the east–west lanes from the Lesser to the Greater Antilles. There was a British prize court in Roadtown, Tortola, and a free port attracting shipping of all flags in Danish St. Thomas. Sailing downwind from Jost, we could pick off an American, French, Dutch, even a British merchantman beating out of St. Thomas Harbour, and take her into Roadtown. There the vice-admiralty court would almost certainly adjudicate her a prize. We could auction the cargo, or run up a British flag and send it on to London or Amsterdam.

I've seen no reports of the prize court's conduct in Roadtown, but Elizabeth Robertson's little classic, *The Spanish Town Papers*, examines the 1,000 prizes adjudicated in the vice-admiralty court in Spanish Town, Jamaica, from 1776 to 1783. She finds virtually no records of ships declared innocent of either trading with the enemy or being an American ship.

Either nefarious purpose justified awarding the captured vessel to her captor. And either could be proved by any available evidence: the ship's papers, flags carried, the testimony of captain or crew, their nationalities, the cargo. Ships' papers were often suspect. Most ships carried multiple flags for disguise and were manned by crews of many nationalities. The crew, seldom told the vessel's destination, held many opinions. Even a barrel of salt or powder could be used as evidence of an intent to deliver it to the American rebels, known to be increasingly desperate for both. To resolve this conflicting evidence, the court need only look to its own interest. A judgment of "prize" netted a percentage of the take; acquittal yielded a small fixed fee.

Oh, to be a British privateer in the 1770s. Or a merchant in a town with a vice-admiralty court auctioning goods left and right at a fraction of their value. Governor Shirley, of the British Leewards, reporting home in the midst of the American Revolution, complained that French produce was being taken to Tortola, "where by some means or other it [is] converted into British produce and shipped in British bottoms to the ports of Great Britain. . . ." The magic lay in the power of the vice-admiralty court to declare prizes.

But the nineteenth and twentieth centuries were unkind to the BVI. The poor soil gave out; the wars ended; economic decline ensued. In 1961, the government officially staked the islands' economic future on the tourist trade. The multitude of small, protected harbors now cater to yachtsmen on charter, the small resorts to tourists who want little more than to drop out of time. Certainly not into history. The combination of tropical rot, insects, fires, and hurricanes has erased almost every trace of the naval drama and human misery that characterized the British imperial period.

The heirs of the British settlers are today in pretty short supply. Unlike the North American colonials, who immigrated for religious and political freedom, the West Indies colonials were in it for the money. They either made it and went home or didn't make it and moved, either to North America or back to Britain. Many believed, for good reason, that more than a few seasons in the tropics would break any European's health. Of their island colonies, the British colonials would have called only Bermuda a "paradise." Or, as one eighteenth-century settler titled his memoirs of the West Indies, *My Paradise Is Hell.* He, and they, left it to the Africans, who had never confused it with anything else.

The British Virgins are still a crossroads. If we just hang out at Jost long enough, we can probably meet everyone in the southwest Atlantic cruising community. Jim and Cynthia on LATITUDE, for example, show up three days after we arrive. We last saw them in Kilmarnock, Virginia, on our way down the Chesapeake.

Jim is a retired political science professor. Because I hang out with some of that crowd too, we have a lot of interests and people in common. Cynthia is a field anthropologist. Two days on Jost and I suspect she knows everybody by name and blood relationship. Our reunion is marred only slightly by their embarrassment at having every boat in the anchorage telling them to call the Coast Guard. A nervous friend back in the States reported them "missing" because they were four days overdue. No search was launched. The Coast Guard definition of "overdue" is that you have failed to arrive at your destination assuming an average passage speed of *three* mph.

In addition to cruisers, Great Harbour attracts a daily turnover of charterers—sailors on rented boats, here for a week's respite from the cold. We've done this ourselves many times. Given our passage from Bermuda, we see new reasons to think it a sensible way to spend time in the islands. What we never realized as charterers, though, was that cruisers regarded us as dangerous, irresponsible greenhorns, not fellow sailors.

On a typical day, our cruisers' anchor watch in Great Harbour begins at 3:30 P.M. Charter boats are pouring in from Tortola and Red Hook and Charlotte Amalie. The charterers have arrived at Great Harbour, Jost Van Dyke, where they are required by the iron laws of Virgin Islands charter-boat culture to spend at least one night at Foxy's. If you didn't do Foxy's, you weren't there.

Meanwhile, we cruisers are eyeing the approaching charter fleet with deep suspicion—perhaps "fear and loathing" would be more apt. Every owner finds something to do on deck between 3:30 and 5:30 P.M. We look busy with our boats, but that's not why we're there. We're there to tell the charterers to keep clear, to put out enough scope on the anchor chain, and not to leave their crappy pieces of lookalike bathtub plastic until they know the anchor is set.

The charter companies' brochures do not feature the steely glares of ill-tempered cruisers. Making peace with them is not covered in the chart briefing. Nor should it be. To the cruising community, a charterer is an inferior being. Strike up a conversation with a cruiser at Foxy's and you will learn the meaning of disrespect. In fact, the charterers will never talk about them to each other any more than they will confess their deepest anxieties and feelings of inadequacy. Because that is the role of cruisers in every harbor—to make the charterers feel like neophytes.

From the charterers' perspective, this is ridiculously unfair. Back home, the friends and family think you're an adventurer. You didn't go to the Club Med and take orders from the recreation director. You're not on a cruise ship where your most meaningful act of the day is to choose what to eat at dinner. You're piloting a boat in strange waters, taking responsibility for your own fate, exploring on your own. That's what we felt like when we were chartering.

Yet in every anchorage, the charterer encounters these incredibly equipped cruising boats. They are almost invisible behind the gear that makes the true cruiser—wind generators, solar panels, jerry jugs, wind vanes, fold-up bicycles, awnings, RIBs. Most of all, it's the jerry jugs—yellow for diesel, red for gasoline, blue for water. Every cruising boat has an emergency store of these precious liquids *because they actually go places where you can't get the stuff.*

As you look at these cruising vessels—sloops, yawls, cutters, ketches, schooners, even junks—wood, steel, aluminum, fiberglass, and ferrocement—there is one obvious commonality in their design. They look nothing like each other or the charter-boat fleet. They tell you what you already know but would rather suppress. This gleaming toy you are on was built for the charter trade. Its role is to pack as many pallid vacationers as possible into its confined spaces and move them maybe 15 miles on a long day, from one night's anchorage to the next. No *real* cruiser would consider buying one of these things. Every last person on a cruising boat believes that in five years, this gleaming steed you're sailing will be junk. They think less of you because you flew down and chartered it, rather than beating your brains out on the Bermuda-to-BVI run like they did. They will not speak to you in Foxy's.

We find it impossible not to participate in this ritual of charterer dissing. It justifies our preparation and anxiety and discomfort. We've sailed 1,600 miles of ocean to get here. What could we have in common with these jerks who laugh too much and need three people on the bow to put out too little anchor line? So what if we were in their shoes last year. We're cruisers now.

Charterers can now be told the truth. If cruisers haven't perfected these vile habits elsewhere, they learn to be obnoxious to charter boats in Great Harbour, Jost Van Dyke, BVI, where the anchorage is always crowded, the holding is poor, and one night at Foxy's is mandatory.

ANNE'S PASSAGE NOTES: FREEDOM

We are lazily puttering about, exploring Jost, doing some boat work, getting real tans, reading, writing, painting, and just hanging out. Heavy-duty exercise means extended snorkeling. There is nothing we *have* to do, nobody we *have* to see (at least not anytime soon), nothing driving anything. Night and day occur. We get hungry and eat. There are land things to be done. We do them or not. We see friends on nearby boats, or not. We sleep. Naps often involve activities more strenuous and pleasurable than sleep. PALAEMON has her demands, and we care for her.

At sea, we forced ourselves into the artificial structure of our three-hour-on, three-hour-off watch system. Even that, though, was an organization of our own making, and we could change it at our whim. We do have an added structural dimension at sea, one that we cannot change, that results from traveling without land-type roadways and markers. Our waypoints at sea are degrees of latitude and longitude. At first I found it disconcerting that the only way to think about the particularly bad squall the day before was in relation to our geographic coordinates. It didn't seem natural to me to think, "Oh, yes. That was when we passed 24 degrees north latitude."

Moreover, I found latitude and longitude confusing. It seemed strange to me that latitude lines, the circles that go around the earth from east to west, measure our position north or south of the equator. Similarly, the longitude lines that ring the earth from north to south (or top to bottom) measure our position east or west of Greenwich, England. But it is a logical system, a manmade grid laid upon the globe.

Universal plotting sheets reinforced my early sense of living within an artificially designated space. The sheets are laid out to cover four degrees of latitude and four degrees of longitude, any four. We began by labeling a stack of them with the latitudes and longitudes we expected to traverse. At the end of each watch, we took our actual latitude and longitude and marked our position on these sheets, drawing a line from the prior position. This process enabled us to visualize our course as we made our way east, then south, and helped us know whether we were trending too far in one direction or another. The plotting sheets are otherwise featureless—no land, no water, just space defined by numbers. Many nights I sat staring blankly at the sheets, my mind foggy from sleep deprivation, trying to convince myself again that I should be measuring north on latitude lines and east on longitude lines.

Eventually the terminology began to mesh with experience. After all, the longitude was all-important in getting to the easterly trades that brought us south. We *had* to reach 65°W longitude before we got to the trades, or we'd be in for a bashing. So 65°W began to take on real meaning. Each degree contains 60 minutes of arc or 60 nautical miles. We began to talk about two-degree boats or three-degree boats, based on the mileage a boat may expect to cover in a day. Two-and-a-half degrees per day is nice progress for PALAEMON. So we might get from 26°N to 23° 30'N on a good day—and find ourselves in enormously different conditions from the day before.

I am surprised at how thoroughly we have absorbed these two very different guiding structures, the lat/lon grid and our watch system, how integral they have become to our thinking. Even now, as we enjoy these hedonistic days, we are keenly aware that, at 64° 45'W longitude, we still have more easting to make when we head down through the Leewards and Windwards toward Trinidad. And our watch system now seems hardwired. With two boats anchored too close to us the other night and the winds up, we reverted to our watch system as naturally as though it had been a way of life for years.

The coordinates of our land-based lives are now almost irrelevant. We have trouble remembering the day of the week. That we should know our latitude and longitude without having to think about it, and not know the day of the week? Sometimes Jerry even gets the month wrong. The tyranny of time is gone.

At anchor, we measure time, if at all, by the sun. We float, only tenuously attached to the earth. We drift about in a chosen space, sensed as a relation to other boats and to the nearest shore. My release from the demands of being in the right place at the right time bubbles up in easy laughter, sometimes in tears of happiness.

18

SUGAR, SLAVES, AND SNORKELS

We move PALAEMON to St. Thomas, U.S. Virgin Islands, to shop and to pick up our younger son Mark, daughter-in-law Mary, and granddaughter Samantha. This island has an odd, unsettled atmosphere. We see a population of waiters, maids, and busboys; cab drivers, clerks, and small-time merchants—people who spend their days catering to tourists, mostly Americans, all apparently rich. This army of service workers does not seem to have a terrific attitude or self-image. The problem is only partly economic. By comparison with much of the Caribbean, St. Thomas is prosperous, a magnet for the down-island unemployed. Half the locals we meet are from somewhere else in the Leewards or Windwards. Most want to go home, but there is no work. Locals beyond middle age often watch their children move on to even greater economic opportunity in the States. U.S. Virgin Islanders seem forever poised between staying and returning home, staying or emigrating to the States. They are American citizens, with no vote in mainland affairs. Their islands are substantially owned by "continental" Americans, who employ, and exploit, off-island aliens to suppress local wage rates.

This sense of transience and threatened identity may be the USVI version of "roots," a continuous thread in the islands' social fabric. When Columbus sent a boat ashore at St. Croix for water in 1493, he began the extermination and expulsion of the true native population, the Caribs. That project took more than a century, and the Caribs gave almost as good as they got, but it ensured that the post-sixteenth-century population would all be newcomers.

The newcomers barely trickled in. Until Francis Drake rediscovered the Virgins in 1595, the European scramble for empire in the Caribbean mostly passed them by. Small settlements of French, Dutch, British, and Danes squabbled over ownership while living under constant threat from Spanish raiding parties based in nearby Puerto Rico. The Spaniards just looted, burned, and went home. Spain viewed the Virgins as too insignificant to warrant settlement.

By the time the Danes purchased St. Croix from the French in 1733, the island had flown five national flags, many of them more than once. Because title could be claimed by discovery, conquest, treaty, or settlement, virtually every imperial European power had a claim to most of the Virgins. Danish sovereignty was not solidified until the British finally gave up their claim to St. John in 1783. The claims of the Indians, of course, didn't count. St. Croix seems to have been the first West Indian island ever purchased by one government from another. America followed this precedent by purchasing the whole group from the Danes in 1917.

It is not just historically contested nationality that makes the character of the U.S. Virgins elusive. "Virgin Islander" doesn't seem to describe an ethnic or national identity today—or, if it does, it is one under continuous threat. The Danes, who can perhaps claim the longest continuous ownership, were never a majority of even the Europeans on the islands. For centuries, the dominant European language has been English, and most place names are Spanish, Dutch, French, or English. Africans have outnumbered Europeans since at least the seventeenth century, but they originally represented perhaps forty language groups, snatched from hundreds of tribal homelands. The West African slaves' common heritage was, like that of their descendants, the heritage of bondage and oppression, an oppositional culture that need not generate any particular positive cultural identity. To know what you are against is not necessarily to know who you are. In his fascinating 1995 lectures, *History, Fable and Myth in the Caribbean and the Guianas,* Wilson Harris complains:

> The exploitation of man by man, inhumanity by man to man, is reinforced, ironically I believe, by ceaseless catalogue of injustice. We need somehow to find an original dislocation within which to unlock a body of claustrophobic assumptions which strengthens itself by promoting a self-encircling round of protest—obsession with irreconcilable difference . . . like a static clock that crushes all into the time of conquest.

I feel that the Virgin Islander is dislocated. But I fail to sense the unlocking of an authentic cultural identity.

Charlotte Amalie on St. Thomas has one of the best harbors in the Caribbean. The Danes valued it and the Virgins primarily as a trading post for ships of all nationalities. It was a haven for privateers, who had to share their booty with the sovereign whose prize courts legalized their conquests. The vendors, cab drivers, guides, and hustlers who today swarm around the incoming cruise ships at Charlotte Amalie follow in the footsteps of the polyglot merchants and stevedores who serviced the bustling trade of the late eighteenth and early nineteenth centuries. During those years of almost continuous war, every ship was a potential prize, and a port favoring no nationality was a privateer's dream destination.

Since then, the U.S. Virgin Islands suffered a century of economic decline, losing half their population between 1850 and 1930. Then came a giddy decade of development. In 1930 there were as many Virgin Islanders in Harlem as in the USVI—20,000 more or less. Between 1960 and 1970, the USVI population doubled officially, and almost trebled, if estimates of uncounted alien workers from Puerto Rico and down island are included. Nearly two million visitors, mostly Americans, now pass through annually, mostly on cruise ships. The number of ships stopping at Charlotte Amalie rivals the glory days of free-port maritime activity under the Danes. I would give a lot to have encountered this harbor in 1800 rather than 2000.

Amid all this change, what does it mean to be a Virgin Islander? Native-born blacks and whites have been a minority since 1965. Continentals, Puerto Ricans, and off-island West Indians now have sufficient numbers to form their own enclaves, establish their own clubs. There is a large measure of political self-determination, and constant political activity, but the USVI is neither an independent nation nor privileged, like Puerto Rico, to choose statehood and become fully "American."

The price of attracting development capital in the1960s was a rapid transfer of the ownership of both enterprise and prime real estate to continentals. The price of making that capital productive was a dramatic increase in imported workers. Little has changed since 1974, when the Organization of Concerned Virgin Islanders protested their "gradual social, economic, and political annihilation." Their prediction that "our children and grandchildren will become strangers in their own homeland" merely seems prescient.

Our attempts to discuss contemporary USVI territorial politics with locals usually go nowhere. Perhaps the subject is beneath the dignity of sensible people. Perhaps we just don't know how to join a conversation that has always been more personality- than issue-driven. But the signs of disarray are not hard to spot. With boatloads of tourist money flooding in, the schoolteachers still have not been paid for the last sixty days of 1999. The government is going, hat in hand, to the U.S. Congress—again. As one islander ruefully puts it, "It's nice to have a rich uncle." But it's not really nice for your government to be a joke and to have to grovel before a Congress that's not yours and that likes nothing better than grovelers. Bureaucrats and territorial governors who don't grovel just get their budgets slashed. Perhaps U.S. Virgin Islanders are now simply too like us for us to see their culture at all.

Hiking the steep rock trails of St. John, we stumble across the ruined terraces that slave labor built into the mountainsides to permit sugar production. The human cost of this feat must have been enormous. The days of major sugar cultivation in the West Indies are now long gone, but sugar was king for nearly a century. Hundreds of thousands of Africans were brought to work and die in Europe's West Indian colonies. Cheaper sugar from more hospitable terrains, and the rise of the European-grown sugar beet, finally doomed the island plantocracy. The abolition of slavery also played a role. But abolition in the West Indies tracks the loss of Caribbean sugar's profitability with uncomfortable closeness.

We trek up to the ruins of the Annaberg sugar plantation on St. John with Mark, Mary, and Samantha. The National Park Service has only recently restored some of the grounds. The blades of the windmill used to crush the cane have long since rotted away, but the stone-and-copper cooking vats remain. The ruined stone walls of the sheds and kitchen still stand. It's an oddly tranquil place. Few visitors seem to come. We are alone with the ghosts of the slaves whose lives were lashed to the backbreaking, bone-crushing demands of the mill.

Sugar cane spoils rapidly once ripe in the fields, and the juice will begin to ferment within a few hours of cutting. Harvest time is a frenzy of cutting, hauling, and crushing cane. The only beast of burden working beside the slaves in this hilly country was the asinegoe, the little donkey that came, like the blacks, from Africa. Asinegoes carried cut cane from field to mill, and their wild, garbage-loving offspring still shatter the Caribbean dawn with a hee-haw that blasts us out of our bunks.

St. John beach donkey.

Two teams of slaves fed the millstones from opposite sides, stuffing in the cane, guiding it out through vertical stone cylinders that crushed the cane between them. To let a hand be carried between the rollers with the cane was certain death. The windmill could not be stopped in time. The slaves struggled through twelve-hour shifts, night and day, four to six months of each year, their bodies fueled by chewing cane and sneaking cups of juice from the holding vats.

I can almost hear the rumble of the mashing cylinders, the cries of the overseer and boiling men, feel the heat of the sun and the fires, sense the near-panic of keeping the mill fed, the real panic of a wind shift when all hands rush to turn the cap of the mill, reorienting the blades before they are shredded from the force of the wind.

The juice from crushed cane sluices down stone gutters directly to the boiling room. Anxious boilers ladle it to smaller and smaller kettles over hotter and hotter fires as the water boils off. The chief boiler must gauge the critical moment. He signals for the heavy syrup to be removed from the vats and poured into clay pots. In the curing sheds, brown muscovado sugar will crystallize at the top, molasses will settle out. If the boiler has misjudged the removal time the set will be ruined. Mostly molasses will result from the cure, to be mixed with raw juice, fermented, and distilled into rum. Sugar sells dear, rum cheap. The overseer will not be pleased.

Little St. John had 109 sugar plantations in 1733, and the owners ran them with the aid of some of the harshest slave laws ever written. The code issued by Governor Gardelin in that same year has to be read to be believed:

1. The leader of runaway slaves shall be pinched three times with red-hot iron, and then hung.
2. Each other runaway slave shall lose one leg, or, if the owner pardon him, shall lose one ear, and receive one hundred and fifty stripes [lashes].
3. Any slave being aware of intention of others to run away, and not giving information, shall be burned in the forehead, and receive one hundred stripes.
4. Those who inform of plots to run away shall receive ten dollars for each slave engaged therein.
5. A slave who runs away for eight days, shall have one hundred and fifty stripes; twelve weeks, shall lose a leg; and six months, shall forfeit his life, unless the owner pardon him with the loss of one leg.
6. Slaves who steal to the value of four rix-dollars, shall be pinched and hung; less than four rix-dollars, to be branded, and receive one hundred and fifty stripes.

7. Slaves who receive stolen goods, as such, or protect runaways, shall be branded, and receive one hundred and fifty stripes.

8. A slave who lifts his hand to strike a white person, or threatens him with violence, shall be pinched and hung, should the white person demand it, if not, to lose his right hand.

9. One white person shall be sufficient witness against a slave, and if a slave be suspected of crime, he can be tried by torture.

10. A slave meeting a white person shall step aside and wait until he passes, if not, he may be flogged.

11. No slave will be permitted to come to town with clubs or knives, nor fight with each other, under penalty of fifty stripes.

12. Witchcraft shall be punished with flogging.

13. A slave who shall attempt to poison his master, shall be pinched three times with red-hot iron, and then be broken on a wheel.

14. A free negro who shall harbour a slave or thief, shall lose his liberty, or be banished.

15. All dances, feasts, and plays are forbidden unless permission be obtained from the master or overseer.

16. Slaves shall not sell provisions of any kind without permission from their overseers.

17. No estate slave shall be in town after drum-beat, otherwise he shall be put in the fort and flogged.

18. The King's Advocate is ordered to see these regulations carried into effect.

Promulgated in the midst of drought and near-starvation, this desperate document helped spark one of the most successful early slave revolts. St. John's slaves, presumably including those from the Annaberg properties where we are now standing, took and held the island for six months. Unable to quell the revolt with British help from St. Kitts and nearby Tortola, the Danish governor called in the French, who sent two well-armed ships and several hundred battle-tried troops from Martinique. The Europeans might contest the territory, but in the face of slave rebellion, they could act as one nation. The French quashed the St. John's revolt lest it spread by example to their rich properties, particularly Haiti. Every rebel was killed or committed suicide.

We talk with the gardener who is re-creating the plantation garden. He is proud of the plants he is coaxing from the rocky soil, protected from marauding goats and donkeys by a high wire fence. A woman sits at a bench weaving a basket. She says she is ninety years old, and the only woman on the island who knows how to collect "basket vine." You have to get it in the right place, she says, and only on the night of a new moon. Otherwise it won't work right; the basket will be brittle; it won't last. Her hands are as large and gnarled as a man's, but her fingers still move quickly. A basket takes shape as we chat. She, at least, seems at home here, although the Park Service apparently uses her as an exhibit.

But we hardly fill our days in the Virgins with historico-political or anthropological musings. With Mark, Mary, and Samantha now aboard, we are more into marine biology—well, OK—snorkeling. The startling thing about snorkeling or diving the reefs of the Virgins is that every fish, crustacean, and coral on our fauna identification card is actually here. We consult weightier and weightier tomes to try to identify the creatures that lurk just a few feet under the surface. We spy some new and unidentifiable animal, requiring further research, on almost every expedition. Inter-snorkeler disputes concerning the size, coloration, location, or shape of the newly discovered species dominate post-snorkeling conversations. Our observational skills may be suspect, but our confidence is unshakable.

Underwater exploration is particularly good around St. John. Much of the Island is a national park, courtesy of the Rockefeller family. Free mooring buoys have been put in to protect the reefs from careless anchoring—by charterers surely, not cruisers. The wildlife is chaperoned by courteous, but serious, park rangers, often uniformed in swimsuits and snorkeling gear rather than the familiar taupe Park Service uniform with its distinctive stiff-brimmed hat.

We are astonished, and embarrassed, to have one of these guys pop up from the water as we are landing JEREMY on the beach, to proclaim, "Excuse me. National Park Service. This is protected turtle habitat. No dinghy landing is permitted." He is quite polite, perhaps because our error is not too egregious—the buoys marking the restricted area were washed away by Hurricane Lenny.

There are turtles. Fascinating creatures. Gliding along the surface, poking up their bald heads and dark, unblinking eyes, they suggest the studied calm of aged Italian peasants. Down on the bottom, they munch turtle grass almost continuously, like so many aquatic cows. I hang above and watch them, wondering why I don't sit and watch cows cropping grass. Perhaps I should; it's very peaceful.

The turtle population is endangered, but its troubles are of long standing. Mariners from Columbus forward found the sea turtle an ideal source of fresh meat. Unrefrigerated beef or pork spoils in no time, and keeping live cattle or

Anne's favorite.

pigs on board is tricky, to put it mildly. The sea turtle, by contrast, is wonderfully obliging and easy to catch. A quick swimmer can do it by hand. The Arawaks reportedly taught the Europeans to use a remora fish on a line. Remora are sucker fish that attach themselves to the turtle's shell, detaching occasionally to pick up a tidbit dropped from their host's jaws. Most larger turtles have one or two of these sucker satellites hanging around. You just send forth your remora and wait for him to catch you a turtle.

Once caught and turned on its back, a sea turtle is powerless to escape—even to move. Better yet, turtles can survive for weeks with just a bit of seawater thrown over them from time to time. The explorers, conquerors, settlers, navies, privateers, pirates, and traders who plied the Caribbean from 1492 until the twentieth century harvested turtles by the hundreds of thousands. That any are left is a near-miracle.

We discover that, as snorkelers, our favorite spots and favorite fauna are as varied as our tastes in ice cream. I like deep holes and caves with huge coral formations, or drifting through dense schools of tiny blue chromis. Anne likes shallow reefs. She is particularly attached to the trunkfish, a bizarre, almost triangular little creature that hovers about by rotating its pectoral fins, warily eyeing anything approaching its territory. The trunkfish looks about as happy to have humans floating over its reef as a cruiser observing the approach of the charter fleet while on afternoon anchor watch.

Mary is in love with everything underwater—large barracudas perhaps excepted. Mark has a project, a search for the green moray eel. He finds one on his last snorkel. He is as happy as a marine biologist who has identified a new species.

His excitement sends me back thirty years, to when Mark was six. We had been fishing for a week in northern Lake Huron, Les Cheneaux Islands. Jay and I had caught northern pike by the boatload; Mark had struck out. On the last evening, Mark and I went out after dinner to try one last time. It

Mark's moray.

was cold, a north wind had sprung up, it would soon be dark. We trolled the weed beds, fished all the usually productive spots. Mark cast and cast. On his seventeenth "final cast," a northern struck; Mark managed to get him to the boat; I penned him in the net.

In my study at home, I have a snapshot of Mark holding that fish. I see that same eager expression when he returns to report his sighting of the elusive green moray. He has grown into a wonderful, gentle man, with the usual load of adult burdens. I want to take the burdens away, to let him be that little boy again. For the moment, he is.

Our granddaughter Samantha (eleven going on thirty-something) hits the water in every anchorage almost before we can get PALAEMON stopped. To our delight, she is fearless, fascinated, indefatigable. She snorkels in spots where I swear she can only be watching the turtle grass bend in the current. Her favorite creature—the sea cucumber—only gives further evidence of her independent turn of mind. Sea cucumbers look like some sort of giant slug. Actually, that is too polite. The most common sea cucumber in the Caribbean is aptly named the "Donkey Dung Sea Cucumber." Its usual color is a mud-brown, although brighter hues are not unknown. It moves almost imperceptibly. Distinguishing a sea cucumber's head from its tail is a challenge.

Samantha's fascination is with the sea cucumber's defense mechanisms. When poked, it responds over a wide range of behaviors: from continuing to be inert, to inflating itself to double its size, to the improbable, and rare, regurgitation of most of its internal organs. This latter trick is apparently not sea-cucumber suicide; it can regenerate the lost body parts. Nor is it just some form of undersea gross-out. This yucky behavior convinces many attackers simply to eat the sea cucumber's visceral offering and go away. I tend to think Darwin's views on natural selection are mostly sound. But I have to admit that believing sea cucumbers just stumbled onto this regurgitation defense by random genetic mutation takes some suspension of disbelief.

When I think about Samantha in the Virgins, I generally have a vision of her ankles and feet disappearing as she makes a surface dive. Sometimes she is chasing a stingray or a turtle, or even taking a closer look at the fantastic array of brightly colored fish on the coral reef. But mostly she is going down to poke another sea cucumber to see what it will do.

Samantha's friend.

Travel lift or trellis?

While my fingers and toes are pretty wrinkled from overdoses of snorkeling, we do not spend all our time underwater in the Virgin Islands. My favorite land activity is hiking from somewhere, almost anywhere, on St. John, to Coral Bay for a hamburger at Skinny Legs. In the competition for best beach bars in the islands, Skinny Legs has to be in the top ten. The food is terrific. The ambience is island-decadent, without the slightest apology to decency. The roof—really a patchwork awning made of cast-off sails and bits of corrugated plastic—leaks dramatically. I'm talking waterfalls here, not drips and drops.

Skinny Legs seems to have tried at one time to be a sports bar with three TV sets. The mountings for two of them stand empty. The sets were stolen because there is no way to lock up the place. To have doors and locks, you need walls all around. Skinny Legs only has two. The third TV set, padlocked into a steel case above the bar, plays constantly, with satellite hookup yet. The cruising clientele demands that the bartender tune it only to the Weather Channel—so they can see how awful it is in Syracuse—or to the CNN business channel, so they can worry about whether their nest egg is going to earn enough to keep them cruising instead of working.

Other enterprises have sprouted up around Skinny Legs. Two or three (it's hard to tell) gift shops sell everything from local arts and crafts to incense and stuffed animals. The Internet and phone shop actually manages to connect us to the 'net or to long-distance phone lines. This, we have discovered, is not a trivial accomplishment within the jurisdiction of the Cable and Wireless, Co., Ltd. A terrific stained-glass artist, for some reason, decided that a studio next to Skinny Legs was the place to be. Well, "next to" may not be quite right. You can't really tell where Skinny Legs ends and something else begins.

So I sometimes take my beer and go bother the stained-glass lady, or spill it on my computer in the phone shack, or take it outside (you're outside if there's no floor) to the horseshoe pit, or sit around with the other cruisers who are discussing the weather and the stock market and maybe trying to decide where to go next. But, hey, what's wrong with here? The boats in Coral Bay with seaweed growing from their bottoms all the way to the turtle grass say, "Nothing!" This is hanging at the mall for grown-ups. Having wasted my youth on school, sports, and jobs, I am making up for lost time.

We're grateful to the Rockefellers for making most of St. John a national park. (OK, it's blood money, but most robber barons and their kin never do anything nice with it.) Nevertheless, we're really glad they never managed to buy Coral Bay and make it into a national park, complete with eco-sensitive campgrounds, labeled trees, underwater snorkel trails, and health-food bars. In Coral Bay we can eat fantastically greasy, unbelievably scrumptious hamburgers at Skinny Legs, stay half-drunk all day, laugh at the weather in the United States, play horseshoes, and feel like we've washed up someplace real.

If hanging at Skinny Legs weren't enough to make us feel like outlaws, the USVI and BVI customs services gladly oblige. Strictly technically, whenever we move PALAEMON from a harbor in the USVI to a harbor in the BVI, or vice versa, we are supposed to clear out of the country we are leaving and clear into the country we are entering.

This means, for example, that if we are at Jost Van Dyke, BVI, and need to go the supermarket—nearest possibility the Marina Market at Red Hook, St. Thomas, USVI—we can expect to spend at least four hours checking in and out to make the round trip. In part this is because there is no customs office at Red Hook. To be legal, we would have to clear out at Jost, go to Cruz Bay, on St. John, to clear in to the USVI and then go to St. Thomas to the market. Then it's back to Cruz Bay to clear out and then back to Jost to clear in (always a pleasure). The total round trip is about 12 miles. Better allow a day and a half to get it done.

Or say we are in Red Hook, USVI, and want to go to The Bight at Norman Island, BVI, to snorkel the caves, look for the green moray eel, and eat at Billy Bones. To be legal, it's clear out at Cruz Bay, clear in at West End, Tortola, BVI, then proceed to Norman. Return trip same, same. This turns a four-hour sail into a day's torture. Why would anyone do it? Almost no one does. We're all outlaws.

I am happy to be carrying on, in this modest form, the tradition of the traders, privateers, and pirates of the age of sail in the Caribbean. And I seem to be winding down. I realized a few days ago that I couldn't find my watch. I have no idea how long it has been gone. It also occurs to me that we are distributing our boat cards less freely than before. We no longer seem to need to be assertive about the cruising-couple identity of PALAEMON's crew. Years ago, an English friend and teacher advised me, "Doing gets in the way of being." I was certain he was right. I am beginning, finally, to understand what he meant.

ANNE'S PASSAGE NOTES: WATCHING SAMANTHA

I see Samantha snorkeling, her bottom in her bright pink suit, her flat feet as she dives. Snorkeling is her passion. She is almost too fearless, wanting to touch everything and go everywhere. She's a natural in the water, despite poor form and no fins ("They *bother* me, Granny Annie"). Her face is luminous, large dark eyes and thick, almost black, curly lashes against peachy fair skin. She is animated, radiant, and full of joy. I love to watch the light on her face, the faint freckles the sun has sprinkled on her nose and cheeks.

I snorkel beside her sometimes, although Jerry, a bolder snorkeler than I, usually forages ahead with her. She holds our hands—something she would hardly deign to do on land—and she wants to share everything she sees. She takes in everything, points me to what I have missed.

I watch her work on her journal, remind her of it sometimes. Both Jerry and I conscientiously pull out books to help her identify shells and other objects she has found. She has been counseled firmly by her mother to keep up her journal, and to bring back samples of things she has seen. She is missing school to be with us this extra week after her parents have gone. A journal plus some sort of special report on her trip is her assignment in lieu of school. From Mary's side glance as she leaves, I understand that I have my assignment as well.

I watch with amusement as Samantha claims all available bunks as her own. She moves each night from one to another. The cockpit is a clear favorite, despite the ever-present risk of an overnight shower.

I sit and watch her in the rope swing that we find on a hike on St. John. The rope is as thick as my upper arm, and Samantha adores it. It is as though some creature put it there just for her. Her hike is over. We drag her a little farther before we realize that her heart is still rope-swinging, the promised views from atop the next rise not nearly so interesting. We return to the rope swing. Only the prospect of snorkeling pulls her away.

Together we watercolor. I do the scenes around us. Samantha makes up pictures—an open book with a candle, and a likeness of the carved wood bear she bought at Skinny Legs, "McBear." Her fondness for him seems to me markedly inconsistent with his plain, not to say homely, appearance. Nor do I quite get her joy in cuddling a wooden object. He turns out to be hard to paint, and we have interesting discussions on perspective and foreshortening, as well as mixing colors. Her representation of McBear turns out to be very McBear-like.

The best moments of all are not visual. Imperceptibly she becomes a boat person, at ease with PALAEMON's spaces and motion. I do not realize her attachment to living aboard until she exclaims that it is so sad that her cousins Paige and Jake and their parents will not stay on PALAEMON when they visit in St. Martin. "They'll miss so much. They'll miss the whole thing. They'll miss this. They'll miss all this. I'm so sad." I had not understood how much of "this" she had absorbed. My heart sings.

I am surprised that I find Samantha so completely companionable. Our interests are hardly the same. I have never been a doll person, and perhaps my worst moment is when she insists that I do a watercolor of Lindsay, her current favorite. But she can hold up her end of almost any conversation, endlessly inquisitive and thoughtful about what she hears. An avid reader, Samantha shows dogged, if not inspired, interest in keeping up her journal.

Our only real incompatibility is her incessant need to vocalize. Jerry and I share quiet and find it restful. A need for quiet is incomprehensible to Samantha. Whistling, singing, talking; she is sometimes silent when reading, but she often whistles. We wish she were a better whistler. Her snoring requires no further practice.

We return to Red Hook, St. Thomas, to put her on the plane for home. We have our last dinner and breakfast at Molly Malone's, an eatery that holds double charms for Samantha—iguanas to be fed and a lovely white cockatoo named Snowflake. Her imminent departure clouds all our horizons.

I am saddened as well that Lily, Samantha's sister, could not

The rope swing.

make the trip. Now eight, nearly nine, Lily has been burdened since birth with severe developmental disabilities. Managing her on PALAE-MON would have been a major challenge and a serious risk. But water fascinates Lily. Though she is many miles away, I have envisioned her often in the past two weeks, splashing happily in the shallows.

Samantha is uncharacteristically quiet on the way to the airport. Tears streak her freckles as we hug her good-bye. Our eyes are watery too, as we turn her over to the flight attendants. For many days afterward, there is a strong missing presence aboard PALAEMON. I see her reading in the cockpit, drawing, playing dominoes, swimming, sitting on the bow staring at the sea. An album of images in my head. Samantha in the vivid colors of herself and the Caribbean.

19

GIN AND THE ART OF BOAT MAINTENANCE

We watch Samantha walk away with her airline chaperon, wearing her back-pack, carrying her beloved Lindsay under one arm. We're waiting for her to turn around and give us one more wave, one more smile. Samantha is talking at warp speed to the flight attendant, who is probably already wondering who will be in charge of whom on this flight. They will soon turn a corner and be gone. At the last moment, Samantha remembers. She turns and waves.

While we wait to make sure Samantha's plane leaves on schedule, we re-visit our sailing plan and flip it again. Our original plan, months ago, had been to sail east from the BVI to St. Martin and then make our way south, island-hopping toward Carnival in Trinidad. But Easter and the Lenten season are so late this year that we realize we can't do Carnival and easily meet our commit-ments to be in the Grenadines in March and St. Martin in April. And if we aren't going to Carnival, Trinidad is not as good a cruising ground as Grenada. And if we are going to Grenada, we should go directly there and then work our way north to the Grenadines and St. Martin. Why take the slow route down through the Leewards and Windwards just to retrace our hops going back north?

On the new plan, we will wait for Jerome and Judith's schedule to clear in early February and sail together to Grenada. We can spend a week there with them, and a few days in Carriacou, before working our way up through the lower Grenadines to Bequia. When we turn north, HERMAN MELVILLE will head south to Trinidad for the hurricane season.

Our new plan means yet more time in the Virgins, but we can put it to good use. PALAEMON has a substantial backlog of projects that should be done before we leave for Grenada. After that, we will either be traveling hard or have other people aboard for several months.

My spirits sink as I confront the "to do" list. I really don't mind puttering about on PALAEMON, doing some project that reduces worry about gear fail-ure, or that makes sailing or living aboard easier or more comfortable. When a task can be done without time pressure, and done when I feel inspired to do it, working on the boat is relaxing and rewarding. A successful project makes me feel useful and competent, particularly if it's something I have never done before and I can accomplish it in about two hours. But few boat projects have even one of these features. Most routine maintenance is time-consuming, boring, and needs to be completed within a particular window of opportunity—such as when we're at a dock with access to parts and unlimited AC power to run power tools. Or when we have a couple of days of low humidity combined with light wind so varnish will dry, and pulling a varnish-laden brush from the can won't spray-paint the decks with a zillion tiny droplets. "New" ventures—improvements and upgrades—usually take six tries and three days to get things working properly. All I learn is that I'm an electromechanical idiot, and that whoever wrote the instruction manual does not count English as his or her first language.

My list includes varnishing and polishing. We apply two coats of exterior wood finish every six to eight weeks to ward off the evil day when all the trim has to be stripped to the bare wood and redone. With drying time, this routine chore takes two to four days. All the metal on PALAEMON is high-grade stainless steel. But stainless it is not. Salt spray creates surface rust that will become permanent pitting if not polished off about once a month. We need about a day to do a good job of rust removal. Cosmetic maintenance thus demands three or four days a month just to stay even.

My engine log tells me that I must soon spend a grubby, uncomfortable day changing fluids and filters and belts. The people who build sailboats and marine engines seem never to give a thought to making maintenance easy. Just to check the transmission-fluid level, I have to empty a large sail locker, take out two plywood panels, and crawl into a space designed for Spiderman. This takes about an hour.

Once I get myself into the appropriate yoga posture and inhale a few cubic yards of diesel fumes, I do other stuff that can only be done from here, like checking the sacrificial zincs in the engine's heat exchanger and the refrigeration condenser. Wherever seawater unites dissimilar metals, it creates low-voltage, but highly corrosive, electrical current. Because the resulting electrical degradation affects base metals first, zincs are put in the way of the current to be "sacrificed" to protect the higher-grade metal components. If I let the zincs get eaten away, the other metals will rapidly fail.

While I am at it, I had better adjust and grease the steering cable. And check the four dozen engine, plumbing, and refrigeration hose clamps that are accessible only from this locker. Hose clamps—those circular bits of steel strapping that hold water and fuel hoses onto their metal fittings—are constantly under attack by engine heating and cooling, vibration, and corrosion. I have now been scrunched in the port-side sail locker for two to three hours with occasional trips into the sunshine to find needed parts, tools, and Band-Aids, and to try to get the kinks out of my back and legs.

Before I leave the locker, I also check and adjust the stuffing box, the contraption for lubricating the propeller shaft where it goes through the hull between the engine and the propeller. With too little seawater cooling at this junction, the shaft will overheat and melt the fiberglass. With too much seawater lubrication, the boat sinks. It pays to keep an eye on the stuffing box. But, of course, it is located where I can't do that—except from the painful position that I am now occupying.

Checking the zincs in the engine compartment reminds me to check the zinc on the propeller hub. That one is underwater, so I have to check and replace it by diving. If I'm very careful, I don't cut my hands on the prop, I don't get any lumps on my head from waves mashing my cranium and the hull together, and I don't drop the screws that secure the zinc. At least I am not in Connecticut, where I have to wear a wet suit to do this job and the water is so murky the whole thing has to be accomplished by feel.

By the end of a day in the sail locker, I am dirty, bleeding, sore, and beat. I am wondering what in the hell made me think I wanted to live on a boat, and Anne is afraid to talk to me. But after a swim, a shower, and two Bombay Sapphires, I feel great. More than that, I feel virtuous, prudent, self-reliant, hardy, adept, and relieved. With luck, I won't have to go back in that locker for another six weeks.

This is, of course, just the routine stuff on my list—maintenance designed to avoid failures. But things fail. The rate varies, but something like once a day seems right. Most are minor, but even the minor ones often take considerable time. I spend the better part of four days in the BVI just battling water pumps.

The pump war begins innocently enough. As part of my standard maintenance routine, I take out the garbage bin from under the sink to tighten the hose clamps under there. But there is water on the floor. Something's leaking. Under the sink are two through-hull drains, two foot pumps (one for seawater and one from the freshwater tanks), one electric water pump (hot and cold fresh water), and eleven hoses. I have to inspect each one because, as usual, the observable water is no longer at the source of the leak.

By process of elimination, the freshwater foot pump seems to be the culprit. Upon removal, the pump reveals its little secret—a cracked housing. Not fixable. It has to be replaced. Fifteen calls later, I am satisfied that there is no replacement in the BVI. I order a new pump from St. Martin. Delivery prediction: one week.

No big deal, the pressure water pump still works. Two days later, water on the floor again. Why? Pressure water pump is failing. No problem. I've got a rebuild kit with all the parts that usually go bad.

So I take out the pump. That sounds straightforward, but this pump is thoughtfully tucked away outboard of the sink. By taking off the door that leads to the cavity underneath the sink, I can get about half my torso squeezed into this very dark, very claustrophobic compartment. I can reach the pump with one hand. Wearing a miner's headlight, I can see two of the four screws that hold the pump in place.

My first attempt at removing this pump requires one hour and forty-five minutes and three Band-Aids. My language becomes so violent that Anne begins reading the CPR section of the first-aid manual. She wants to be ready when the heart attack comes.

I take the bottom off the pump. *Voilà!* The pulse-dampener diaphragm is clearly bad. This rubber gizmo helps make the water flow in a steady stream rather than in spurts. Moreover, I have a new one in my spares kit. I put it in and reinstall the pump. One hour—I am getting better.

I turn on the pump and water floods out the bottom. It's much worse than before. Why? I repair to the electric pump manual. There, in the fine print, may be the solution: "Some newer models require brass grommets in the pulse dampener diaphragm to achieve a good seal." Some newer models of what—pumps or pulse-dampener diaphragms? The old diaphragm had no grommets. But maybe the new one needs them. Do I have any? Eureka, they're in the rebuild kit.

I take out the pump again. Thirty minutes flat. I'm getting good at this. In my haste, I did break one of the electrical connectors, but I can fix that. I disassemble the pump and put in the grommets—nine tiny little devils that lacerate my fingertips as I force them into place. Pump reassembled and reinstalled—including electrical repair—less than forty-five minutes. Bloody marvelous. (In British territory, I say things like that.)

I turn on the pump. It still leaks—less, but it still leaks. In one of my repair bins I have some rubber goop called "Instant Gasket." It is supposed to stop leaks. I take out the pump, disassemble it, smear Instant Gasket everywhere that it could possibly leak, reassemble, and reinstall. The elapsed time is so trivial I am beginning to hope that there is a category for this sort of thing in the *Guinness Book of World Records.*

But I can't turn on the pump to test it. Instant Gasket needs twenty-four hours to cure. For the next day, we will have to get our cooking, drinking, and washing water from the foot pump in the head. I cleverly installed this pump only two weeks before we left Connecticut, never dreaming it would ever be our sole access to our potable-water tanks. (I also cleverly installed it to prevent closure of the seacock that I had to pull and reinstall in Wilmington.) As I am about to turn on the electric pump the next day, I can see that Anne is poised to jump overboard. If it doesn't work, all bets are off. But it works. Total repair time only about eight and a half hours.

This repair lasts less than a week. In the end, I have to buy a new pump. Actually two. The first one is defective right off the shelf. It switches itself on every fifteen seconds whether or not we are running any water. Replacement thus requires two more removals and reinstallations. But by now I can do it in my sleep.

The pump problem was minor. A bit of leakage under the sink. But we must still deal with some larger issues before we push offshore again. The aluminum python is still loose inside the mast. Capturing that electrical conduit and re-securing it with pop rivets, while not damaging the wiring, is not a job for an amateur. Even a guy as talented as I am! This is a job for Isaac Fonseca, rigger extraordinaire and proprietor of Wickhams Cay Rigging in Tortola. We had already made a date with Isaac for two days after Samantha's departure.

As we motor into Roadtown Harbour to keep our date with Isaac, the engine fails right at the mouth of the harbor. The fuel plague is back. Fortunately, there is an anchorage in the outer harbor that we can negotiate under sail. Dodging the freighters and cruise ships, we get the hook down and start looking for someone to come pump all of the fuel out of the tanks. We need to start over with clear diesel. There is no telling how much junk is in there just waiting to rise up from the bottom of the tanks whenever the going gets rough.

It is Thursday. The most hopeful response I can wheedle out of the two places capable of doing a pump-out is, "Might be able to do it next Tuesday." Time for improvisation. We carry a small portable fluids pump that can be attached to PALAEMON's batteries. If we can find containers sufficient to hold the remaining 20 gallons of diesel, we can pump out the stuff ourselves. There are 18 gallons of diesel in jerry jugs on deck, so putting in clear fuel at anchor is no problem.

A few inquiries ashore elicit the puzzling response that we should check out the wood-fenced enclosure behind the Moorings charter base. Behind the fence, scores of 5-gallon plastic fruit-juice containers sparkle in the Caribbean sunshine. Moving furtively, like the container thieves we are, I vault the fence and throw over four pineapple-juice jugs. No one seems to notice our crime. But we cannot remain inconspicuous. Our only path back to JEREMY BENTHAM leads through the Moorings hotel and reception area. We waltz through as nonchalantly as possible while carrying four large, bright-blue containers; toss them into the dinghy; and beat it back to PALAEMON.

Under cover of darkness, we return the four containers, now full of contaminated diesel. Their disposal location is ecologically sound but unconventional. Not every cruising secret can be told.

The fuel fiasco galvanizes me to undertake a project that I have been contemplating, and avoiding, for weeks. The engine fails from contaminated fuel because the primary fuel filter gets clogged and refuses to allow fuel to the engine. That's how it's supposed to work. But opening the filter canister, replacing the filter, and re-priming the engine takes about ten minutes. Had PALAEMON's engine failed while motoring into Roadtown's packed inner harbor, the results would not have been pretty. Ramming a boat or a dock or going hard aground would have been our likely options.

To avoid a calamity of this sort, I have decided to re-plumb the fuel lines. Henceforth we will have two primary filters. If one filter clogs, I can switch to the other by turning two levers—the work of thirty seconds. I have thought carefully about this project, drawn diagrams of the arrangement of hoses and valves, and collected all the materials, some sent from Bruce and Johnson's Marina, our wonderfully reliable yard back home in Connecticut. Mark Friel, the main engine guy there, offered to bring the parts himself and help with installation. He would need a round-trip plane ticket, of course, and his clock would be running from the time he left the yard until he got back. I thanked Mark for the offer and asked him just to ship the parts.

The re-plumbing takes me a day. Everything fits where I thought it would. I really do have all the parts. I am not swearing or throwing things. I am not even bleeding. Anne keeps looking in from the cockpit, where she's painting, to see whether I am alive. She finally can't stand it and breaks a cardinal rule. "How's it going?" she asks. "Great," I reply. She shakes her head in wonderment. Maybe the Caribbean really has mellowed me out.

Then there is the matter of the GPS chartplotter. Since its twenty-four-hour nervous breakdown two miles from home, it has behaved perfectly. But, now, suddenly, the plotter blows its fuse every time I hit the power button. After four fuse failures, I call Raytheon Electronics in New Hampshire. They advise shipping it to them and promise to repair and return it within two weeks. They not only keep their promise, they charge nothing for replacing the power panels in a six-year-old machine because, in their words, "It should not have failed, unless struck by lightning." So far as we know, it has not been.

When reinstalled, the plotter comes on, but it provides no location information. Is the GPS bad, too? Yes, says Cay Electronics, the Raytheon dealer in Roadtown. The internal wiring is fused together, as if from some massive electrical charge. Whatever killed the GPS may have fried the chartplotter, too. They were installed with a common power source. Could we have been struck by lightning and not noticed? We haven't spent *that* much time at Skinny Legs. We buy a new GPS and install it with the GPS and chartplotter power supplies separated.

This is a tricky job, so I get help from a Cay Electronics technician. As I watch him splice the tiny, low-voltage wires with a solder gun and waterproof them with plastic wrap, I try not to think about the half-assed job I did on Otto's wiring with crimp connectors and electrical tape on the way down from Bermuda. Should I get this guy to take out Otto and redo my splices? No, damn it, Otto's not broken.

While in Roadtown near supplies and electrical power, I decide to get one more task off my list—installing a stopper for the mainsheet. Coming down from Bermuda, Anne was adjusting the mainsail when a 40-knot blast ripped the mainsheet from her hands. Despite the figure-eight knot in the end of the line, the sheet went zipping through the fairlead and out of reach from the cockpit. The mainsail was now out of control, the boom was swinging wildly, and the mainsheet was writhing around the deck like a scorched sea serpent. The slithering sheet wrapped itself around the starboard cowl vent and yanked it out of the coach roof. Not satisfied to leave the job half done, the enraged Dacron reptile coiled itself around the port-side vent and ripped that off, too.

I managed to crawl forward and secure the mainsheet without getting brained by the boom. The cowl vents, our only ventilation when the hatches are dogged down at sea, somehow had not gone over the side. It was 1:30 A.M., but I decided I had better put them back on. Drilling properly spaced holes for the fasteners while galloping through squalls in the open ocean is not the work of a few minutes. Not one of our best nights at sea. With the mainsheet led through a stopper, we will not repeat that particular episode.

And so it goes, as the days pass and our list dwindles. I have by now spent so much time crouched below the companionway working on something or other in the engine compartment that Anne has done multiple sketches of my back and rear end. She could do a show called, "Amazing Contortions of an Engine Mechanic," or perhaps borrow Elaine Scarry's book title, *The Body in Pain.* The sketches remind me of childhood visions of my dad, inside the back of a malfunctioning washing machine or television set. The original "Mr. Fixit."

Dad actually liked doing this stuff. He trained as a technician in the early days of radio. He had an intuitive grasp of how mechanical and electrical gizmos work, and he tinkered with them endlessly. He volunteered to fix neighbors' appliances. Kids for blocks around brought over their bikes, and later their motorbikes and cars, to solicit his services. Meanwhile, he wanted me to "help" by standing around in case he needed me to hand him a wrench or a screwdriver. "Helping" bored me silly, and Dad's explanations of what he was doing were of zero interest. I just wanted machines to do what they were supposed to do, and if not, for Dad to fix them while I did something else, almost anything else. Now, here I am, fifty years later, looking at my dad's backside hovered in front of PALAEMON's engine compartment. But it's mine.

ANNE'S PASSAGE NOTES: RAVING

Mashaw males rave. I see this phenomenon mostly when they are fixing things that are broken, or improving things that are not. As Jerry has often said, his dad raved. All his uncles rave. Both sons rave. Jay, the elder son, smiles easily about it, explaining that raving clears the head and enables concentration on the task at hand. Mark, the younger, has a little less humor about himself. He bridles at the indignity of this "stereotyping" of Mashaw men. Of course, raving is not *limited* to Mashaw men—they just seem to have a certain flair for it.

On PALAEMON, engine projects are candidates for big-time raves. So are computers, electronic devices, even barbecue grills, but these usually produce lesser raves than the engine. For one thing, engine failures are often serious. If they are not fixed, we soon will have no electrical power, no lights, no means of communication, no refrigeration. For another, engine projects are miserably uncomfortable. And bloody. Jerry always cuts himself. Hose clamps, with their razorlike edges, are among the worst hazards, but hardly the only ones. Jerry can skin himself on a well-polished piece of teak. The horrors available in the engine compartment are too numerous too mention. Also, you never know until the end whether you will have all the right tools and parts. Finally, you rarely know that what you are doing will work. For all these reasons, engine projects generate high anxiety, and correspondingly intense raves.

We have had our moments on PALAEMON in our home waters, with Jerry pretzeled into the engine, raving away, and me doing all the wrong things—asking what's happened and, heaven forbid, forgetting myself and laughing when the end wrench inevitably drops—as though of its own volition—into the bilge. It *is* funny, the rage, so out of proportion to the event—great burbles of laughter rise from deep within me, half choking me, demanding to be let out. Woe upon me if I give in to them at the time—the raving index (fury plus decibels plus hyperbole and threats) notches way up. Moreover, the rave turns away from selling the boat (always "the boat" in these circumstances, never PALAEMON) or aborting the sail and aims directly at me. Even though I know nothing personal is intended, I much prefer not to be the object of a good Mashaw rave.

On this trip, most of the raving has not been *so* out of proportion to the incident. The wrong nut lost in the bilge (such as the nut that secures the screw that secures the alternator to the engine) is not a laughing matter. A replacement may be hundreds of miles, and perhaps weeks, away. Moreover, I admire Jerry enormously for the creativity and perseverance he brings to our various engine dilemmas. So I work very hard at finding ways to help, and I head for the foredeck to hide any laughter that cannot be repressed. Or, if I can't get out, I stick my head in the towel locker to stifle my mirth. Jerry can enjoy a good laugh about it later, but not at the time.

I now see a common pattern for engine projects. He begins. This means the companionway is blocked and tools are strewn everywhere, along with parts and manuals. Jerry is almost immediately covered with grease and dripping blood from one or more appendage. I bring Band-Aids, although he will rarely accept them. ("Take them away; I'm just going to cut myself again anyway"—the raving index is pretty high by now. He *will* accept paper towels. Perhaps paper towels are more manly, because they can sop up oil and grease as well as blood?) I occupy myself with minor projects that will keep me out of the way but still at hand. Cleaning the head, perhaps the V-berth; applying felt pads to bin doors that have proven noisy underway; polishing brass or other metal—those sorts of things. Sometimes Jerry raves early on, and then mostly stops.

Then, usually, as his son suggests, he settles in, the raving index down, although I can easily set it off again if I am stupid enough to ask how things are going, or when he thinks he will be finished. But I rarely make this mistake. If I run out of things to do without interrupting him, I settle down heartlessly with a book in whatever space I can clear of tools and parts. Whatever I'm doing, after the initial rave and as long as I'm quiet, he soon begins asking me to find things for him—the socket wrench that matches a nut, or a nut to fit a specific machine screw, an additional manual, a piece of hose. Then he begins to talk about what he's doing. Soon we are involved in what may or may not turn out to be a productive discussion about the problem. I don't have his instinct about engines, but I have distance and some aptitude for mechanical things. Besides, it helps to talk. His fixes virtually always work, and at the end of the effort he is tired and has injuries to nurse, but we are able to be happy together about the success.

But that is not quite the end of an engine-induced rave. I also have intense anxieties about engine failures, and while Jerry has exorcised his by raving and fixing, I haven't. So, a day or so later, I can't resist asking whether he still wants to sell "the boat" and fly to Florence. Sometimes I get a laugh; sometimes he can only manage a stiff smile that doesn't quite make it to his eyes. No matter. I have released my emotional pressure valve.

Jerry repairs the engine.

20

IN SEARCH OF THE CARIBBEAN

We varnish and polish and lubricate moving from anchorage to anchorage in Gorda Sound, the birthplace of our sailing dreams. From PALAEMON's cockpit, the roof line of the Carrows' house, where we stayed in Leverick Bay—a cross like an Anglican church—pokes up above the hibiscus and bougainvillea. We walk the beaches and visit the restaurants that we remember from that time. Much has changed. Charter boats now outnumber cruisers; new resorts have joined the old. Cruise lines now enter the Sound. Anchored in mid-Sound, they treat their more adventurous passengers to water skiing and paragliding. The remainder waddle ashore to the beach bar on Prickly Pear Island. Some play beach volleyball under the watchful eye of a man I hope is a cardiologist.

When we were last on this beach, it was an empty sand spit as deserted as the rest of the island. A Swiss couple was restoring a wooden dinghy they had towed up from Bequia. We looked longingly at their big cruising ketch while I tried not to look at Erica's impressive bare breasts. Very distracting if you're not accustomed to toplessness. We talked about the trip they would soon make to Venezuela to buy ship's stores. We wondered that they could talk so casually of sailing more than 400 miles to get better and cheaper groceries.

Then, a land-based week on Gorda Sound was an unimaginable gift. Now, after a few hours ashore, I feel restless, caged. I am heavy on the land, light on the sea, even at anchor. I am ready to head offshore again.

But I am no longer impatient. I have discovered how to manage the restlessness problem that plagued me while we headed down the east coast. Just as I need physical activity at home to leaven my relentlessly-intellectual, academic work, I need to balance the physical pursuits of sailing and snorkeling and the manual tasks of boat maintenance with intellectual exercise. Reading good novels, poetry, biography, whatever, is not enough either. I need an intellectual project, and in the Virgins, a big project has begun to take shape. I want to understand the Caribbean and its peoples, how what we are seeing got to be the way it is.

I had begun reading some Caribbean history before we left home. The broad outlines of what has gone on here from the Age of Discovery to the present are clear enough. Spanish conquistadors followed rapidly in Columbus's wake, looking for the gold and silver he never found. They discovered a bit in Hispaniola and Cuba, then hit the mother lode in Mexico and Peru. Spain's New World wealth was not only the envy of the rest of Europe—if the other powers failed either to limit or to match Spanish wealth, they would soon be speaking Spanish.

Thus began 300 years of struggle. War, piracy, privateering, trade, and settlement were the technologies of a competition deployed by England, France, Holland, Denmark, Portugal, and Spain—not just in the West Indies, but also in Africa, North and South America, the South Pacific, Southeast Asia and the Far East. These were truly the first world wars.

War in the Caribbean seldom stopped, even when hostilities ceased elsewhere. Most European peace treaties of the sixteenth and seventeenth centuries contained an explicit or implicit proviso limiting their territorial effect to *"la ligne de l'enclos des amitiés"* (from the Treaty of Vervins, 1598). Peace did not include activities "beyond the line"—roughly all the world west of the Azores and south of the Tropic of Capricorn. The West Indies played a huge role in European economic and political struggles. The islands were used first for strategic naval purposes, raiding Spanish shipping, after which the climate was exploited for the wealth that sugar could bring. Settlers (such as the British and French) as well as traders (such as the Dutch and Danes) profited handsomely.

The mines were worked out, and Spain's naval power was crushed. The European sugar beet, and cheaper cane sugar from more fertile regions, assassinated King Sugar. By the mid-nineteenth century, a Caribbean that had been the center of a worldwide contest for wealth and power lay dozing in the tropical sunshine, an economic and political backwater. The European exodus left in its wake a cluster of destitute microstates and quasi colonies, a power vacuum that sucked them inexorably into the American sphere of political influence. By the mid-twentieth century, the balmy climate, combined with failure to participate in the Industrial Revolution, produced a potential tourist mecca whose possibilities are now exploited—often for the enrichment of foreign firms and local politicos.

That the West Indies islands are now overwhelmingly black, with few Europeans and hardly a trace of the pre-Columbian Indians, is a by-product of the way the historic European contest for global dominance played itself out in the Caribbean. Massive infusions of non-European labor were required to work the mines and the plantations. Hard labor, vicious treatment, and new diseases rapidly dispatched most of the indigenous peoples. Blacks could be imported in seemingly limitless quantities from West Africa. Most of the Europeans died or went home. Unlike North America, where they came to settle and develop the land in a climate similar to the one they had left, they colonized the West Indies in order to exploit a climate ill-suited to the European physical constitution.

But these broad outlines of Caribbean development are tantalizingly vague. Who were these Amerindians whom Columbus described in the journal of his first voyage as "very well-built people, with handsome bodies and very fine faces . . ." who "became so friendly it was a marvel" but who seemed to "have very little and be poor in everything?" What was their relation to the fierce, allegedly cannibalistic Caribs whom Columbus's men encountered on St. Croix in 1493? How could they all have disappeared by 1530, less than four decades later? Why were they so technologically primitive, essentially a Stone Age people, in 1492?

And why did imported West Africans become numerically preponderant in the Caribbean, but not elsewhere? The American South was a plantation economy, and slavery was abolished in the British Caribbean three decades before the American Civil War. Yet blacks never outnumbered whites in any North American colony save for a brief period in South Carolina. Why were West Africans, transported thousands of miles from their homelands, more disease-resistant than the indigenous Amerindians? Why didn't European colonization jump-start Caribbean development like it did North American? Why is the British colonial legacy in the United States or Hong Kong so different from its legacy in Antigua? Why do present-day Puerto Ricans have sixteen times the annual income of their neighbors across the Mona Channel in the Dominican Republic? Why did Haiti have the Western Hemisphere's only successful eighteenth-century revolution for independence outside of the United States? Why is it now the developmental basket case of the Western Hemisphere?

Understanding the Caribbean, even bits of it, is a huge project. I find that I have started on it or stumbled into it with no adequate background for the task and no particular sense of direction. Pondering the Virgin Islands has induced a rabid, but poorly focused, curiosity. So while waiting for HERMAN MELVILLE's schedule to clear, I begin with biology or population ecology or something like that. I am led in that direction by Jared Diamond. For days I intersperse PALAEMON projects with immersion in his *Guns, Germs and Steel.*

Diamond's book is a world historical revelation, and it gives me a completely new perspective on what might be true about the Caribbean.

Diamond asks himself a simple question: Why did the Spanish sail to Mexico and conquer the Aztecs instead of the other way around? Within that question lies the bigger one that he hopes to answer: Why have societies progressed at differential speeds? What, across the whole of human history, divides the rich from the poor, the developed from the underdeveloped, the economically successful from the economically unsuccessful?

His answer is both sophisticated and simple. Early starters will surpass late starters. Early starts depend critically on natural advantages, particularly plants and animals that are susceptible to domestication, for only domesticated agriculture and husbandry can create the surpluses necessary for the rise of commerce and learning. Late bloomers can catch up, but only if the technology transferred from early starters is adaptable to their environment. Taking cows and potatoes from England to Massachusetts helps jump-start development. Taking them to the barren Bahamas doesn't.

Diamond marshals strong evidence for his thesis. The "fertile crescent" of the Middle East, roughly the biblical Garden of Eden, was enormously richly endowed with good candidates for animal and plant husbandry by comparison with almost anywhere else in the world. These domesticated sources of wealth transferred happily east and west to similar climates in much of Europe and North America, quite unhappily north or south.

Technological advantages were not just an economic head start. When cultures collided—European with Amerindian, for example—they made the difference between life and death. Steel armaments annihilate any nonsteel defense technology in their path. More important, most human diseases come from domestic animals. Humans who live with these animals for generations develop immunity; hunter-gatherers will be felled by a bacterium that doesn't give a shepherd a runny nose.

As I read Diamond in light of what I already think I know, the almost necessary sweep of Caribbean island history opens before me. Naturally occurring domesticable animals—zero. Plants—a few fruits and vegetables, mostly tubers. Mineral deposits—salt, a trace of gold. Result—a late start. Ability to absorb European technologies—very limited. Transportability of agriculture—ditto. Temperate-climate flora and fauna mostly perish in the tropics. Ability to withstand European diseases (or armaments)—virtually none. Result—the peaceful Amerindians, the Arawaks or Tainos, who were enslaved by and lived in close proximity with Europeans, perished.

Europeans did not find a happy home here, either. Their crops mostly didn't work, large animals (horses and cows) could not find sufficient fodder, and the colonizers had poor resistance to tropical diseases. Creating wealth by transferring European technology to the Caribbean was not a winning developmental strategy. Some wet islands were good for sugar cane when cultivated by Africans. The enslaved West Africans died in droves, but, unlike the Amerindians, they could be replenished by capture and transportation.

In short, until the age of rapid, large-scale transport of people and goods, these small islands were suited to precisely the sort of hunter-gatherer economy that the Caribs and Arawaks had established. There are abundant fish and a sprinkling of edible wild fruits and vegetables. Temperatures are mild throughout the year. One of Diamond's most illuminating insights is that a hunter-gatherer culture is not just a primitive evolutionary stage. In some environments, it's the best you can do. Add in beautiful beaches and clear waters and you have exactly the sort of place that late-twentieth-century Americans and Western Europeans would like to go for a vacation—provided you lay on some resorts and a few shopping malls.

Diamond is painting in broad strokes here. But his argument resonates with much that is known about the agriculture of the West Indian colonies and about the way Europeans, West Africans, and Amerindians reacted to the diseases that they exchanged.

European crops and domestic animals were not a success on most West Indian islands. Indeed, the economically successful crops—tobacco, cotton, indigo, logwood, cocoa, and, of course, sugar cane—were either domestic to the islands or brought from other subtropical territories. The Europeans couldn't even feed themselves from the crops and livestock they brought with them.

Henry Powell led the first English settlers to uninhabited Barbados in 1627. He went immediately to Dutch Guiana (now Suriname) to trade with the Arawaks for food crops. Happily for the Barbados-based English colonists, their adjacent indigenous neighbors were not just hunter-gatherers. The Arawaks on the north coast of South America, and their close relatives, the Island Arawaks or Tainos, had distinctive subsistence-agriculture techniques. Thirty Arawaks returned with Powell to Barbados, to see the "far place" that figured in Arawak legends. Barbados was not far in miles, just dead to windward. Powell's helpers, or captives (it's not so clear which) taught the Barbados settlers how to cultivate native fruits and vegetables, to make cassava bread and to catch fish. When Powell returned to England, the grateful settlers grabbed the land that Powell had given the Arawaks and made them slaves.

The sugar technology that ultimately dominated the Caribbean economies was developed by the Dutch in the 1620s and 1630s, but in Brazil, not Europe. When they were driven out by the Portuguese, the Dutch moved their machinery and know-how north to the British and French West Indies, encouraging the English and French to grow sugar while they took up their historic and lucrative role as financiers and traders. And slavers. The Dutch had followed the Portuguese into the slave trade. By spreading the sugar monoculture through the West Indies, they increased demand for their human cargoes.

Which leads back to the question of the resilience of the West Africans in the West Indies. Why did Africans replace the Indians who had worked the Spanish mines of Hispaniola and the white bondsmen who originally worked the fields of Barbados? Indeed, why did blacks rapidly become the dominant race, in numbers, throughout most of the Caribbean?

The simple answer is that huge numbers of West African slaves were imported to work on the sugar plantations; the Indians died and most of the Europeans died or went home. But why did the Indians essentially all die out from European diseases while many blacks survived? And why did the Europeans die from tropical diseases that often gave blacks little difficulty?

The answers are, at best, reasonable but untestable hypotheses. The Indians clearly had no immunity to either European or African diseases. Yet some might have survived the European infections—measles, mumps, chicken pox, smallpox, and venereal diseases—and raised a next generation who would have encountered these pathogens in childhood, had mild cases, and developed immunity. That this failed to happen resulted from two other factors. The second wave of diseases, those brought by the West Africans, infected them too rapidly to permit a second-generation adaptation. The demise of the Arawaks or Tainos was astonishingly rapid. By 1530, they had all but disappeared.

In addition, enslavement weakened the Indians by overwork and malnutrition and introduced many to a local disease—yellow fever—to which they had no immunity. By moving thousands of Tainos or Island Arawaks from the small islands of the Bahamas, and from the coasts of other islands, to the interiors of Hispaniola and Cuba, the Spanish exposed them for the first time to the conditions that sustain yellow fever. In the Western Hemisphere, tropical yellow fever is endemic only to the forests of the West Indies, and South and Central America. It is essentially a disease of monkeys. It devastates nonimmune human populations only when in close contact with monkeys and each other. For the usual mosquito vector for yellow fever, *Aedes aegypti*, has a lifetime range of only a few hundred yards! Herded together into the mines of Hispaniola and Cuba, the Tainos perished as if they were immigrants to their own lands.

By contrast, the West African slaves already had at least some immunity to both European and tropical diseases. Yellow fever is also endemic to West Africa. As a childhood disease, yellow fever is often as mild as measles or chicken pox. And untold generations of adaptation to malaria had long since produced the special blood-cell shape in West Africans that combats malaria but also produces sickle-cell anemia. European diseases were also familiar in West Africa. They had had direct, if limited, contact with Europeans and their diseases for hundreds of years. West Africans also raised a number of the same domestic animals that incubate many human pathogens.

Finally, meager as it was, the West African diet actually improved slightly by transportation to the West Indies. Within two generations, the average height of African creoles was 3 inches greater than their contemporaries who remained at home in Africa. By contrast, the Indian slave diet was much worse than their usual well-balanced menu of fruit, vegetables, and fish.

West Africans' tropical-disease immunity gave them one advantage over newly arrived Europeans; the capacity to produce disease-resistant subsequent generations provided the second advantage. Millions of African females came to the West Indies, about one female for every two males. Planters encouraged, indeed insisted on, slave propagation. Most Europeans, by contrast, were in-dentured male servants and soldiers. They came in their teens and twenties, prime years for contracting infectious diseases, and they left no purely Euro-pean descendants. Creole—that is, island born—West Indians encounter yel-low fever as children and often shrug it off within a few days. In its virulent adult form yellow fever is known locally as "strangers' fever." Because most Europeans were indeed strangers—newly arrived indentured servants or seamen—they were carried off in huge numbers.

British naval vessels sometimes lost 60 to 70 percent of their crews within a year, 40 to 50 percent was common. Soldiers in barracks did worse. The British had a penchant for locating soldiers' housing on agriculturally useless vacant land near forests and swamps. If *Aedes aegypti* couldn't go to the En-glish, the English would go to it. Europeans had much the same experience in West Africa. The eighteenth-century records of the Royal African Company show that half the Europeans sent to West Africa died within a year. A mili-tary assignment to West Africa or the West Indies was almost the equivalent of a death sentence.

The pre-Columbian people of the West Indies are virtually all gone. Most

Europeans who came to the Caribbean never intended to stay, although many were interred before they could leave. Some survived, remained, and reproduced—the ancestors of the current white minority. The West Africans, who never wanted to come, died by the hundreds of thousands from disease, overwork, malnutrition, abuse, and neglect. Yet by virtue of massive importation, some natural advantages, and the capacity to reproduce—despite appalling levels of stillbirths and infant mortality—their descendants have inherited the Caribbean islands. It is perhaps not too much to say that the West Indies is black by disease rather than by design.

21

IMAGINING GRENADA

The more we look at the chart of the Lesser Antilles, the more we convince ourselves that a sail from the British Virgin Islands to Grenada will be a fast and easy offshore passage. The rhumb-line (direct) course runs just east of south. Since we have been in the Virgins, the trade winds have been consistently north of east. The wind angle looks perfect—just behind the beam, giving us slightly following seas and very little roll. As we approach Grenada, the islands themselves should provide some protection from the rollers marching west all the way from Africa. The only things we have to miss are the Saba Bank, St. Croix, and an island called Isla de Aves—a tiny Venezuelan possession inhabited by thousands of nesting seabirds and a few fishermen. Because none of these "obstructions" is within 20 miles of our rhumb line, I could do the navigation on this passage the old way, with a sextant, and *probably* not hit anything.

While we have been waiting for Jerome and Judith, the wind has been clocking toward the south and is occasionally south of east. But we are assured by our Caribbean forecaster, David Jones, that these aberrational conditions are about to disappear. The winds next week will still be substantial, but from the northeast.

When the wind backs from east southeast to east, we leave, anticipating its further movement to the north. As we clear Peter Island, PALAEMON's bow bashes into steep seas still marching in from the southeast. Spray flies back past the dodger, green seawater courses down the leeward deck. No roll, but rough as hell. Three hours out, Jerome and Judith radio that they are turning back. Confident that the discomfort is temporary, that the promised wind shift to the northeast is only hours away, we press on.

For the first twenty-four hours, Anne is as sick as she has ever been on a passage. As the sun sinks, we can see line squalls on the horizon. The squalls lie across our route most of the night, packing gusts of 35 to 40 knots. It begins to look like another fast, rough, wet, and mostly miserable trip. We're thinking of starting a charter company, "Offshore Discomfort Specialists." I can see our ad in *Cruising World* magazine: "Want to get some offshore experience in crummy but not life-threatening conditions? Come make a passage with us!"

Although we have lost Jerome and Judith, we are traveling in company with Larry and Shirley Ladd. So we still have someone with whom to talk on the radio, commiserate about the weather, and discuss cruising plans. Their 50-foot catamaran, INSPIRATION, has a top speed nearly twice PALAEMON's. But, as Shirley explained when I suggested that they would quickly leave us in their wake, you only sail at that speed in a cat if you like riding bucking broncos twenty-four hours a day. Larry and Shirley take it slowly and heave-to every thirty-six hours to sleep, shower, bake bread, eat a good meal.

The Ladds' approach to passagemaking suggests that they feel at home on the open ocean in a way that we originally thought we might. But for us, *passage* is still the critical feature of passagemaking, at least in the conditions we have experienced thus far. We just want to get the passage done, relax in a harbor. Shirley and Larry are headed to Trinidad for Carnival, then on to Venezuela, along the north coast of South America, through the Panama Canal, and into the Pacific. They are in the first year of a seven-year circumnavigation, not a measly ten-month sabbatical.

When not sleeping, barfing, or talking to the Ladds, we try to imagine what we will find in Grenada. We have two sets of descriptions. They do not fit together very well.

The cruisers' grapevine describes a near-paradise. A dozen well-protected harbors define the southern end of the island. They are just south of the hurricane zone, so we could even stay there through the summer, as many cruisers do, without having our insurance canceled. Fish teem in the cuts between the reefs, local markets provide an unparalleled abundance and variety of home-grown fruits and vegetables. The deep interior is an eco-hiker's dreamland of lush rain forests, waterfalls, tropical birds, and troops of screaming monkeys.

Another vision of Grenada competes with the cruisers' account. Like most Americans, we had paid the island little notice until the Reagan administration decided to invade it in 1983 to keep the Caribbean safe from the spread of Cuban communism. Like many Americans, we have remained skeptical whether this show of U.S. muscle was really necessary. Given Uncle Sam's checkered history of supporting "stability" in Latin America and the Caribbean, we can imagine an island controlled by oligarchs, seething with popular unrest, but dissuaded from further attempts at grassroots reform by the credible threat of another American "peacekeeping" mission.

We have a copy of George Brizan's political history, *Grenada: Island of Conflict.* Brizan's title mirrors his plot line. His picture of Grenada is of an island locked in perpetual civil strife. Brizan's pre-Columbian account parallels the standard story told of most islands in the Windwards and southern Leewards. The gentle Arawaks moved up from the Amazon through the Guianas and Venezuela to inhabit the Lesser Antilles. They were followed centuries later by the warlike Caribs, who pushed Arawak civilization north and east to populate the larger islands of Hispaniola, Puerto Rico, Cuba, and Jamaica.

Some aspects of this story are now thought to be quite wrong. In the revisionist view, the Lucayans of the Bahamas and the Tainos of the larger Caribbean islands were not Arawaks at all, although related by ancestry, and they had been in the northern Caribbean long before the Caribs began their push up the Lesser Antilles. Indeed, there is some question whether the Island Arawaks of Grenada were Arawaks from South America rather than Eastern Taino relatives. Whoever they were, the Caribs either drove them out or killed the men and appropriated the women.

Then came the Europeans. The Spanish claimed Grenada—Mayo, or Concepción, as they alternately called it—along with all the rest of the Caribbean, but they were only transient visitors. A British group of 200, financed by London merchants, attempted a settlement in 1609 but were driven off by Carib warriors. In 1638, a French party from St. Kitts met the same fate. In 1650, a well-supplied and well-armed French expedition established a beachhead, built a fort, and planted tobacco. Seeing the handwriting on the wall, the Caribs began a guerrilla campaign that developed into a full-scale war. With help from their compatriots in St. Vincent, they held out until 1654, when they were all but completely exterminated. The last Carib warriors are said to have thrown themselves into the sea at Le Morne des Sauteurs ("Leapers' Hill") to avoid an ignoble death at the hands of the pursuing French.

The Caribs lost the battle for Grenada but imposed such high costs on its then-owner, Governor DuParquet of Martinique, that he had to sell out to the Comte de Cerillac. The new owner sent a governor so oppressive that many settlers fled to Martinique. The remainder revolted, set up a "people's court," and condemned the governor to be hanged. He objected that as a nobleman, he had to be beheaded. The colonists agreed, but, unable to locate a skilled executioner, they finally shot him instead. At this point, the Crown intervened, transferred ownership to the French West Indies Company, and, when that was dissolved in 1674, took over direct control and administration. *La Grenade* became fully French.

The French established the usual plantation system, but Grenada was so well suited to cocoa and tobacco that sugar became chief among equals, not king. Unlike their British neighbors, only Haiti among the French colonies succumbed to sugar monoculture. Nevertheless, by the mid-eighteenth century, West African slaves outnumbered whites in Grenada by ten to one. Having thus planted the seeds of future social unrest, the French hung on for nearly a century. They ceded Grenada to the British at the Treaty of Paris in October 1763.

The British continued standard colonial policies—that is, the colony was to be run for the benefit of the homeland. They also attempted to impose British culture, thus adding Franco-British cultural competition to the simmering racial division that had emerged among blacks, mulattoes, and whites. The Anglo-French conflict included an almost intractable religious animosity between the Catholic French and the Anglican British.

The conflicts between British and French settlers were so strident that the usual form of eighteenth-century British colonial administration became unworkable. Normally, a British royal governor appointed a council that served as a sort of upper house of the British colonial legislature. An assembly was elected to serve as a lower house. This was not nearly as democratic as it sounds. The council and assembly were largely advisors to the governor, and the franchise was so limited by race, gender, and wealth requirements that the system was essentially oligarchic. Perhaps the most striking example of the limits of British colonial democracy is provided by an eighteenth-century British Virgin Islands election in which Jost Van Dyke, with a population of nearly 500, had only three residents qualified to vote or fill its two seats in the colonial assembly. Perhaps they drew straws.

Even quasi-representative oligarchy was too democratic for Grenada. The governors could find few willing and fewer able to serve on the council. English settlers objected to French participation in either the council or the assembly. The only actions that seemed to unite either body were votes opposing the governor's proposals or attempts to have him removed. The hopes and recalcitrance of the French settlers were kept alive by almost perpetual war between Britain and France. Indeed, France recaptured Grenada in 1779, only to return it to Britain by the Treaty of Versailles in 1783.

A frustrated British government gave up the pretense of democracy and resorted to "Crown Colony" administration, a system that placed virtually all powers in the hands of the governor who was advised by an elected, but effectively hand-picked, local assembly. By 1792, French settlers had been barred from political participation in island affairs, the revenues of Catholic church properties were being confiscated, and marriages ceased to be recognized unless conducted in Anglican churches. French colonists migrated elsewhere or plotted revolt.

In 1795, Julian Fedon, a "free coloured" Grenadian who owned a substantial plantation and numerous slaves, freed his slaves and called on all free coloureds, slaves, and Frenchmen to rise against the British in the name of the French Revolution and its stated ideals of liberty and equality. France and England were at war again, and Fedon's rebellion was supported, both in planning and execution, by three military commissioners who were sent by the French National Convention in 1794 to command French military operations in the Windwards. Fedon's aspiration was to return Grenada to France, which would, under the new laws of the French Republic, free the slaves and give citizenship rights to all free men.

Although Brizan fails to mention it, it is more than a little ironic that the rebellion of the oppressed francophone community against British rule and slavery in Grenada should have been led by a slave-owning mulatto Grenadian under the banner of the French Revolution. The mainland French bourgeois revolutionaries were economically allied with the colonial planter class and active participants in the slave trade. Civic rights for free blacks and coloureds, and the abolition of the slave trade and slavery itself, were not on the French revolutionary agenda. France granted political rights to free coloureds only as a strategic maneuver to thwart the rebellion in Haiti and abolished slavery in the French colonies only after abolition had become a *fait accompli* in St. Domingue.

In short, revolutionary France no more embraced abolitionist thought, or political equality for "free coloureds," than Great Britain. The banner of the French Revolution came to signify these things in Fedon's francophone Grenadian rebellion only because of the impact of the Haitian rebellion on French revolutionary legislation. In any event, after fifteen months, the loss of thousands of lives, and the virtual destruction of the Grenadian economy, Fedon's revolt was crushed. Had it succeeded, Fedon would later have had to rebel against France, which quickly reinstated slavery when Napoleon I assumed control.

Britain and the British slave plantocracy held the reins of power in Grenada through Emancipation Day, August 1, 1838. And, in Brizan's account, not much changed until the 1930s, when class conflict, effectively mobilized by organized labor, was added to ethnic, racial, and religious animosity. Class solidarity apparently had the adhesive force to bind disparate factions together. The power of the oligarchy began to crumble. Grenada moved slowly toward popular rule.

Britain attempted a staged withdrawal, gradually introducing more democratic constitutional arrangements. But for several centuries, Grenadians had only experienced one form of government—rule from the top. As in countless other postcolonial regimes, reform democracy degenerated into one-party kleptocracy. Economic development, education, and public works languished, while political power became more and more concentrated, and all opposition was suppressed.

Grenada entered the late twentieth century suffering from the usual third-world economic maladies. It supplied raw agricultural products and some minerals to developed nations, while importing high value-added goods and services from abroad. Most investment was also foreign, with management fees, interest payments, and profits leaving the country for elsewhere. Those Grenadians who had the greatest potential tended to emigrate to advanced economies where their skills and aptitudes found broader scope.

These sorts of political and economic conditions are the usual breeding ground for "people's movements." Grenada was no exception. Amid mounting unrest, Britain granted the island independence in 1974—perhaps "fled the scene" is more descriptive. In 1979, the government left behind by the British exodus was overthrown in a violent revolution, and a "People's Revolutionary Government" was installed. While the PRG had seized power in the name of the people, it ruled through a party elite and largely by decree. Henceforth, political competition was within the party. A "noble," "principled" oligarchy—the party—replaced the old colonial one. Through internecine bickering, the people's revolution self-destructed in only four years.

The American intervention of 1983 was, strangely enough, designed to reinstate the more pragmatic and popular elements of the People's Revolutionary Government, who had been ousted by hard-line Marxists within the party. The reactionary Ronald Reagan scurrying to the aid of the Grenadian People's Party is at least as curious as Fedon's embrace of a French revolution that was either pro-slavery or, at best, uninterested in the question. Perhaps relishing the political irony, the vast majority of Grenadians welcomed the outcome of the American intervention (including the foreign aid that quickly followed), although substantial numbers doubted that the invasion itself was really necessary.

I had had a firsthand account of the American liberation effort from George Coburn when we motored our old PALAEMON up the east coast from Norfolk to Branford. According to George, he had led a platoon ashore twenty-four hours before the main military force landed. He found a tense but manageable situation. Indeed, George's understanding was that the hard-core

Marxist cadre had reconciled itself to turning over power to the moderates, and that they and their Cuban "advisers" had virtually all decamped.

When the U.S.–Caribbean coalition then started landing troops bristling with firepower, the locals panicked. The untrained militiamen with whom George had been negotiating started shooting. George dislocated his knee jumping over a stone wall to avoid a bullet, and he recognized instantly that his career in the Special Forces was over. He spent the next several days helping cruising sailors whose boats had been shot up, then went home and retired from the U.S. Army.

Since the invasion, parliamentary democracy has held on, but Grenada has not thrived politically or economically. Indeed, given a political history that seems to equate politics with oppression, theft, and betrayal, most Grenadians reportedly prefer to have nothing to do with politics at all.

So where are we headed? To an island paradise? Or to a political and social volcano that might blow its top at any moment? Should we be comforted by the knowledge that a strikingly similar story could be told about most of the Caribbean ministates, and that none is currently erupting into social turmoil?

Sometime during the week before we left the Virgins for Grenada, our SSB was tuned as usual to the daily chatter on the 8:15 A.M. Caribbean safety and security net. This net is a long-standing institution directed by Donald, aboard DAISY D, usually somewhere in the western Caribbean, and Melodye Pompa, aboard SECOND MILLENNIUM, mostly hanging out in St. Lucia. For fifteen minutes every day, before David Jones breaks in with his Caribbean weather report, cruisers from Cancun to Trinidad report matters of interest to the cruising community and seek local knowledge. Missing boats are listed, muggings and dinghy thefts are described, changes in local regulations are reported.

On this particular morning, some cruiser in St. George's Harbour, Grenada, reported that the St. George's Merchants Association had yesterday formed a new committee. Its task was to help eliminate burglary and robbery on cruising boats. Attuned by Brizan to the complex reality of Grenadian politics, we were uncertain how to interpret our invisible informant's report. Was this a sign that the citizens of Grenada were determined to maintain good order and hospitality toward visitors? Or was it evidence that the duly constituted law-enforcement agencies were incapable of maintaining the basics of a civil society in the face of economic hardship and political unrest? Were we bashing our brains out just to experience Brizan's island-of-conflict theme firsthand?

22

REALITY WITH NUTMEG

One cruisers' story about Grenada is certainly true—you can smell the island before you see it. The sweet aroma of spice reached us nearly 40 miles out. The last six hours of sailing were terrific. As the squalls that had plagued us lifted, Grenada emerged out of the mist—soaring green hills sprinkled with the bright orange-and-red blossoms of the poinciana (or flamboyant) trees and of the African tulip trees that Grenadians call "flame of the forest." Once sailors' amnesia works its magic, these may be the only six hours we will remember.

As we close in on our waypoint at the south end of Grenada, the rain gods thoughtfully provide a ten-minute downpour in which we can wash ourselves and PALAEMON. The sun pops out just in time to show us the reefs, and we make our way slowly against wind and current into the still waters of Secret Harbour at Mount Hartman Bay.

The sheltering hills are ablaze with flamboyants and mimosas, pink and yellow poui trees, and African tulips. Beneath the finery in the treetops lie bougainvillea and hibiscus in luminescent purple and red and orange. The gold of the allamanda, the pinks and reds of the oleanders, ixora, and the delicate pride of Barbados march together along the hillsides. Unless we encounter an armed uprising ashore, the cruiser's view of Grenada is going to beat out George Brizan's perspective without much contest.

The beauty and serenity of Mount Hartman Bay are more

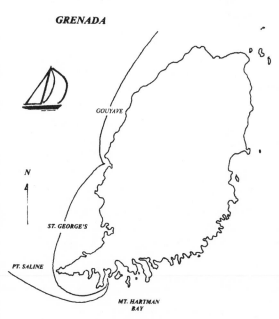

The Spice Island.

than usually welcome. Earlier this morning, we had a close encounter of the panicky kind with a Venezuelan freighter. In the gray dawn mist and showers, I had difficulty judging the freighter's course. It was clearly closing on us, but with its running lights obscured, I was uncertain whether we were headed for a collision or for a close, but reasonable, port-to-port passage. The radar was telling me that it would be one or the other, but not which. Repeated and increasingly frantic radio calls to the freighter's captain produced nothing. When PALAEMON and the looming freighter were less than a mile apart, he finally broke radio silence.

We then had a little misunderstanding. I asked him for his speed and bearing (the direction he was headed). He apparently thought I was asking for the bearing between his ship and us. When he gave me that, I, of course, thought I had just been told that we were on a collision course that would put PALAEMON under his bow in about three minutes.

I yelled for Anne and we scrambled to come about in the steep seas. Seeing us do this, the freighter captain began shouting over the VHF, "No, no, no, I have changed course to avoid you." We had now nullified his collision-avoidance maneuver and were rushing to intercept his ship. Another scramble brought us back onto our original course and out of danger. If you have trouble getting going early in the morning, try a little freighter-dodging to get your blood flowing.

After anchoring, our plan is to make immediate peace with Grenadian officialdom by clearing customs and immigration. We have the hook down by 3:30 P.M. We can just make the customs shed before it closes at 4. We have anchored close in, so we can row ashore. Boarding waves made off with JEREMY's gasoline tank as we submarined through heavy seas on the way down. When I take the pump up to the foredeck to inflate JEREMY, I get a rude shock: I can't pick him up. Seawater has made its way *inside* his buoyancy tubes. We had so much water on deck that it forced its way through his inflation valves.

Showing rare good judgment, we decide that we are in no condition to wrestle with a water-filled dinghy. If the customs officials want to give us a hard time for failure to clear in on the day of our arrival—Grenadian customs officers have a particularly nasty reputation—we will just take our medicine. We opt for a drink, an omelet, and sleep.

Rapping on PALAEMON's hull startles us out of the bunk twelve hours later. A smiling young man wants to sell us some freshly baked bread. Not a bad way to start the day. Things are looking up. When I ask him where I might buy a new gas tank for JEREMY BENTHAM, he offers to bring us his spare one. We can use it until we find something better. Pretty friendly for an island that Brizan had led us to believe might be populated exclusively by disgruntled, unemployed, fire-breathing revolutionaries. Political history is not social destiny—a nonequation for which, I suppose, most countries can be thankful.

We spend our first day reinflating JEREMY with air rather than water, paying homage to the customs and immigration offices (conveniently located 6 miles apart), and finding a gas tank for the dinghy. After sending the necessary "We made it" e-mails and putting PALAEMON back together, we reward ourselves with dinner at the elegant Sea Harbour Resort, overlooking Mount Hartman Bay. The resort rewards us with entertainment by Grenada's premier steel band and a performance by a limbo dancer of almost magical ability. He looks 7 feet tall, yet he eventually makes his way under a bar set no more than 8 inches off the floor.

As we watch this astonishing performance, I begin to understand Wilson Harris's puzzling claim that limbo is a continuing connection between the West Indies and West Africa and a building block for an authentic Caribbean cultural consciousness. Limbo is West African, but not a dance of the African mainland. Geographically, limbo hails from the middle passage—an art born of playfulness and defiance in the cramped confines of the slave deck. Vertical clearances were almost always less than a man's height. To bend forward or crawl is servile. In the limbo posture a man looks upward while simultaneously demonstrating powerful control over his own body.

Musically, limbo also connects Africa with the West Indies. It is performed both to drums, the traditional African instrument, and pans, the West Indies' unique instrumental contribution to world culture. The body of the limbo dancer makes a physical reference to African animism that resonates simultaneously with the West Indians' history of slavery and emancipation. For, as he goes lower and lower, the limbo dancer becomes a spider, the trickster and changeling of animist mythology—a gatekeeper between man and the gods, an escape artist who crosses over from one form to another.

When I read Harris's account, I couldn't quite get the picture. That was because I had never seen a limbo dancer who could go low enough that the angles of his legs and arms and swiveling head make him a spider—a spider that pops out from under the pole as a man, free to dance upright. In the midst of a show staged for tourists, I begin to glimpse, as Harris suggests, a Caribbean consciousness that celebrates itself.

Grenada is an almost continuous delight. Part of its charm is surely attributable to Darius—cab driver, tour guide, and fount of local knowledge for those cruisers lucky enough to wash up in Secret Harbour. Every morning, Darius appears at 8:30 under a tree up the hill from the dinghy dock. (He parks up there to avoid the cabbies down below, who are understandably grumpy about the fares they are losing to Darius's cut-rate bus service.) Darius leaves at 9 to take everyone who wants to go into St. George's. Everyone. Darius's van seats eleven. His record load is twenty-two. On the way into town, we must reach consensus on where and when Darius will meet us for the return trip. With this combination of physical proximity and participatory democracy, we get to know our neighbors in Mount Hartman Bay very quickly.

St. George's drapes itself around a splendid harbor. Brightly painted houses and shops tumble down steep hills to the waterfront. Boats are everywhere—moored, tied to the stone wharf on the western shore, pulled up onto the beach. Although some smaller cruise ships stop in St. George's, its port remains a working harbor—home to the Grenadian longline fishing fleet, interisland traders, and cargo carriers. The restaurants are cheap and good, and the outdoor market is a hoot. Grenadians seem to specialize in niche marketing. The woman whacking out fish steaks with a machete plies her trade next to a guy dealing exclusively in bathtubs. Vegetable stands run to two or three products. The vendor with tomatoes has onions, but you have to see the guy with potatoes if you want scallions. Not to be upstaged by the bathtub king, another Grenadian entrepreneur seems to have cornered the market in oscillating fans. Next to him is the nutmeg department store—everything comes from the nutmeg tree, but the products range from the spice itself to jams, jellies, and costume jewelry.

On our first visit, I am after fish. It is here in abundance. Big hunks of marlin and tuna and mahi mahi hold down tables along the sidewalk. Underneath are tubs of baitfish and squid and lambi. I point at the big piece of marlin. The proprietress grabs it by the tail and slings it up onto a concrete slab. She sets the machete on the fish and I push it to where I want her to make her cut. She slices the dark meat down to the bone, then grabs a baseball bat and whacks the machete sharply on the back of the blade. Beneath a shower of marlin blood, a perfect steak flips onto the table.

I learn to stand back a bit from Grenadian-style fish-steak carving. Returning from my first purchase, I look a little like Rocky Balboa after he's gone a few rounds with the hanging beef carcasses in his brother-in-law's meat-packing plant. I should have realized that the fish carver was not wearing a rain slicker on a bright day because she was a weather pessimist.

We find Grenadians an attractive mixture of dignity, charm, and helpfulness. Would you walk into even your favorite lunchtime restaurant, for example, and ask them to put your bloody Ziploc bag of marlin steaks in the refrigerator while you eat? The barman at the Nutmeg in St. George's complies without batting an eye. When we leave he insists on packing the steaks in a bag of ice so they won't get too warm on the ride back with Darius.

Darius and one of his sons take us on an expedition into the interior. We drive up through agricultural smallholdings and lush rain forest. The two are not very distinct visually. Grenadians have discovered that their main crops—cocoa, nutmeg, and bananas—seem to do better when grown in combination rather than separately. This multiculture is sprinkled over the hillsides among the natural flora, particularly flamboyants, in no apparent pattern. We bounce along pitted tracks, climbing out of farmland into rain forest alive with screaming parrots and screeching monkeys.

Darius stops from time to time and sends his son to grab a banana or some cocoa off a tree. The cocoa seeds are bitter as hell, but inside their coconut-size casing, they are covered with a deliciously tart, fruity meat. The taste is something like a cross between a kiwi and a lime. Darius also stops repeatedly to talk to whoever is on the road or sitting on a porch, mostly women with whom he has flirtatious conversations. Darius claims thirteen children. When we inquire after his wife, his response is vague.

In *Don't Stop the Carnival*, Herman Wouk's hilarious account of a Broadway-producer-turned-Caribbean hotelier, all vehicular accidents are caused by taxi drivers suddenly stationary after having encountered a friend, relative, or paramour who cannot be passed by without a chat. Anybody following Darius had better keep a sharp lookout. More than once, a driver following too close behind us—the accepted Grenadian distance seems to be about 4 feet—is saved from disaster only by the emptiness of the road ahead as he swerves to avoid Darius's rear end. There is no shouting, arm waving, or recriminations. Grenadian drivers really seem to believe that a miss is as good as a mile.

Anne is seldom comfortable with other people's driving. With Darius, she alternates between seeing the sights and covering her eyes to avoid panic. The roads are hairy enough; Darius's penchant for unscheduled stops almost puts her over the edge.

We spend part of an afternoon at the cooperative nutmeg factory, learning about the history, handling, and anatomy of this remarkable plant. Although Grenada now provides about 40 percent of the world's supply of nutmeg, Grenadians stole their plants from Indonesia in the nineteenth century. The Dutch jealously guarded their virtual monopoly on nutmeg production in the East Indies by dipping all seeds destined for export in lime juice, to prevent germination. But when the East Indians turned to the West Indians for help with sugar production, some Grenadian plantation managers who visited Indonesia smuggled home a cache of untreated nutmeg seeds. Nutmeg remained only a household crop in Grenada until an Indonesian nutmeg blight provided the incentive for commercial production. Suddenly, the "spice island" economy was born.

For Grenadians, this was great good luck, both economically and socially. By the 1830s, the sugar trade in the British West Indies was collapsing. Nutmeg rapidly replaced sugar as the major money crop in Grenada, although islanders had always grown cocoa, bananas, coffee, and tobacco as well. Nutmeg not only cushioned the economic decline, it, like the other Grenadian export crops, can be grown efficiently on relatively small acreage. "Spice" production absorbed at least some of the sugar-plantation workers and reinforced the yeoman-farmer and small-estate agricultural pattern that already existed outside the sugar plantations. The sugar plantocracy had a long period of dominance in Grenada, and an island elite persists. The upper reaches of Grenadian society were always in competition—not just with bondsmen and indentured servants but also with a class of independent small farmers, a part of Grenada's French-Creole heritage. Unlike most of the British West Indies, the basic elements necessary for the creation of both a petit bourgeoisie and a working-class consciousness have persisted throughout much of Grenada's difficult political history. Thanks in part to nutmeg, the collapse of the sugar economy did not herald the collapse of Grenadian society.

Nutmeg is the bison or elk of the fruit kingdom—every part of it has some independent use. The hard exterior shell surfaces pathways and provides mulch for gardens. Mixed with charcoal, it gives a distinctive flavor to Grenadian barbecued meats. The soft fruit is turned into syrups, jams, and jellies, as well as a spicy liqueur. Remove the fruit and you see the nutmeg's second spice. Wrapped around the nutmeg seed is a thin outer layer of mace. The seed itself yields both spice and oil for pharmaceuticals, cosmetics, and a host of sedative and antiseptic preparations. The nutmeg graces the Grenadian flag and

The nutmeg.

flavors everything from soup to tarts to ice cream. No Caribbean rum punch worthy of the name would fail to have a grinding of fresh nutmeg on the top.

Trial by water determines whether a nutmeg seed is spice quality or will end up in a tube of lipstick. The denser, higher-quality seeds sink, the less good seeds float. Nutmegs are tested like English criminal defendants before the rise of the jury system. If the water accepted you, you were innocent; if you floated, you were hanged. Low body fat must have been a real advantage if you were contemplating a life of crime in medieval England.

The nutmeg processing plant for all of Grenada is in the fishing village of Gouyave. Here, scores of Grenadians separate the nutmeg into its constituent parts; cure, sort, and bag the product; and prepare everything for shipping to the world market. The nutmeg co-op is a triumph of preindustrial production. Everything is still done by hand amid gossip, shouts, and laughter. A modern operations engineer would replace 90 percent of these workers with machines and computers. Even Henry Ford probably would have managed to dispense with half of them. As we wander about the cavernous wooden structure, there is no obvious way to tell employees from family or friends who have just stopped in for a chat. The ambience is more like that of a fair or festival than a factory. Production may not be very efficient, but the feel of a festival is better than the feel of a factory.

But let's not wax too rhapsodic. Part of the festival air may result from the simple fact that we can't understand a word that is being said. Virtually all Grenadians speak perfectly good English, the island's official language. But much noncommercial conversation is in the island patois, based on French. The British ultimately triumphed here politically, but the social ambience of Grenada seems more French Catholic than Anglican. And as a native Louisianian, I learned long ago that the otherworldly charm and animated Creole babble of a New Orleans or Lafayette oyster bar does not mean that *les bon temps* in fact *roulent* twenty-four hours a day.

With preindustrial technology comes preindustrial compensation. At one workstation where workers scrape the thin layer of mace off the nutmeg's inner core, a woman has mounted her own minor protest. Her words, in white on the unpainted wooden wall above her, read, "The Lord looked at my work and found it good. He looked at my wages and just hung his head and passed on by."

While we feel we have found paradise in Grenada, it is still a very poor country. Annual per capita income is about $3,000. The economy has improved somewhat since the early 1980s, and the political situation seems quite stable. Two major political parties alternate in office, sometimes in coalition with smaller parties. The locals whom we engage in political conversation complain mightily about the taxes and what they think they are getting (or not getting) for them. They have recently voted in a new government. They do not expect the tax burden to decrease, but they have hopes that some of it might find its way back into public projects benefiting the whole island, not just the politicians and their friends. They love to point out the potholes in the roads and ask where the petrol taxes are going. So what else is new? However difficult Grenada's road to stable political democracy may have been, these sound like the sentiments of citizens almost everywhere.

George Brizan is surely correct that his island is born of struggle, with a history punctuated by political, social, and economic conflict. But that could be said about almost any former West Indian colony. In Grenada, the crucible of struggle seems to us to have melded a distinctive culture. Grenada's polyglot background, its diversified agriculture, its modest reliance on tourism, and its population of small farmers, fishermen, and small businessmen have somehow come together into a coherent whole. Unlike the USVI or the BVI, Grenada feels to us like its own self—a self we are reluctant to leave.

Rather than weighing anchor and sailing away, we feel like going house hunting. But we do not need to hunt. Up the hill from our anchorage is an extraordinary structure built into the top of the hillside. The roof is the hillside itself, complete with flowering plants and an occasional wandering goat. The house is open to the east for the morning sun and cooling winds, completely enclosed to the west for protection from the summer heat. It has fabulous views of the bay and the Atlantic beyond, passive solar heat for hot water, and a dock for PALAEMON.

There are two minor drawbacks. The first is a $6 million price tag. Such things are negotiable, of course, but still, at our current rate of capital accumulation, it would be out of our price range until about 2050.

The second small problem is a potentially defective title. According to our informants, the house was built by a retired mogul pushing seventy, with a twenty-eight-year-old wife, not his first. Six weeks after moving into this love nest, the mogul died, leaving it to his wife. Six months later, the grieving widow married the building contractor. No one with whom we talked doubted that she had killed her husband. We have no idea whether this delicious gossip is true. But for the locals, the only controversy seems to revolve around which of the many easily available poisonous plants on Grenada she slipped into his callaloo soup.

At any rate, there is an ancient principle of Anglo-American law that no one will be allowed to profit by his or her own crime. Inheriting a house from your murder victim fits comfortably within this principle. Anyone purchasing the property could find, as the lawyers say, "a cloud upon the title."

Unable to buy our dream house, we decide to leave Grenada. Well, not really. Our time is running out and the wind has moved slightly south of east— a real advantage for us, since we need to head east of north to make our way back up the Windwards. Having been beaten up by southeasterlies on the way down, we can at least get a lift from them on the way back. Leaving means that we overlap in Grenada with Jerome and Judith for only about eighteen hours. We are becoming hardened passagemakers. If we have to choose between time with our friends and a fair wind, we will take the fair wind.

ANNE'S PASSAGE NOTES: HALFWAY

It is early February when we drop the hook in Secret Harbour, Mount Hartman Bay. In sea miles and in months, this is our halfway point, and I feel deeply ambivalent. When we leave Grenada, PALAE-MON's bow will be pointed north.

I announce immediately that I want to stay in this harbor for the full time—roughly a week—that we have in Grenada. I want land exploration, no sailing. Grenada's beauties are reputedly more land-based than water-based, but more important, I am exhausted with the sea and its anxieties. I expect opposition from Jerry. But he only raises his eyebrows and says, "You mean you don't want to sail for a week?" "Right," I say, my chin sticking out, still expecting opposition. Instead, he smiles.

So we explore the land. The flowers are spectacular, glorious mounds of vivid color, their fragrance intense, and always laced with the aromas of spice. After the dry Virgins, the lushness of Grenada is overwhelming. But it is the people who most compel me. They seem to belong to their island, and their island to them. The markets are much as they have been for years. The tourist business is still small. The steel-pan music is the real thing. The fishing and spice businesses are real, if not thriving. Yet, as has happened in so much of the Caribbean, the young are beginning to leave, and Grenadians' hold on their culture, their identity, their island seems fragile to me. Strip commercial development is beginning along some main roads, industrial parks are under construction. The new will almost inevitably crowd out the old as the economy modernizes.

I do not like to think about what the future holds for these lovely people, and Darius, our most consistent local contact, is not optimistic. I also feel some sense of missed opportunity. Exploring different cultures was at least in part what we came for. Yet we spent so many weeks in the relative cultural wasteland of the Virgins, and have so little time here. I do not regret our time in the Virgins. The beaches, the snorkeling, the family and friends were wonderful, and good for us. Jerry relaxed and got his intellectual juices flowing again. I started to paint. But at the turnaround point, here in Grenada, it seems as though we have only just begun.

The clock, anxieties about the route home, the stark symbolism of pointing PALAEMON north—all loom over me. After a day of silent and unproductive introspection and an occasional, "What's wrong with you, anyway?" from Jerry, I shelve my fretting. PALAEMON, for now, has few demands. I let myself explore and enjoy the island and its people.

But the clock lifts its face again all too quickly. When the wind veers slightly south of east, we prepare to set sail, even though we might have stayed another couple of days. We have too many sea miles behind us to ignore the wind when it and the sea conditions say "go." I do not want to go. I have been afraid before. I have wanted to postpone the inevitable, even though I knew we needed to move. This is different. I am enticed by the islands ahead, but I do not want to turn north, nor do I want to leave Grenada so little explored. We linger over our good-byes to Judith and Jerome, even as we turn our faces to the sea. Anchor weighed, gear stowed, PALAEMON's bow points to the north for the first time since we motored to Bermuda to hide from Lenny. The sea conditions are lovely. Despite my sadness, a familiar anticipation teases my senses.

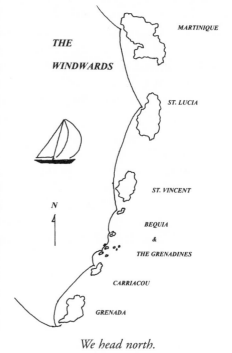

We head north.

CHARMED BY CARRIACOU

The sun is sinking into the sea by the time we finally settle in a small bay on Grenada's west coast. A fishing skiff piled high with nets lies nearby. From this perch, we can make Carriacou in a few hours tomorrow, arriving while the sun is high, the reefs and shallows clearly visible. Anchoring has been difficult, driving us farther and farther north, searching for decent holding. Lenny's angry waves demolished the coast road and swept its broken remains out to sea. Boulders and chunks of concrete and asphalt litter the bottom just off-shore. Almost everywhere the big CQR anchor touched bottom, I felt the rumble of metal on stone through the chain.

As I go forward at first light to weigh anchor, the fishing gang is out, scouting just off our bow. The spotter and I nod a greeting. I wait to bring in the anchor, not wanting to spoil a set. The spotter stands in the bow of the skiff. His crew sits silent, motionless, waiting to play out the long net. If they make a set, they will haul from shore.

Most island fishermen work on the "shares" system—a third for the seine owner, a third for the seine, the remainder to the crew and others who

Seining crew.

materialize on the beach to help haul. The tidy idea of distribution by thirds is almost always complicated by local custom, kinship, debts, favors, gifts. The fish disappear into buckets and tubs. The sharing-out is almost instantaneous, apparently conforming to some clear, unspoken understanding that remains utterly mysterious to an outsider.

A set can produce anything from a few pounds of small fry to hundreds of pounds of jack, mackerel, and tuna. Modest catches are the rule. The spotter rarely sets on nothing, yet nothing is all I ever see until a net is hauled ashore, alive with writhing silver treasure. It is as if these guys can feel the fish surging beneath the opaque surface of the sea.

Encouraged by the seine crew's example, I put out my trolling line. I haven't hooked anything since a yellow fin tuna stripped my reel of 200 yards of 60-pound-test wire on the passage from Lookout Bight to Wrightsville Beach off the Carolina coast. When I cranked down on the drag to keep him from taking everything, he snapped the wire as though it were made of sewing thread. I could use heavier tackle, but what the hell would I do with a 200-pound tuna?

Our passage to Hillsborough, Carriacou's port of entry, is uneventful. No high winds, no gear failures, no fish. We don't even have to clear out of Grenada and into Carriacou, which is politically a part of the nation of Grenada, Carriacou, and Petite Martinique. This is hardly a union of equals. Grenada has a population of 100,000, Carriacou is an island of 8,000, Petite Martinique has only 800.

Carriacou is reputed to be the friendliest island in the Caribbean. It may be. It's not just that people are responsive when we go ashore and ask directions, they outshine even the ever-attentive Bermudians in their solicitation for a stranger's possible disorientation. Perhaps I walk around looking more lost and confused than most, but within our first thirty minutes in Hillsborough, a half-dozen locals inquire whether I need assistance. Carriacouans are gentle guides. I sometimes elicit offers of help from strangers even in New York City, but the subtext there is something like: "I-can-see-you're-from-the-sticks-maybe-I-can-keep-you-from-getting-killed-by-the-next-taxi-and-besides-you're-blocking-traffic." That's not the tone on Carriacou.

Carriacou also has a reputation for being extremely laid-back. The ratio of rum shops to gasoline stations is a hundred to one. On the other hand, going to a Carriacou rum shop is sort of like going to a gas station. There is usually only one brand per shop—homemade, or "House Blend." You bring your own jug and plop it on the counter, the behavioral equivalent of "Fill 'er up." You can get high test and low test, and from the smell of most of this stuff, I suspect you could run a car on it. I know it's cowardly, but I just can't bring myself to try the local product. When somebody offers to sell me a fifth of rum for less than a dollar, I begin to fear that the phrase "blind drunk" might have to be taken literally.

I am also a little wary of small-batch West Indian distilling equipment. Seventeenth-century British planters and indentured servants used to complain of a mysterious West Indian disease they called "Dry Belly Ache." It turned out to be lead poisoning. The British West Indian settlers drank such prodigious amounts of rum that the lead leaching from their distillery piping reached toxic levels in their innards. Nothing usable gets thrown away in the West Indies. Some of that pipe may still be in use.

Carriacou joy juice fuels a lot of activity in Hillsborough, where we are moored. Facing west, Hillsborough was clobbered by Lenny's waves. Half of the main street that skirts the bay has disappeared, along with the dinghy dock we were planning to use. Homeowners and shopkeepers are putting their properties back together as best they can. The usual Caribbean practice of building if and when you can get materials is underway. The main street itself is being rebuilt by hand, mostly with volunteer labor. When I say, "by hand," I mean with no earthmoving equipment, not even an electric cement mixer. The effort is prodigious, progress painfully slow.

The hand-crank cement mixer is set up at Hillsborough's main intersection. On a typical day, nearly everyone in and around the town will pass by or through this spot across from the ferry dock. Customs and immigration have a corner on the water side of the street; the loading ramp and taxi stand have the other. Across the construction site that *was* the street is the main market—a few hundred square yards of tables and baskets laden with vegetables and fruit, some hand-sewn bags, and leather sandals. A general store holds down the second inland corner. The East Indian proprietor stocks everything from baby powder to boogie boards, shirts to syrup.

Shoppers, taxi drivers, stevedores, and a few tourists leap over piles of ground limestone, sand, and gravel, and tightrope-walk the edges of the cement forms to avoid falling into the wet concrete. Two young guys take turns at the cement mixer; three others load the mixer, water the load, tip it into wheelbarrows. Two barrow men wheel the fresh mix to where the form crew has laid out the next wood-edged square and lined it with rusted reinforcing wire and a few pieces of iron rod. Men with rakes and shovels fill the form and make a first cut at leveling the cement. Two older men direct the others, smooth the mix with a two-by-four across the top of the form, finish it off with hand trowels. Maybe twenty in the crew. They can probably lay four squares a day, 40 feet of road.

Spontaneously organized communal projects ("maroons") are as uncommon in most of the contemporary West Indies as a traditional neighborhood barn-raising in twenty-first-century Iowa. But in Carriacou's almost classless society, maroons like this one persist. The low priority of Carriacou or Petite Martinique's public works at government house in Grenada adds incentive to tradition.

In Grenada they say, "They're all the same in Carriacou." That is hardly true, but Carriacou's culture is distinctively egalitarian. When the sugar industry collapsed, all the planters—all thirty or so—packed up and left. The slaves and free coloureds of Carriacou were emancipated and politically empowered at a stroke, left to build a society for themselves. Rather than falling into the "wage slavery" that characterized most postslavery plantation economies, in which a few big landowners controlled employment for everyone else, Carriacouans became independent small farmers, fishermen, boatbuilders, seamen, and artisans. A generation and a half ago, wage labor was almost nonexistent on Carriacou.

Even before the end of the slave period, Carriacou's social and economic organization was peculiar. In 1833, on the eve of emancipation, an "English Visitor" reported to his hometown journal, the *Bristol Mirror:*

> The model of all slave islands seemed to me to be Carriacou. . . . Mr. Maclean [is] the principal proprietor there. . . . [The] total population is about 4,000 of whom 3,200 are slaves. Mr. Maclean has either of his own, or under his management, about 2,200 slaves. The principal production by which the Negroes make money is poultry, which they breed and send down by small vessels, which are constantly running up and down between that [island] and Grenada. . . .

> But the great excellence of the management consists in the very complete system of task work which is introduced into every department of labour. . . . They set a certain quantity of work to each Negro daily; suppose to make two hundred holes for planting canes. The whole gang has the same quantity, and works in the same field. They generally commence at 5 o'clock, that they may finish early, and . . . have the rest of the day to themselves.

It generally happens that if one or two are weaker than the rest, and have not finished their task at the same time with them, the whole gang will remain and complete the work of those that have been behind. . . . In a short time the plan will be still further improved, by setting a weekly instead of a daily task, so as to allow them two or three days a week to themselves; so that they can never have any difficulty in raising money to purchase their freedom.

As it is at present, it is not at all uncommon for a father to purchase his wife and children, to send them to work in his ground, still himself remaining a slave, that he may retain his house and ground. The consequence of this treatment is that during the last seven years, the slave population—now about 3,200—*have been increasing at the rate of 60 per annum*—the total in seven years being 421. . . . These are facts which I can vouch for . . .

The "English Visitor" emphasized his last point about slave increase, indeed seems to have anticipated disbelief, because it was virtually unheard-of in the British West Indies. Slave populations in Barbados, St. Kitts, Nevis, Antigua, and Jamaica had to be reinforced by constant importation from West Africa. Sugar's appetite for black bodies was almost insatiable.

While anthropologists, ethnographers, and ethnomusicologists prefer to study traditional peoples untouched by Western ways, Carriacou's unique West Indian culture has generated something of an ethnohistorical cottage industry. The seminal text is M. G. Smith's *Kinship and Community in Carriacou*, based on fieldwork done in the early 1950s. Smith carefully documents Carriacouans' history of improbable, but successful, cultural straddles: families "voluntarily" half-slave and half-free, African rites combined with European customs, French Creole culture ordered by British governance, Christianity piled on top of ancestor worship, science supplementing magic, emigrants whose only loyalties were to the island they had left, permanent marriage that winked at generalized male promiscuity, paternal responsibility from absent fathers.

Carriacou "folk" have no reticence about going to the medical center for treatment of an illness. But, if you want to know *why* you got sick, you visit your *obeah man*. Carricouans' parents hang around after death, constantly making demands on their children. They will agree to stay in their graves only after months of propitiation, the erection of a tombstone, and the giving of a "stone feast." Nothing less will do. The prevalence of such beliefs among their Christian flocks horrifies the Carriacouan clergy. For the average Carriacouan, his parents' failure to disappear as soon as they are buried seems like a perfectly plausible understanding of purgatory. That a "good father" cares for his children by marriage as well as his acknowledged children by other women makes perfect sense to people who live in a community where women have vastly outnumbered men for nearly two centuries.

Carriacou is also one of the few remaining sites of traditional boatbuilding in the lower Caribbean. A handful of Scots washed up on Carriacou more than a century ago and started building boats on the beach. Instead of sailing away when the boats were built, the Scottish boatbuilders sold them, took orders for more, and married islanders. This enterprise continues, in a low-key, Carriacou kind of way. Many of the traditional sail-powered fishing and cargo vessels that ply the waters from St. Vincent to Grenada are Carriacou-built. And, as the English Visitor's report to the *Bristol Mirror* noted, Carriacouans have been trading by sea for centuries. M. G. Smith's survey of occupations in L'Esterre in 1953 showed twenty-nine out of thirty-six male heads of household making a living from boatbuilding, boat ownership, work as a seaman, or fishing.

We catch a bus ("the red one," a typically helpful resident informs me) over to Windward, the "Scots" settlement where Carriacou boatbuilding got its start. Hulls in various states of completion, restoration, and collapse are strung along the beach, waiting for their owners to get more building material—or the money with which to buy more building material. No one is at work today. Some of these projects will require decades to complete. But on Carriacou, to own a sloop, better yet a schooner, or their contemporary engine-driven equivalents, demonstrates a man's capacity to fulfill his family responsibilities. Just to have a boat under construction is a sign of maturity and seriousness of purpose.

Carriacou boats are built by eye—no plans and no models. Having struggled through the construction of one 10-foot dinghy and one 15-foot skiff, both with plans and instructions, I find this building-by-eye technique pretty impressive. The hulls are fair and graceful. Most are built for interisland transport (the bigger the load, the better) and for maneuvering among the reefs and shallows. Their economic niche is to go where large cargo vessels cannot. This compromise between load and nimbleness yields a distinctive, broad-beamed, shallow-draft design. The masters of Carriacou coasters are terrific sailors. We watch them tacking back and forth through the reefs off Windward, banking off a steady trade wind, sluicing through narrow cuts—waters we would consider nonnavigable even under power in a dead-flat calm.

Our wanderings on the Windward beach are enlivened by conversation with Ray, our volunteer escort. At various points, Ray claims to be from Los Angeles, San Juan, Glasgow, and the Bahamas. I would not bet a lot of my net worth on Ray being Ray, or only Ray. He looks like he took one too many acid trips in Haight-Ashbury in the 1960s and then quietly aged. His clothes and hairstyle are straight out of Berkeley Plaza, circa 1968.

Ray is full of information, all of it suspect. He may be right that the recent fish kill off Grenada and Carriacou results from mining pollution up the Orinoco River in Venezuela, pushed more than 200 miles northeastward by mammoth floods in South America. But when Ray tries to give authenticity to this story by claiming to be a marine biologist, I begin to tune out. He has already described himself as a naval architect and a classical guitarist. He would have that guitar now, he says, but Foxy took it as security for his bar bill twenty years ago, before Jost was spoiled by tourists. Did we happen to notice whether Foxy was playing a black guitar? If so, it was Ray's.

Ray is also a very special sort of artist. He paints trees. Not pictures of trees, the trees themselves. Ray lives aboard his partly finished boat on the beach at Windward, and every tree within a hundred yards of his habitation is evidence of his commitment to improve on nature. There are blue trees, orange trees, bright green and magenta ones, whatever paint Ray can scrounge. These arboreal insults actually begin to grow on us after a while. (Sorry, pun intended.) Given the dim prospect that Ray's particular art form will become a commercial success, he supports himself as a more conventional painter of houses and boats. Again, the articles themselves, not pictures of houses and boats. He seems to be paid mostly in food, rum, and the leftover paint with which he pursues his true artistic calling.

There is another artist on Carriacou whom we hope to meet on purpose. Canute Caliste, or Mr. Canute Caliste, as he signs his canvases, has been painting on Carriacou for the last seventy-six years. He started at age nine. While we do not generally like primitivists, Mr. Canute Caliste's work is intriguing. In the illustrations, we have seen human figures often float or fly above land or sea, recalling the West African slave legends of flight both to paradise and home to Africa. The story is still told on Carriacou of the Igbo people who marched off a slave ship at L'Esterre landing and into the sea to walk home to Africa. According to legend those who had avoided salt and had honored their ancestors found they could walk on the water or simply take flight toward home. Some version of the story of the flying Igbos is part of slavery's oral tradition in most of the West Indies, although it is thought to have originated in South Carolina. Whatever its origins, the image of, or the longing for, flight is a constant theme in West Indian stories and songs.

Mr. Caliste is said to live up the hill from L'Esterre Bay, so we chug off there in JEREMY BENTHAM, hoping to find him. We arrive on the flawless, seemingly uninhabited beach to find two people sitting in the shade of a sea grape. One, a robust, bare-chested conch fisherman, is cleaning his catch. The other is a black goddess in a flowing, ankle-length dress of cotton batik. A thousand braided tresses cascade down her back, and her perfect hands end in exquisitely polished nails. This couple could have just stepped out of a Carriacou tourist-board poster—if there *were* a Carriacou tourist board.

We ask whether they know where we might find Mr. Canute Caliste. The conch fisherman gives us a shy smile and replies that "this beautiful lady" surely can help. The "beautiful lady" seems accustomed to such compliments from conch fishermen on the beach in the middle of nowhere. Well, maybe just this conch fisherman. We look at her expectantly, hoping for directions to Mr. Caliste's house. Instead, she reaches into the folds of her dress and whips out a cell phone—one of many Caribbean moments in which we have zipped from the eighteenth century to the twenty-first in a nanosecond. Or vice versa. After punching in a few numbers and receiving no response, she announces: "I thought so, he's not home. He's in Grenada for his art show."

We thank her, and explain our errand, our disappointment at not getting to see some of his paintings. She replies that she has some, if we would like to look at them. They are up at her beach bar.

We notice for the first time that while we are in the middle of a fabulous, otherwise-deserted, mile-long beach, we are not in the middle of nowhere. In the shadow of the palms and the sea grape stands a beach bar, next to a tiny beauty shop. We're beginning to get the picture here. Ali is the twenty-first-century entrepreneur, complete with her ever-ready cell phone. The conch fisherman is an eighteenth-century holdover, still fishing the traditional way from a small sloop, diving for conch, cleaning them on the beach.

We walk up the beach with Ali, expecting to see a few of Caliste's works hanging on the walls of the bar. Instead, she returns from inside with a roll of canvases. Mr. Caliste has not

Ali's friend.

spent all his time painting for the last seventy-six years. Our hostess is one of his twenty-three children. Caliste has had three wives. Since Ali assures us that he is in perfect health, we suspect he may be in Grenada looking for a fourth.

Ali's obvious pride in her father's age, his number of children, and in her mother (because she "gave him" eleven of them), suggests that some of Smith's midcentury observations on Carriacou's culture remain true. When he did his fieldwork, precisely these attributes gave a person status in society. Whether Mr. Caliste had these "wives" simultaneously or seriatim is unclear, but he seems to be providing for his children, as a good Carriacouan father should, by endowing them with paintings. And, like Ali, many Carriacou women of Smith's era carried on independent trades, sold garden produce, perhaps distilled rum and ran a rum shop. Without enough men to go around, nearly half of all Carriacou women lived mostly on their own, raised children whose fathers were in Grenada or Trinidad earning the family a living, or were married to someone else.

But sitting on the beach with someone of the opposite sex would have been scandalous behavior in the 1950s, unless the couple were married or betrothed. Somehow we don't think Ali and the conch fisherman's relationship has reached either of those stages. Owning a small fishing sloop is probably not sufficient evidence of good economic prospects to convince Mr. Canute Caliste that Ali's friend is an acceptable suitor. Carriacouan fathers of his generation have high standards for what makes a man a serious marital prospect.

We sit at a picnic table, peeling Caliste's canvases one by one from Ali's stack. His work is representational and fantastical at the same time, a lyrical mixture of almost anything: scenes of Carriacou, representations of the devil, children flying kites, and especially floating forms he calls "The Maids"—mermaids he has summoned from the sea. Ali says her father claims them as his inspiration. The canvases glow with the strong hues of the Caribbean—vivid greens, deep blues, violet reds, vibrant yellows.

There is nothing tentative about Mr. Canute Caliste's paintings. Yet, his images of the mundane and special occasions of Carriacou life hint at the fragility of his culture, as if the artist means to hold on to his vision of Carriacou by the very boldness of his brush.

We had hoped we might find a painting of the "Big Drum Dance," the distinctive Carriacouan festival at which each "nation" of the island—some fifteen different West African ethnic or linguistic groups—is represented. In an order dictated by ancient custom, dancers sing each nation's songs. No one on

Carriacou speaks these languages any longer. Only the songs remain, some of their meanings completely lost.

Big-drum rituals were common five decades ago—indeed, almost mandatory for marriages and births, burials and boat launchings, any event that signaled a major change in a family's composition or fortunes. But only a few islanders remain who can perform the

DETAIL FROM "THE MAID CUNTRY" BY MR. CANUTE CALISTE

Mr. Canute Caliste's Maids.

nation dances. Modernity intrudes. Carriacouan society is changing. We are disappointed that we do not find a "big drum" painting among Ali's canvases. Her father has done some, but they have become rare, like the dance itself.

If Ali's bar had been open, I would have tried her rum. Rather than walking away with one version of "The Maids," we would probably now own the largest collection of Mr. Canute Calistes in the world—outside of his immediate family.

24

LIVING IN THE BOAT-BOY ECONOMY

As we head north, the image of Caribbean sailing that has danced in our heads since we left Connecticut becomes our reality. The islands arc across the latitudes of the eastern trade winds, which provide steady, beamy breezes for easy passages south or north. The upthrust of the ocean floor has scattered islands just far enough apart for romps in the open ocean. PALAEMON dances over rollers pushed from the Atlantic into the Caribbean by easterly winds that stretch all the way to the Sahara. Transatlantic cruisers tell us that when the trades are really blowing, boats as far west as Barbados turn pink from the red dust of the African desert.

Climbing the island chain from Grenada to Carriacou to our next stop in the Grenadines, we must sail slightly northeast. That's why we bailed out of Grenada so abruptly when the wind clocked toward the southeast. This geography also explains the British-inspired "Windward Islands" name. To get from Trinidad or Grenada to their other possessions in the Lesser Antilles, the British (or anyone else, for that matter) had to sail to windward, into the prevailing northeasterlies. This British terminology is, as usual, eccentric. The "Leewards" are to windward of virtually the whole Caribbean Sea. The Spanish called all of the Lesser Antilles the "Windwards" and reserved "Leeward" for the islands off the Venezuelan coast that really *are* in the lee of something. But history and conquest, not logic, determine whose names prevail.

We revel in the warm winds and easy sailing, mostly avoiding the two navigational traps the Windwards lay for the unwary. The first is to imagine that the nice 15-knot wind that is carrying us along the lee (west) side of an island will continue when we leave its protection. As we clear the northern head of each island, the wind suddenly leaps to 20 to 25 knots, sometimes 30. If we forget to reef down before the headland, we have an interesting few minutes getting things under control.

The second is to forget the strong westerly current, the rivers of ocean flowing through the gaps between the islands. We sometimes sail 15 or even 20 degrees east of our rhumb line in order to maintain a course toward our destination. We watch—with feelings of great superiority—as boats (mostly charterers, surely) failing to respect these currents are swept off to the west. We encounter them later in the day, sails furled, laboring back east under power.

There was also the remote possibility that the volcano lying 60 feet below the surface on the route from Grenada to Carriacou would pick the time of our passage to form a new Caribbean island. But this particular hazard has been quiet since 1989, so I don't think it counts as a serious navigational hazard.

From Carriacou, the Grenadines are only 30 miles. Politically a part of "St. Vincent and the Grenadines," this group of tiny islands—from Union in the south to Bequia in the north—is a magical realm of volcanic hills and reef-protected anchorages. The *pièces de résistance* are the Tobago Cays— uninhabited, unwatered oases of limestone and sand, cactus and coconut palms, sprinkled haphazardly behind a massive reef stretching miles into the Atlantic. Twenty square miles of sandy shelf only 2 to 3 fathoms deep; alive with coral patches, fish, and lobster; the sandy bottom so bright PALAEMON casts a crisp black shadow on the seabed.

Our first stop is Salt Whistle Bay on the island of Mayreau, a picture-perfect, horseshoe-shaped cove with deep sand beaches, fringing palm trees, and excellent snorkeling around the points. At Salt Whistle, we can lie on deck and watch modern yachts beating their way up the narrow channel to the To-bago Cays, or fishermen coaxing plywood-patched, ragged-sailed sloops in to the beach where they clean their catch. Ashore is a restaurant where each table is a separate stone cabana providing the ultimate in ass-numbing private din-ing. But it is better to eat on the boat, for in the Grenadines, we enter the "boat-boy economy."

As with "newsboys" in an American city, boat boys are not boys. They're grown men running independent businesses out of sleek, brightly painted skiffs. Ray's favorite tree colors—orange, lime green, yellow and indigo—are well represented in the boat-boy fleet.

These "boys" play different economic roles in different places. In St. Vin-cent and St. Lucia, they have a bad reputation. Their principal business seems to be extortion—offering pilotage, anchorage, and "boat-watching" services made necessary only by their interference and implied threats.

The safety and security net reported today that some boat boys in Do-minica are currently running a dinghy-napping scam. Each morning for the past week, several cruisers peered over their sterns to discover their dinghies missing. "Somehow," they broke loose from their mother ships in the night and floated away. But these vagrant craft have been rescued by the heroic efforts of local boat boys, who now have them on the beach. For a "finder's fee"—the going rate seems to be U.S.$50—the dinghy savior will return it to its owner. There is talk of vigilante action tomorrow. If anyone's dinghy is missing, fifty cruisers are said to be prepared to go fetch it from its "savior."

On prior charter trips, we have not found dealing with these characters too difficult, provided we took a firm stand. That's the approach we take now in Salt Whistle Bay. We choose one guy from the circling swarm, tell him clearly what we need and do not need, and then tell him that he's our guy only as long as nobody else bothers us. We also lock PALAEMON's every hatch and locker when away. JEREMY is tethered with a kryptonite cable of the type used by building contractors to secure expensive power tools on insecure job sites. With only these precautions, we can live quite harmoniously with even "bad" boat boys.

In the Grenadines, we encounter no bad boat boys. They may look fierce, with their Rasta hair and ragged pants, but they are polite, efficient, and highly competent. And they provide real services. Part of the joy of the Grenadines is to be anchored off islands or reefs that have virtually no people and no supplies. But if we want to stay for more than a day or two, we will need some things. Well, *want* them anyway. Enter the boat boys. They will zip off in their quick craft to larger settlements and bring back whatever we order—fruits and vegetables, baguettes, ice, gasoline. They also provide a taxi service should we need to send someone to the airstrip at Union Island without having to move PALAEMON.

Eating aboard is a particular joy in the Grenadines because the boat boys are also purveyors of fish and lobster—grilled. A skiff comes alongside PALAEMON in the morning, a selection of lobsters scrambling about in the bottom. We give the proprietor a time in the evening when we would like to see our lobster split, grilled, and ready for eating. At the appointed time, the lobster will return—perfectly done, complete with a choice of lemon or garlic butter, for a scrumptious dinner in the cockpit. Watchless, the boat boys of the Grenadines make their delectable deliveries on schedules that would be the envy of a Domino's Pizza franchise.

Grenadine boat boys give each other, or themselves, striking names—a sort of trademark, easily remembered by an otherwise inattentive clientele. Many are descriptive. "Bushmon," our main man in the Tobago Cays, does look like he just emerged from the jungle, perhaps after an unhappy encounter with a tiger. But beneath the fierce exterior, he's a charming guy with a wonderfully droll sense of humor.

"Yellowmon" is the only white man in the boat-boy business in the Grenadines, perhaps in the Caribbean. With his long blond hair and bright yellow boat, Yellowmon stands out in any anchorage. Why one guy calls himself "More Fresh," however, we never quite fathom. Perhaps he is advertising quick service. Or maybe "More Fresh" has some special significance in the boat-boy patois that we are missing.

Although the boat boys are clearly competitors—they stage a high-speed race to be the first to any boat entering an anchorage—there is a complex system of economic cooperation as well. If Bushmon gets more custom than he can handle, he lays off some of it on a competitor. So when we tell Bushmon that we would like some ice at 9 the next morning, we're never sure who might show up with it. The one thing we must never do, however, is to accept the ice from a competitor who is not really Bushmon's deputy. If we behave in this unreliable fashion, we might find that neither Bushmon nor anyone else will provide us with decent service.

As at the Grenada market, there is a high degree of specialization in the boat-boy economy. Bushmon and Yellowmon do lobsters, ice, fruit, and vegetables. But they do not do T-shirts and arts and crafts, or fresh bread. These are someone else's concessions. There is also a guy who specializes in dealing with local fishermen and lobster divers. He lives in a tent on one of the Tobago Cays with a lobster "pound" floating off his beach. From this vantage point, he brokers lobsters and fish between the fishermen who do the catching and the boat boys who service the retail trade.

Courtesy of boat-boy entrepreneurship, we could anchor for weeks in the Tobago Cays with no obvious access to any market. Our every need would be supplied by one or another enterprising chap in a swift boat. Although there's obvious collusion on prices, they're not that bad. The organization of this market clearly requires further study. I plan to apply to the National Bureau of

More Fresh.

Economic Research for a grant as soon as we get back home. The project should not require more than three to five years—on-site, of course.

The only tedious feature of this plan is that I will have to learn Grenadine boat-boy patois. That will be a challenge. Although based on either English or French vocabulary—and I claim to have mastered a bit of both—the patois of the Lesser Antilles is really a different language. West African slaves came from as many as 100 different language groups, and they were often purposefully separated from others in their own group as a precaution against easy organization into rebel cells. Patois emerged as a means of common communications across differing West African linguistic heritages, using the words of the masters modified to fit West African linguistic traditions.

Originally, all West Indian patois was exclusively oral, as were most West African languages. This was reinforced by West Indian colonial slave codes. It was a crime in many colonies to teach a slave to read or write. As in most exclusively oral languages, gesture and tonality often substitute for vocabulary. Many word variations from the written base language are simply unnecessary in the patois that borrows from it.

West Indian patois, for example, economizes mightily on pronouns. "Him" is an all-purpose third-person pronoun. Oral context will easily distinguish among "he," "she," "it," "his," "hers," even "they" and "their." "Me" serves for "I," "mine," or "my," and actually corresponds closely to "I" in a number of West African languages that use "mi" or "mo" for the first-person singular. Economizing on words theoretically should make the job easier for the student of patois, but it doesn't. For, as in spoken Chinese, tonality and emphasis give multiple meanings to a single word. And, as with Greek, island patois is highly concrete and metaphoric. "Eye water" means "tears" or "crying"; "big eyes" means "greed."

Perhaps the most challenging aspect of boat-boy patois is the open syllable form. Few West African words end in consonant sounds. West Indian patois therefore drops most English or French ending consonants. "Do le de ge we" means "Don't let them get wet." These are all perfectly familiar English words, but when Bushmon shouts them at his fumble-fingered assistant, I am clueless. Moreover, the patois shifts from island to island both between French and English (Spanish in some places) and among the African words that have been retained. Barbados patois (Bajan) uses a fair number of Igbo terms; Cubans have mostly retained words from Yoruba.

I am reminded of a story my Uncle Herbert tells about why he has lived in southwest Louisiana for forty years and never learned Creole patois. On his first night in Lafayette, he went to the high school football game. Seeing him sitting alone in the stands, a friendly Cajun waved him over, welcomed him to town, and asked him what language he wanted to speak. Herb asked what his choices were and was told, "English, Lafayette French, Houma French, Breaux Bridge French, Lake Charles French . . . ." Allowing time for language training, I may even need seven or eight years in the Grenadines to do my boat-boy-economy project.

Visions of the Tobago Cays.

In a way, being in the Grenadines is a throwback to the era in which the grocer, the baker, the milkman, and the pharmacy all delivered. My grandmother, once she had a telephone, could buy all the necessities for her household without ever leaving the house. But she was not sitting as we are, in crystal-clear water with a panoramic view of ringing reefs and high volcanic islands. Ordering from boat boys goes well beyond convenience shopping; it's a different activity altogether. Although my MaMaw would have washed out my mouth with soap—literally, I've experienced this—for calling any earthly setting "paradise," the Tobago Cays come awfully close.

25

Bequia Sweet, Sweet

It's February 25 and we're sailing from Mayreau up to Bequia. We're about to get into the crewed-charter business. Ted and Jan Marmor arrive on the twenty-ninth for ten days. Bruce and Susan Ackerman show up thirty-six hours after the Marmors leave and will stay until March 18.

If we wanted to test whether we might live in the Caribbean full time and run crewed charters for a living, the next three weeks would provide close to laboratory conditions. Our pals are great company, but they are not accomplished sailors. They help with food preparation and other things, as instructed. "As instructed" means that, without "instruction," they are passengers. We are responsible for the boat—and for them.

We are surprised at how much more anxious we become about routine movements when guests are aboard. Simple things like getting in and out of a bouncing dinghy. Moving, slippery boats are hazardous. Seamen and stevedores do not file all those compensation claims because they are trying to maim or kill themselves. I am not denying that admiralty law is deeply solicitous of crew safety. Cases on unseaworthiness are often worth reading just for their comic value. I once worked on the defense side of a case in which our client's boat was said to be unseaworthy because a seaman was on deck without a life vest. The plaintiff was the estate of the guy who failed to wear his vest—contrary to posted instructions—fell overboard, and drowned. The plaintiff won.

Seamen have received compensation for legs broken after jumping out of second-floor windows of brothels in a police raid, on the ground that it was a foreseeable hazard of shore leave. The only unseaworthiness claim I can remember in which the claimant lost was a suit by a ship's cook who intentionally cut off his own hand with a cleaver. He argued that the ship was unseaworthy because it employed a crazy cook.

As my repeated attempts to cut off my fingers with the windlass suggest, I have tried most of the ways to beat myself up aboard PALAEMON. Anne has watched me try them. By painful experience, we have learned how to move with the boat. Indeed, we now wobble about like drunks on land. Well, Anne has learned. Confident assertion that I will avoid injury is certainly misplaced. But we worry about our friends, who have had much less experience at sea. We will tailor activities and passages to limit risk.

The real test of running a crewed charter would be to do it with strangers, but we don't need or want a test. Getting up with a smile pasted on my face every morning, and keeping it there all day, would wear me out. Watching incompetent strangers beat up PALAEMON would drive me nuts. Having virtually no time alone with Anne would make me grumpy. Anne's a nicer person than I am, but I don't think she could handle it, either.

We had a reinforcing conversation with a couple in the BVI who were in their first year of running "one-couple" crewed charters on their 51-foot sailboat. The boat was perfectly designed for the task—two comfortable staterooms, two heads—but they were beginning to believe that they weren't. Their current clients, for example, were a husband and wife on a twenty-fifth-anniversary cruise, the husband's surprise gift for his spouse. The wife, it turned out, was afraid of the water, was seasick even at anchor, and did not swim—meaning, also, that she could not snorkel. What her thoughtful husband believed she was going to do on this charter was anybody's guess. How she had remained married to a guy who had such profound insight into what would make her happy was a deeper mystery. This improbable couple was ashore as we talked. The captain and mate were dreading their return, and they were thinking seriously of returning to the day-charter business. It's boring taking folks to the same places day after day, but the day charterers go home at 4:30.

Even with folks we love to have around, such as the Marmors and the Ackermans, Anne has a few nonnegotiable rules. Ted may only smoke cigars in JEREMY BENTHAM tethered at least 30 feet downwind of PALAEMON. Bruce may not make reference to Heidegger, or even less densely incomprehensible philosophers, before breakfast. Because Bruce, Ted, Susan, and I are all colleagues in related fields, we are absolutely forbidden to talk about work or faculty politics. These rules make everyone better off. Anne's determined enforcement of them suggests that she might have the makings of a crewed-charter captain after all.

We chose Bequia to meet our friends because we want to show them the Grenadines. There are direct flights from New York to St. Vincent. The ferry from there to Bequia takes hardly an hour, and from Bequia we can visit the whole of the Grenadines in a week's time. Well, we actually plan to skip Mustique. Neither Princess Margaret nor Mick Jagger ever invites us up

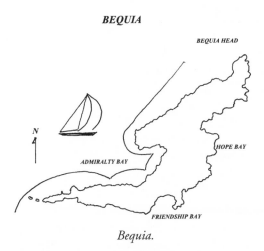

Bequia.

for a drink, and a hamburger on Mustique costs $20.

Should our touring plans collapse because the weather turns nasty, Bequia is a terrific place to hole up. The principal harbor, Admiralty Bay, is nearly 3 miles long. The bay is ringed by sandy beaches, palm trees, small hotels and restaurants, open-air markets, ship's chandleries, and brightly painted houses—all set against a backdrop of volcanic hills and lush forest. Like a host of Caribbean anchorages, Admiralty Bay is open to the west for sunset watching and the pursuit of the elusive green flash.

Pursuit of the green flash is one of my favorite sports. This strenuous game is played while drinking rum in the cockpit and watching the sun drop into the sea. Some players fuel the contest with other beverages, but I prefer the classic approach. As it plummets through its last 10 degrees of arc, the sun is magnified by the thickening atmosphere of the earth, and its color shifts from yellow through gold and orange to fiery red. The rim dances with exploding gases and the lower limb presses a dimple into the horizon, as if supported by the surface tension of the sea. The dimple ruptures; the ball descends; but, unwilling to slip beneath the waves, the sun's upper limb clings to the horizon. Abruptly, the rim drops over the edge of the earth; the fiery circle is gone; only the horizon remains, stark and straight, etched by the meeting of still-bright sky and the sea, now suddenly dark. A line marking the end of the world. Beyond, "there be dragons," as the old charts say. And, on some rare days, at just this moment, a brilliant flash of green appears just where the sun lost its grip on the water's edge. It lasts a second or less before the fading glow of reflected sunlight returns and the sky drifts toward twilight.

The green flash is not a mere optical illusion, the common experience of seeing green after staring at red. It is the result of some odd refraction of light, a transient atmospheric anomaly as yet unexplained. The possibility that tonight's sunset will yield a green flash adds a tinge of happy anticipation to the faintly *memento mori* melancholy of drawing down the curtain on another day, however gentle the Caribbean night.

Admiralty Bay has much more going for it than grandstand seats for the green flash. Here the boat-boy economy has perhaps reached its apogee. Stocking up for our charters, we cannot just have food delivered, we can have it delivered from Doris—which is as good as having the stuff flown in from Zabar's in Manhattan. Need diesel fuel? Call the Daffodil or Lighthouse Marine barge to come fill us up. Drinking water? Same deal.

At Lighthouse Marine Services, Ann not only brings ice, she takes back our substantial bag of accumulated laundry. Four hours later it returns sparkling and neatly folded for the princely sum of U.S. $8. Ann is the princess of marine services, laughing dark eyes parked over one of the sweetest smiles in the Caribbean.

My Anne is partly amused and partly annoyed by Ann's coy acceptance of the Bequian male ego. Whenever a man is in the delivery skiff with Ann, he must operate the engine, yet none is anywhere near as skilled as she is. One of these jerks almost puts Ann and our laundry into the bay as he crashes the Lighthouse Marine skiff into PALAEMON's stern. Ann only giggles while saving herself and our clothing. Leaving, she rolls her eyes at us as if to say, "That's the way it is. What can I do?"

Ashore are restaurants and bars of every description, a bountiful open-air vegetable market, and a splendid institution called the Bequia Bookshop. There, Heather Reynolds, the proprietress, sells nautical charts and scrimshaw along with the books. But if you want the latest in pulp fiction, you can just go somewhere else. The Bequia Bookshop exists to improve the Bequian mind. Heather's stock runs strongly to Caribbean authors, mostly expatriates such as Jamaica Kincaid and Maya Angelou, and to Penguin classics. She also serves up strong views on reforming the Bequia school system and unprintable opinions on the local government. The Bequia Bookshop provides a front-porch reading area where we can sample the stock, hang out with our own books, or swap reading recommendations with other layabouts.

Bequia tempts us to do a "Best of Bequia" guide. But we realize that we would end up listing almost every feature of the place and would have to resort to a Michelin Guide star system to highlight the really special stuff. Gingerbread topped with ice cream at the Gingerbread Hotel is a clear four-star entry. It's hardly surprising that so many cruisers hang out in Bequia. The diversity of the flags of origin on boats in Admiralty Bay is rivaled only by those we observed in St. George's, Bermuda. We invite two couples over for drinks and end up with two Americans, an Italian, an Austrian, a Brit, and a Dutch man in the cockpit. Anne and I are the only ones who have been so boring as to take a spouse of the same nationality.

The cruisers' ethnic diversity mirrors Bequia's population. Admiralty Bay must have attracted the earliest Spanish, Portuguese, and Dutch explorers and traders. Heather has a copy of an Eastern Caribbean chart from 1673 that shows Bequia clearly but fails to notice St. Vincent, which is about a hundred times larger and only 8 miles away. France laid claim to Bequia in 1664 but ceded it to the British a hundred years later. The French settlers held on long enough to give their family names to a large proportion of Bequia's mostly black population. More Ollivierres live on Bequia than any other clan.

Nor are black Bequians only West Africans. Here, and in St. Vincent and St. Lucia, the Europeans failed to drive out the Amerindians. The Caribs dispatched the Arawaks but intermarried with both slaves and free blacks to form the "Black Caribs." How many of today's black Bequians are descendants of Black Caribs is disputable. The last large group clearly identified as Black Caribs was forcibly transported from St. Vincent to Roátan, off the Honduran coast, in 1796.

But there is reason to believe that Black Carib bloodlines run deep here. They may even be pre-Columbian. This much is well documented: The Black Carib warriors of St. Vincent and the Grenadines were so effective at repelling Europeans in the early years of West Indies settlement that the colonial competitors agreed by treaty at one point to leave St. Vincent, St. Lucia, and Dominica to the Amerindian population. Serious European settlement on St. Vincent did not begin until 1719. Meanwhile, some West African slaves escaped from other islands to the Carib strongholds. Others arrived by surviving the wrecks of their slave-ship prisons on the reefs that guard St. Vincent's and Bequia's Atlantic shores. Black Caribs are thus, according to the standard account, the progeny of Carib unions with West Africans who had been freed either by escape or by shipwreck.

But this story fails to solve a puzzle: Blacks from St. Vincent were reported fighting side-by-side with Caribs against Martiniquian French for control of St. Lucia before the first reported wreck of a slave ship on St. Vincent in 1635. And a 1730 British census reported 6,000 Negroes and 4,000 Caribs on St. Vincent. A population of 6,000 mostly free Africans on an island where limited settlement had begun only eleven years earlier is not easily explained by runaways and shipwreck survivors.

The puzzle would disappear if, as some believe, Africans were in the

Windwards, and elsewhere in the Caribbean and South America, before Columbus arrived. Pre-Columbian figures with African features, as well as pre-Columbian cave writings in a form of Arabic, attest to a pre-slave-trade African presence. Several ancient sources record two large sailing expeditions, one comprising 2,000 vessels, sent out by the Mandingan Emperor Abubakari II between 1307 and 1312 to "discover the limits of the Atlantic." And Las Casas states, in his version of Columbus's third voyage, that Columbus was told by the Portuguese in the Cape Verde Islands that West African traders had stopped there "headed toward the lands of the west with merchandise." Similar reports were provided by Amerindians on Hispaniola, who reported to Columbus that they sometimes traded with black men who came from the southwest, apparently somewhere on the north shore of South America. The "Garifuna" (the common local name for Black Caribs, and itself a word of Mandingan origins) of St. Vincent and the Grenadines may have been the descendants of Carib intermarriage with both African escapees and pre-Columbian African explorers. A tantalizing theory, but the evidence is fragmentary.

That Bequians are seamen is not in doubt. Ships and the sea have defined Bequian life. At 7 square miles, and with only modest rainfall, Bequia was not a hugely successful sugar producer. Segments of the island still carry sugar-estate names—Paget Farm, Friendship, Spring, Belmont, and Hope—but sugar did not displace other crops such as indigo or the more enduring Bequian occupations of shipbuilding, fishing, and interisland trading.

Over the years, Bequia shipwrights built more and larger interisland traders than those produced by the Scots on Carriacou. In *Clean, Sweet Wind*, Douglas Pyle catalogues eighty-three schooners built between 1920 and 1960 in St. Vincent and the Grenadines—most of them in Bequia. The small interisland traders built today come out of Carriacou, but a majority of the graceful schooners seen throughout the lower islands are probably Bequia-built.

"Bequia-built" is now almost synonymous with "whaleboat." William Wallace, Jr., a Bequia-born Scot, introduced Bequia to whaling in 1875. Bequia whaling boats were copied from the small, double-ended harpoon boats carried by the American whaling ships that roamed the globe in the late nineteenth century. Bequians, by contrast, only needed to go a few miles offshore to intercept migrating pods of whales. They modified the American design to create boats that could be launched off a beach, were fast under sail to intercept a passing pod, and rowed well to pull a captured whale home. As a proud Bequian skipper once explained, "She flow off de water, mon, and she jam the sea. She break the toid. She got Bequia backbone and plenty, plenty fast to

Waiting for the Race.

chase the whale." Given the obvious dangers of harpooning and killing these mammoth beasts—however splendid the 25-foot Bequia whaleboats—the Bequian proverb, "Whaling is a set of brave thinking and poor men," seems to capture the combination of need and bravado that makes a whaleboat man.

From 1880 to 1925, Bequia was awash in whales. Whale meat was the mainstay of the Bequian diet, and the sale of whale oil and whale meat was the backbone of the cash economy. By 1887, so many boats were chasing whales that the whalers had to hammer out a detailed ordinance to regulate competition at sea. While numerous articles of the ordinance required cooperation and noninterference, article 1 left intact the natural rewards of skilled boatbuilding and good seamanship:

> If a whale is seen from the shore and the boats of two companies shove off and give chase, the boats which get nearest to the whale have preference.

Virtually the whole island was involved in hunting whales, building boats, working in the shore stations butchering whales, rendering oil from the blubber, and curing whale meat.

Then overfishing by a high-tech Norwegian concern operating out of southern Grenada killed the fishery. Whaling continued, but it never recovered to re-create the days recalled by Eldon Hazell's calypso that begins:

> Blows! Blows! They shout
> When they see the whale spout
> Everybody's eyes fixed on the sea
> With blows, blows in their mouth

The last whaleboat captain in Bequia, Athneal Ollivierre, hung up his harpoon only a couple of years ago. When Nathalie F. R. Ward published her history of the Bequian whale fishery in 1995, taking the title, *Blows, Mon, Blows!* from Hazell's ballad, there were two boats still working under an international quota system that gave Bequia two humpbacks per year. Hazell had something to say about that, too, in a song called "Pen Them Up":

> Why all this fuss that they making,
> When we kill just two whale.
> But listen your radio and,
> > It's people you hear getting killed.
> > (Chorus)
> > And they kill the mink for its fur,
> The rhino for its horn,
> The elephant for its tusk
> Crocodile will soon be gone,
> So tell them big men,
> Two whales is just enough.
> > If them whales is their property
> Well, tell them pen them up.
> Pen them up (we love it boil),
> Pen them up (we love it dove),
> Pen them up (we love the oil),
> Pen them up (with potato).
> If them whale is their property
> Well, tell them pen them up.

> We don't do no mass destruction,
> Only the blood and guts waste,

It's a part of our tradition,
So tell them I say keep their place.
(Chorus)

While Bequia boatbuilders still build and race fishing boats, yachts, and small freighters, whaleboats are produced only as models for sale to visitors. The models are exquisite, perfect in proportion and detail, enameled jewels. Watching the strapping men who carve the models, we see them as emblems of a shrunken present. In our romantic imaginations, these Bequian carvers should be sitting on the beach beside their whaleboats, waiting for the shout of "Blows, mon, blows," not hunched over sticks of wood in the back of a shop—safe, silent, waiting for tourists off the ferry from St. Vincent. Given the outrageous risks of whaling, the carvers probably take a different view.

Anchored in Admiralty Bay waiting for our friends, we are happy and sad, and mildly anxious. Although we have chartered with both couples before, we feel that we will be seeing them anew in a habitat that is now ours, not theirs. Ted and Jan and Bruce and Susan are all accomplished and energetic. We can see them exploding into our little Eden with an eastern, urban bounciness that will overwhelm our serenity—a sort of Pooh-meets-Tigger mismatch.

Our fears are groundless. We marvel at Ted and Jan's immediate adaptation to Caribbean time. Ted is perhaps the highest-energy person I have ever known. Sometimes I feel that I should cling to his ankles to keep him from levitating from sheer, pent-up adrenaline flow. Yet after a day on PALAEMON, he's as laid-back as a boat boy. He sleeps ten hours a night instead of his customary five or six, and he naps at almost any moment that we aren't hustling him off to do something aquatic or gustatory. I find him conked out on deck, in the cockpit, in the main saloon. One night after dinner, he topples over onto the cockpit seat almost in midsentence. We laugh until we are crying; Ted slumbers on.

Jan, who can be serene in the midst of chaos, seems as though she has been on the boat from the beginning. We wake every morning to find Jan painting in the cockpit or on the foredeck, trying to capture the special softness of the early Caribbean light. Her customary gentle smile has become beatific.

When we feel we must indulge in exercise, we take hikes up over the hills, our labors rewarded by views of the sea and nearby islands. On the windward side of Bequia, Hope Bay provides a spectacular empty beach with Malibu-style rollers. We hike over with Ted and Jan so that Ted can reenact body-surfing scenes from his California youth. Our middle-aged bodies pummeled by three or four waves, we decide to sit on the sand and reminisce about our teenage exploits rather than trying to re-create them. I suspect this is what we would have done as teenagers, too, but the image of my intrepid younger self, built up over many years of storytelling, banishes the thought. Whoever first said that we imagine the past and remember the future was truly a wise person.

Bruce and Susan carry more of their environment with them. Their heads seem fuller of things at home, with less room to absorb the wholly other. Yet, within two days, Bruce has moved into his silliness mode, summoning cascades of "Oh, Bruce's" from Susan in response to his horrible jokes and public displays of affection. Our anxiety evaporates like the morning haze. Bruce and Susan declare the Tobago Cays the most beautiful place on earth. We feel bereft as we watch their plane lift off from the little Union airstrip to return them to St. Vincent and then home. We have canceled the sail back to Bequia and the ferry; the wind is howling at 25 to 30 knots out of the northeast.

Although our "charters" were filled with bonhomie, we can't quite shake the feeling that we are changed in some way that distances us slightly from our old friends. They have brought with them a flavor of the lives we left behind. It is a gift that lets us see more clearly how we now respond to different enthusiasms and concerns. We see some clear space separating us from our onetime selves.

Sunset in the cockpit is no longer a spectacle, but a ritual—almost a sacrament. We have become accustomed to allowing our minds to idle; to empty out and take in, in no order that we seek to control; to experience beauty and calm, and anxiety and fatigue, as a part of our daily routine; to expect to share without speaking; to understand without explaining.

Watching our friends in the markets, we discover that we no longer hate shopping because we no longer separate the commercial and the personal. We encounter shopkeepers, market vendors, and boat boys as persons, not as the inhabitants of roles, as clerks or salesmen or owners. We are not embarrassed not to buy, but find it unsatisfying, even rude, not to talk. We have become quasi villagers, alert to the multiple dimensions of casual human contact.

We talk for an hour with a man on Union who is building a fishing skiff in an ancient form, starting with a dugout canoe. We discuss his choice of material, the shaping of ribs and thwarts with only an axe and a machete, the advantages and limits of the hull form. The dugout canoe is, after all, the mother of all boats. And the canoe form reached prodigious size in the West Indies. The Caribs traveled in nothing else and had boats that would carry seventy warriors. Appearing suddenly in their dugouts, they raided and razed European settlements from Grenada to Puerto Rico for more than a hundred years. Early-nineteenth-century visitors to St. Vincent and the Grenadines reported with seeming amazement in their travel journals that they were transported from settlement to settlement and island to island in 30- to 40-foot canoes bearing passengers and cargo, propelled by oars or paddles and steered by a coxswain using a paddle hung on the stern.

Our friends wander off baffled at our intense engagement. We are in a seminar whose very existence is hidden from them. I wonder, not for the first time, about our return. When I go home, my days will be populated with papers and arguments, laws and holdings and analyses, not boats or the brute and beautiful realities of the physical world. Can I summon my old enthusiasm for exploring words, for searching out an author's methodological and normative commitments, for evaluating the soundness of empirical findings? Can I find some way to combine the analytic and the aesthetic, to channel and focus critical capacity while remaining open to mystery? I have always compartmentalized easily between work and leisure, analysis and contemplation, mental and physical activity. My soul now resists these productive habits.

Stranded in Union, waiting for the winds to abate, we spend hours observing and appreciating the skill of the schooner crews who ferry tourists on

"Boat seminar." Union Island dugout canoe.

day trips to the Tobago Cays. They move 50-ton vessels among the reefs with the insouciance of Fred Astaire guiding a partner among the tables to that spot on the dance floor where they will glide free, as if on the wind. The winds still are high, but the schooner captains have bills to pay. If the flights from St. Vincent come in, they will take the tourists to the cays—and bring them back safely.

After three days, we head north again to spend a last few days in Bequia. In our charter and noncharter modes, over the weeks of late February and March, we have repeatedly rounded the protective headlands on the southwest side of Admiralty Bay and beat our way toward the anchorage off Port Elizabeth. Now, as on each occasion, we have a feeling of coming home. Like proud homeowners patrolling their property on returning from vacation, we are eager to see whether anything has changed, whether everything is still as we left it.

We look to see whether FOLKLORIC, a rusting steel cutter, is still in port. FOLKLORIC stays most of the season in Bequia, providing a floating platform for Flora to paint and sell her artwork, and for her husband to work on his sculpture. He doesn't get much of the latter finished because he is constantly welding FOLKLORIC back together. It's a good thing he works in steel rather than wood or clay or marble.

We look for Dennis, our favorite Bequian boat boy, in his gleaming runabout, THE MENACE. Dennis provides us a mooring if we want, and if not, that's OK too. Given the amount of rope he smokes, everything is pretty much OK with Dennis. We could stay high in Bequia just by mooring downwind of the Frangipani Hotel's dinghy dock, the usual gathering place of the boat boys. It's not clear how much of the Rastafarian way of life Dennis subscribes to, but he's got the dreadlocks and ganja part down cold.

Doris is always glad to see us, as she should be, given the amount of food we have been ordering to feed our friends. She probably thinks we are setting up a charter operation in Bequia, and are likely to speed her toward a comfortable early retirement.

The guys who run the vegetable stalls are still fighting among themselves for customers and driving the more timid away. Two steps into the covered market area, we are attacked by six or seven vendors thrusting mangoes, pineapples, christophenes, taro, and plantain into our hands. If we reflexively take one of the proffered goodies, its owner immediately claims ownership over us too and begins to ply us with his other wares. In order to keep these guys at bay until we see whose stuff looks best and decide what we want, we have to keep our hands in our pockets and shout rudely above the aggressive sales pitches that we're not buying anything until we've had a look around. This causes everybody to sulk as though they have just had their proposals of marriage rejected. To salve their hurt feelings, many then ignore us when we are ready to buy, and we practically have to beg them to sell us something.

Lots of Caribbean markets are competitive, but I begin to get the impression that this particular, mostly male coterie is more interested in beating each other at a private game called "Capturing Customers" than in selling fruits and vegetables. My suspicions are reinforced the day the only guy with limes refuses to sell us any—at any price—because we bought our other produce from his competitor at the adjacent stall. We send Jan back later, and she is bullied into unneeded mangoes in order to get at the limes. It's a small price to pay. I really need those limes for my rum and tonic while pursuing the green flash.

Many female vendors have abandoned the mayhem of the central market to set up independent stalls along the main street. Because we can buy from them without engaging in a food fight, it is worth it to pay their slightly higher prices. Others obviously feel differently. The central-market vendors are still in business. Perhaps we just haven't discovered the knack of dealing with them.

As with many aspects of business behavior in the United States, I think the key to understanding the hypercompetitiveness of the Bequia central produce market lies in sociology, not economics. I mean, all those corporations buying other corporations in lines of business that they do not understand and can't manage effectively cannot be about creating "shareholder value." Too many acquisitions turn out to be flops. It's got to be about creating the biggest empire for CEOs who are playing the "my-firm's-bigger-than-your-firm" game. That the game sometimes also makes the shareholders richer is just dumb luck. That's my theory, anyway.

After a bout of vegetable-shopping-as-warfare, we feel the need to make sure that Arthur is still at the Frangipani Bar serving up his soothing rum punches. We take one and sit by the beach to watch the activity in the harbor. As the afternoon wears on, acquaintances from other boats wander by and chat. Sleek Caribbean blackbirds scrabble around the table cadging a handout. They cock their heads and stare at us with unblinking eyes, complaining in their distinctive three-note cry because we are not giving them any French fries.

Bequians say that the blackbird's call is really three words: "Bequia sweet, sweet." And it is.

ANNE'S PASSAGE NOTES: ISLAND MARKETS

I buy as little as I can in conventional stores and spend my shopping time in open-air markets. There the colors, fragrances, bargaining, fragments of song, and hawking calls, the rugged competitiveness among vendors—all carry the richness of life being lived. Our excursions for provisions have taught us the pattern of old-style island communities. Most stand in uneven semicircles, their main streets edging the harbor. The shallows and the beach are home to a hodgepodge of native boats, cruisers' dinghies, and trading vessels. A ferry dock and a handful of other docks service beach bars and restaurants that seek boat and island trade.

Banks, hardware stores, grocery stores, bakeries, liquor shops, and pharmacies line the side streets one or two blocks back from the harbor. A store's name may tell little about its inventory. The "hardware store" may sell beer, canned juices, soda, and secondhand books along with plumbing parts and a few boating supplies. The "pharmacy" may offer baked goods and rum, while batteries, hats, and canned goods adorn the shelves at the "bakery."

On volcanic islands, the roads turn vertical past the first or second block inland. Streets meander up the hillside, following the easiest paths around rocky impediments. Whether shacks or houses, bits of garden show behind or near all but the poorest dwellings. The most prosperous are rich with flowers. A school and a church stake out flatter terrain; off to leeward somewhere, a garbage dump smolders. On the leeward side near the summit, sheltered from the brunt of the trades, a hotel or restaurant clings, looking out at the sunset.

But the open-air market is not up here. It is near the water, its stalls spilling out in every direction, tables awash with fruits, vegetables, and spices. The produce bears little resemblance to that found in a North American supermarket's gleaming, orderly bins. Nothing is polished; nothing is without blemish. This stuff is grown for taste, not show. I am offered dozens of things I have no idea how to cook. But everyone has ample advice. I remember particularly the patient older woman who poked about among her goods till she thought I had all the ingredients I needed to make her particular variation of callaloo soup: a bunch of callaloo (a spinachlike green), onion, chunks of pumpkin, okra, garlic and chilies.

I have bought and cooked one of just about everything—taro, christophene, plantain, strange tubers whose names bounced off my ears. Familiar foods, such as grapefruit, tomatoes, mangoes, seem the best—perhaps because they look so much worse and taste so much better than their namesakes at home. A scruffy, orange-size island grapefruit is not a thing of beauty. But the quality is there, judged by heft, the weight of water and sugar that it bears.

I am a grumpy shopper in towns where cruise-ship hordes have driven the food markets away from the waterfront, to be replaced with uninspired boutiques and jewelry stores—souvenir T-shirts their staple crop. A noisy, confused market down by the water where it ought to be does my heart good. I buy nutmeg, ginger, tomatoes, untried tubers— more than I can possibly use—for the simple joy of being there, a willing captive of the market's colors, sounds, and smells.

26

SKIMMING OVER THE SURFACE

We sail out of Admiralty Bay into a deep emotional low. We have a little less than two weeks before we are scheduled to meet Jay, Lisa, Paige, and Jake in St. Martin. We need to travel nearly 300 miles, and we want to do it in day trips, rather than long passages.

Our choices are to do either a "Cook's tour" of St. Vincent, St. Lucia, Martinique, Guadeloupe, and Antigua—two days here, two days there, moving all the time—or to bypass most of those islands, using them only as anchorages, and spend a week in one place. We decide on a week in Antigua before moving on to St. Martin.

This perfectly sensible plan is somehow burdened with steamer trunks of negative emotional baggage. We want to see the kids and grandkids, but we are grumpy about the arrangements. Because this is the seasickness-prone side of the family, we will meet them at a resort that has an attached marina. They can do the resort thing and we will join them from our perch at the dock, seemingly a perfect compromise.

But we do not like to be in marinas. We like to swing to the wind and feel the motion of the boat. That's not possible in the bay near their resort, which is open to ocean swells and much too rolly for comfort. If we want proximity to the kids, we have to do the marina. And we hate resorts. Resorts feel to us like expensive minimum-security prisons. Resorts seem to be organized to try to keep us within *their* enclosed space, doing *their* activities, while *they* define what it means for *us* to have *fun*.

The prospect of a resort vacation at St. Martin reminds me of the four days we spent with Samantha at Disney World. The Disney folks have got mind control, not just crowd control, down to a truly fine art. They define your wants and needs and then satisfy them at a pace that drives out all independent thought—while simultaneously emptying your bank account. The whole thing is brilliantly orchestrated, and everything, not just the trains, runs on time. The totalitarian environment really got to me. Disney World is what fascism would be like if run by efficient capitalists. It's great if you have a bunch of high-energy kids to keep entertained, but after three or four hours, I wanted to organize a revolt.

This resort thing is just a little black cloud, not the real weather-maker that is unsettling the emotional atmosphere on PALAEMON. Our basic problem is that we are now headed north in earnest. After we leave St. Martin, a month from now, we will have 2,500 miles to cover in about ten weeks. At the outside, we need to be back in the Chesapeake by early June in order to minimize the possibility of playing hurricane tag again. We are heading home. This adventure is going to end.

I have the moderately comforting prospect of slipping back into my old job routines. But, given my growing ambivalence about whether I want to do it, whether I even *can* do it, this security blanket seems rather ragged and thin. I have been months away from the professional pursuits that have structured my whole adult life. I was not afraid when I left that I would miss them. My unease was that I would not—that I could leave it all behind without the slightest pain, with no thought of projects yet undone, masterpieces left unwritten. That has largely been true.

I have somehow never seemed to myself to fully inhabit my own professional life. I have been blessed with a successful career, well beyond my original aspirations. Yet there remains a disjunction between "it" and "me." I notice the gap most acutely when lecturing in an unfamiliar locale. Well-meaning hosts introduce a person I scarcely know, praise a book that I hardly remember. I am embarrassed in conversation with eager minds who want to discuss my ideas, or claim to. I can't bear to tell them that a book or an article completed, published, has little or no further claim on my interests or emotions. I have divorced it, left it behind—I suspect for no good reason. I feel like a guilty parent, asked about a child he no longer really knows.

My students are often a joy, but I have only a tenuous belief that what I try to give them will be useful. My ambition is for them to attain that knife-edged intellectual posture a former colleague once called "exuberant skepticism"—a passion to serve justice without ever being certain what it is. I preach an uncomfortable religion. Most students want a cause. They come into law school mounted on white horses, willing to ride them hard to pursue the right and the good. Some find or maintain their passion. Many leave as cynics, the intellectual refuge of disappointed idealists. I find the passionate dangerous, the cynical useless. I fear that my "exuberant skeptics"—there are some—have gained a faith that may fail to sustain them.

Most of the time, I can't tell whether I am having much effect on the students at all. I am surprised when a student tells me she is really enjoying a class. I wonder why, but I seldom ask. The reason may not be comforting. Manuscripts sometimes arrive from former students with cover letters claiming that I first opened their eyes to this or that problem. Could I look at the draft, give them comments? Some are good, but I often cannot identify what the author thought I had to do with either the subject or his vision of it. Others are unintended parodies of my former, half-forgotten work. Some attack me directly. Here, at least, I can see the influence. I hope that their attacks are the working-out of intellectual commitments, that I am not just a foil for the strategic pursuit of academic ambition. Hiring committees have an unwarranted partiality for young scholars who attack even semicanonical texts.

A year otherwise engaged has always held the danger of shaking me loose. What if I can't reenter that old life with any conviction? What if the exuberance is gone, and only the skepticism remains? Will practicing the rituals of teaching and scholarship bring it back? Or will I be beached on a desolate shore listening to the rustle of the dry grass of intellect, searching for a spring of passion that has dried up while I was away?

Anne has retired; there is no well-rehearsed role for her to resume. She is going to have to figure out what she wants to do with the autonomy that retirement provides. At the moment, she has no clear idea what she is going to do with her talent and energy. She has started painting again. Will that become a passion? Can it be enough? She wants to take her time, to try things on for size, not make any hasty commitments. Given a free hand, one of our friends would have her managing six worthy charities within a week. Her retirement plan is eminently sensible but deeply unsettling. Being reasonable may be the least emotionally satisfying activity available to humans.

Both of us are a little frightened at the prospect of not being within 20 feet of each other most of the time. Before we left, some of our friends and acquaintances speculated that their marriages would never survive a year squeezed into the relatively confined space of a 38-foot sailboat. For us, they had it backward. We can get on each other's nerves, but our complaint has always been too little proximity, not too much. PALAEMON is just right.

These going-home and "dashing-through-paradise" thoughts also cause us to question how well we have come to know the Caribbean, or any of its places and peoples. The answer, we suspect, is that our understanding is as shallow as a Bahamian bank. We have been basking in the sunny side of the Caribbean, hardly penetrating the deep shade that lies just behind the palm trees and sea grape.

St. Vincent skiffs at work.

As we ghost past St. Vincent in the lee of the mountains we talk about Miss Phyllis, our taxi driver and tour guide when we chartered there five or six years ago. Phyllis was doing OK, but she was not sanguine about the prospects for her island. She had watched her daughter emigrate to the United States in the late 1980s, along with almost 10 percent of the total population of St. Vincent. This was not a "bright lights, big city" exodus, but one fueled by pervasive lack of economic opportunity.

The transient population we first encountered in St. Thomas seems to be replicated all up and down the island chain. The only difference is that many "down islanders," like Miss Phyllis's daughter, are now in the Virgins. Even on Carriacou, where the community exerts a particularly strong hold on islanders' loyalties, men must often emigrate to work. Most who are home have had to spend time abroad to get the money for a wooden house, the absolute prerequisite for marriage on Carriacou. In our cruisers' heaven of Bequia, per capita income is less than $3,000 per year. That's nearly 400 percent of the per capita income in Haiti—but still.

The globalization of trade and empire from the time of Columbus's explorations to the French Revolution made the West Indies a commercial and military crossroads. Contemporary globalization may leave them in the economic backwater they have inhabited since the end of the colonial era. Like that local bank we used to have, none of these islands is big enough to make serious economic progress in the twenty-first century. But attempts at

Caribbean economic and political integration have all fizzled. Most of the islands are still trying to solve the problem of nation building. It is virtually impossible to develop state identity and strong national institutions while simultaneously pursuing supranational regional integration. So each micro-state struggles alone against the region's common problems—illiteracy and overpopulation and the loss of its most energetic and entrepreneurial youth to emigration.

They are also competing with each other like crazy for American, European, and Asian tourist cash, building resorts and hotels at rates that the eco-logical infrastructure may not be able to support. Tourism clearly helps bring in hard currency to redress chronic balance-of-payments problems, but less of it stays around than meets the eye. Much of the tourist industry is built on for-eign capital, and the profits are repatriated abroad. Contemporary competi-tion for offshore financial intermediaries is waged almost wholly in a "we-have-the-lowest-taxes" mode that turns a game of "beggar thy neighbor" into "beggar thyself."

This is not the Caribbean experience that most inhabitants want to talk about with strangers. Phyllis and Darius have been special in their willingness to provide a glimpse of their worries, probably not in their perception of what is going on.

So what do we really know about Bequia, or Grenada, or any of the other places that we have come to love? How are they going to recover from Lenny before the next storm tears out roads and flattens roofs? Judging by the progress we saw it will be years before the highways on the west side of Grenada are completely rebuilt. Considering the low-tech construction meth-ods, it seems unlikely that the main street in Hillsborough, Carriacou, will be completed before the next hurricane season starts.

We anchor at St.-Pierre, on the northwestern tip of Martinique. Lenny so dec-imated the town that we can't bear to go ashore. Storm surge wrecked the ferry dock, along with much of the first block of the town. Rebuilding is going on, but the job is massive. And this is a French island, where thousands of French workers and millions of (pre-euro) French francs have been provided to speed restoration efforts.

St.-Pierre is no stranger to natural disaster. It was one of the busiest ports in the Caribbean in the late nineteenth century. Indeed, with a population of 30,000 in 1900, it was a center of fashion and art—known as the "Paris of the Caribbean." In 1902, Mont Pelee erupted, wiping out the entire town and all the ships in the harbor. The sole survivor was the lone inmate of the local jail, a one-room affair with extremely thick walls and virtually no windows. We sit looking at the few posts that remain of what the guidebook describes as "a beautiful new dock for tying your dinghy," and at the boarded-up remains of what had been the St.-Pierre waterfront. We wonder whether the resilience of a population that rebuilt St.-Pierre at the beginning of the twentieth century remains strong enough to do it again, even on a smaller scale, at the beginning of the twenty-first.

Bobbing disconsolately off St.-Pierre, we are also anxious about Judith and Jerome. They came up from Grenada to Bequia to see us off, arriving deeply out of sync with each other. Jerome's head was in boat projects and sailing back south to Trinidad. He seemed unconsciously to be signaling to Judith that HERMAN MELVILLE was his main interest in life, that she was just along for the ride. Judith was elsewhere too, missing New York. She wanted to be at the opera. She was fed up with fighting the seawater that was finding its way into HERMAN MELVILLE from some unknown spot to drip relentlessly on their bunk. They assured us that they would visit us in Connecticut in the summer. As we left Bequia, we had no idea whether they would be coming together or separately.

In short, we are in a funk. We are also becoming fugitives from the law. Having slipped in and out of Marigot Harbor in St. Lucia without paying our respects to customs and immigration, and repeated the same drill in St.-Pierre and Iles des Saintes, we decide to get legal by checking in and out of French territory at Deshaies, on the northwestern tip of Guadeloupe.

Deshaies itself is somewhat down at the heel, but it has its charm. Steep limestone cliffs define a protected harbor. Tropicbirds soar above them in the updrafts. The anchorage is deep, nearly 40 feet, but from the surface I can see the set of the CQR in the ocean floor. In the sensible French fashion, most shops ashore are devoted to the provision of good food and wine. The customs office belies the French reputation for cultivating officious bureaucrats. On the door is a note, "Away today. Be back probably Friday"—tomorrow. Some fellow cruisers in the harbor suggest that we take that "probably" seriously. The sign once said, "Tuesday," then "Wednesday," now "Friday." Several compulsively law-abiding boats have been waiting five days to clear out.

But, we luck out—sort of. Not only does the customs officer return on Friday, he returns by skiff to visit all the foreign-flagged boats in the anchorage. He is complete with a driver and a subordinate. This is a man who has made a happy life in the French bureaucracy. The driver's only function seems to be to run the motor; the subordinate does all of the paperwork. The beautifully uniformed and beribboned customs officer sits serenely in the bow of the skiff, giving orders to the other two. In a moment, he will surely light up a Gauloise—in an ivory cigarette holder.

This procedure is wonderfully colorful and Frenchified (no one speaks any English), but for once, clearing in and clearing out is less formal than we would like. After much arm waving and head shaking, I finally understand that this dapper official only wants his subordinate to write our names and passport numbers, along with PALAEMON's name and documentation number, in a little spiral notebook. That done, he bids us *au revoir,* signals his driver with a dip of his cap, and speeds off to the next foreign vessel. No stamping of passports, no issuance of clearing-in papers, and no issuance of clearing-out papers.

This has been a congenial encounter with officialdom, but how are we going to explain to the customs officials in Antigua that we have spent seven days traveling from Bequia to Antigua without visiting a single island en route? Sailboats are slow, but if we had not been stopping along the way, we could have *floated* from Bequia to Antigua in seven days.

Oh, well, at least we can try to explain in English. Charles de Gaulle is the only Frenchman I ever heard who spoke slowly and ponderously enough for me to understand most of what he was saying. My own conversational capacity in French barely rivals that of a three-year-old native speaker. Parisian policemen—not a group renowned for their English-language skills, or their desire to accommodate Americans—have begged me to switch to my mother tongue. I am ready to go to Antigua, speak English, and engage in some serious attitude adjustment.

27

TRANSITIONS

Clouds pour over the peaks that ring Deshaies as we weigh anchor and depart Guadeloupe. The trades are kicking up and the sea is unsettled, perfectly reflecting our state of mind. We are headed home, but we have not even been able to choose a route. The original plan was to go from St. Martin to Puerto Rico and then spend some time in the Dominican Republic. From there, we would island-hop our way up through the Bahamas to Bimini, and reenter the United States at Fort Lauderdale. There are a lot of things to be said against this plan. Fort Lauderdale to the Chesapeake means motoring up the ICW. We could avoid that by going outside in the Gulf Stream from Fort Lauderdale to North Carolina. But, if we are going to go offshore from Fort Lauderdale to Beaufort, why not stay in the Bahamas all the way north to Freeport and then sail offshore to North Carolina from there? And, if we are getting back into four- and five-day offshore passages, maybe we should just hang around longer in the Caribbean, sail back to Bermuda, and then go direct to Long Island Sound.

We decide to decide in Antigua. By recalling encounters we have been having with new and old cruising buddies, we are somewhat comforted that we are not the Caribbean's most neurotic nauticals.

In Bequia, we caught up again with Jim and Alice on MOONLIGHTING. When we left them—or rather they us—months before in Jost Van Dyke, they were headed to Puerto Rico, and then perhaps straight to Venezuela. Instead, they had come back to the Virgins and worked their way south through the Leewards and Windwards. From Bequia, they were headed to Trinidad, or maybe Venezuela, to wait out the hurricane season.

We saw Howard and Lynda, part of the "Bermuda 87," aboard RESOLUTE in Deshaies. When we last talked with them in the Virgins, they were going to work their way down through the Caribbean and lay over in Venezuela for the hurricane season. Instead, they are now returning north, preparing to leave in early May from Antigua to head for the Azores and then Europe.

The ever-present thought of open-ocean sailing also has me thinking about whether or not PALAEMON is ready. Her standing rigging is old and has not been checked by a pro since we left Connecticut. Since then, it has taken a real pounding. I check the rigging every week, but I don't know whether to be glad that I am finding nothing or suspicious that I am missing something.

The fuel gremlin is back again. My dual-filter system is keeping us from having a cataclysmic loss of power, but something needs to be done to clean out the fuel tank. In addition, the engine is beginning to overheat at lower and lower rpms. The easy answers—clogged intake filters, failed water pump, and the like—have all turned up negative. More serious investigation is in order. We roar into historic English Harbour, Antigua, surfing down rollers from a blustery southeasterly, with projects to do and decisions to be made.

In the eighteenth century, Antigua was Britain's most important Caribbean possession. It did not produce the most sugar or treasure, but English and Falmouth Harbours on Antigua's south shore provided the Royal Navy with immediate access to the trade winds and anchorages adequate to shelter a whole fleet from a hurricane or a hostile naval force. The points defining the entrances to English and Falmouth Harbours are almost close enough to heave a rock across. A few cannon on the heights and these anchorages become virtually impregnable.

Lord Nelson was naval commander here for a time, reportedly succeeding an inept captain who had blinded himself in one eye while chasing a cockroach with a fork. Nelson hated Antigua, its then–governor general, and most of the plantocracy. In his letters he declares, "English Harbour I hate the sight of," and describes it as a "vial [sic] hole." His poor opinion of the place seems to have resulted from dual antagonists—the mosquitoes by which he was "woefully pinched" and the merchants who detested him for enforcing the British Navigation Acts, keeping the port closed to all trade not carried in British ships.

Those who traded with the North American colonies and sympathized with the rebels were the most inflamed by Nelson's taste for strict legality. Governor Shirley had for years winked at scores of American ships trading in St. Kitts, Nevis, and Antigua, using British registration papers issued prior to the Declaration of Independence. Nelson seized rebel ships and cargoes and proved their true colors by the testimony of their crews. An economic elite dependent on the North American trade could hardly be expected to appreciate Nelson's efforts on behalf of the Crown.

Indeed, they sued him in the colonial courts for the value of their seized cargoes. While Nelson ultimately prevailed, the Caribee plaintiffs' influence at the British admiralty so poisoned the minds of the royal command that it took the ever-ambitious Nelson nearly a decade to repair the damage to his reputation. Nelson suffered the added indignity of having to remain aboard his flagship for nearly three months lest he be arrested and jailed by the enraged locals.

The planters had a point. The British West Indies were as dependent on the North American trade as North America was on the West Indies. Perhaps more so. While the American rebels needed the West Indies trade to obtain hard currency—or at least letters of credit with European factors that could be redeemed in manufactured goods—the West Indians were dependent on North America for food. By the end of the trade embargo attending the American Revolution, an estimated 30,000 West Indian slaves had died of starvation, and every Antiguan plantation was in receivership.

The dockyards that serviced the Royal Navy of Nelson's day were deserted long ago, but they have been restored, and Antigua is once again a choice location for the repair and refitting of sailing vessels. Cruising megayachts, like those we snuggled up to off the seawall in St. George's, Bermuda, have replaced the merchantmen and ships of the line of Nelson's day. Many stay afloat economically on crewed charters. We have arrived a week before Antigua Sailing Week and the Classic Yacht Regatta. Beautiful traditional yachts are pouring in from all over the Caribbean; the harbor gleams with varnished wood and polished brass. We are in a great place to get our rigging and engine problems scoped out, if we can get anyone's attention.

The rig is duly inspected, found to have one cracked terminal, and declared unfit to sail outside the harbor. The latter cheerful pronouncement is based largely on the age of the materials, not any identification of specific weaknesses. The rule of thumb among riggers and surveyors in the Caribbean seems to be that wire over seven years old is scrap. Most of our rig is seventeen. We are not thrilled with this report.

We decide to replace everything. It never happens. A number of the parts have to be airfreighted from Fort Lauderdale. After measuring, ordering, and preparing a blizzard of customs forms to avoid paying import duty, we wait with less and less patience for materials that never arrive. They are always slated to be here the next day, or the next, or the next. In the end, we replace the cracked terminal and decide to trust the rig to get us home. It has gotten us here. While the rigging is old, PALAEMON's prior use in New England coastal waters has probably put less strain on it in sixteen years than in one year of Caribbean cruising. So we tell ourselves.

The engine temperature is another matter. We need to get that temperature down to a reasonable range. The local experts do not turn out to be mechanical geniuses. A technician from the best (reputedly) diesel repair shop spends nearly a whole day on PALAEMON. He fixes several things that don't need fixing and creates two new leaks in the freshwater cooling system. I am ready to stuff this guy in the heat exchanger and run the engine temperature up to 195 degrees.

Luckily, we have been befriended by Monty and Betty Nation on TANDEM VINCITUR. Monty is not, as their boat's name might suggest, a retired Latin teacher. He is a retired head maintenance supervisor for a large trucking firm. Before that, he had been a race-car driver. What Monty doesn't know about engines—well.

Monty gives me some useful and unwelcome advice. An overheating engine is almost always the result of poor fluid flow through some part of the cooling system. To find the problem, I should just take apart every piece of the cooling system, one link at a time, and test to see whether I am getting good water flow through that segment. If so, put it back together; if not, fix it. Sounds simple. It's not.

A marine diesel engine has two interconnected coolant systems. It takes in seawater, but it does not run that through the engine, for the good and sufficient reason that salt water inside your engine is a recipe for corrosion. Instead, the raw water from the ocean is used to circulate around a separate and self-contained freshwater system that cools the engine and also heats the hot water in the hot-water heater. The seawater also cools the condenser on PALAEMON's refrigeration unit and discharges into the exhaust line to cool the engine gases and to charge the water-lift muffler that quiets engine noise.

This is a damn complex system with lots of parts. I begin to sense that much of my time in Antigua will be spent crammed into my favorite sail locker communing with the engine's cooling system.

Working in the Caribbean heat in a cramped engine compartment—removing and reconnecting hot, slick hoses, most of which have hardened onto their nipples, while fitting and refitting multiple sizes of sharp hose clamps— is so much fun I can hardly begin to describe it. At the end of the process, my hands and arms look like I have been whipped with barbed wire, and my good humor has gone somewhere south of Antarctica.

Poor Anne. I really lose my cool. I threaten to sell the boat; I compare our trip unfavorably with a year spent in Kosovo during air raids and ethnic cleansing. I curse the designers of the engine, the builders of the engine, everyone who has ever worked on the engine. I ask repeatedly what we're doing on this boat instead of living in our friends' apartment in Florence; I profess my hatred for all things mechanical; I ask why I need a law degree and a Ph.D. in order to be a plumber. The Caribbean has slowed me down and mellowed me out, but I have not had a personality transplant.

Yet the results are not all negative. I have found three problems and fixed them. The engine is again running within its normal temperature range. And I'm sure this has been a character-building experience. But I think my character is about as good as it's going to get. It does lead me to one firm resolution: I will never, ever again grumble about an auto or boat mechanic's service rates. Provided, of course, he fixes something rather than making it worse.

We do our fuel-tank-pump-out number again, this time with jugs bought from a Rasta man. He asks that I return the jugs filled with the contaminated fuel. I am afraid to ask what he is going to do with it.

I do not spend the whole of our time in Antigua banging my head into sharp objects in the engine compartment and cursing the gods who put me there. For one thing, our friends Janet and Paul Herzog on HERZ II are parked just across the way, getting their teak refinished. We have some great times eating and drinking with them, particularly at Catherine's, which serves the best mussels south of Nova Scotia. That's because Catherine flies them in from Nova Scotia and then does those wonderful things to them that only French cooks know how to do. Catherine makes a lot of other great stuff, too, all served up with a Gallic charm that makes you feel like you're eating at a friend's house rather than in her restaurant.

We are also reunited with Mark and Andrea, the crew of BRAVEHEART, the "gold-plater" that was docked next to us in Bermuda. We had last seen them in the Virgins, reluctantly setting out to take their owner to Foxy's for the New Year's Eve party. They are now waiting for him to arrive for Antigua Race Week. As usual, they have BRAVEHEART, looking like she has just rolled out of the building shed for commissioning. She should surely take the "Best Maintained Boat" trophy this year. Last year, she only came in third. I can't imagine what the other boats must have looked like.

So we eat and drink, hang out with friends, wait for parts that never arrive, do some touring, and spend a day at the Saturday market in St. John's. It is almost as good as the Grenada market, but more conventional. The fruits and vegetables, and the local crafts, are fantastic, but nobody seems to be selling only bathtubs or oscillating fans, or hacking up marlin and tuna with a machete.

We also make a firm decision about our itinerary. We buy charts for the

Puerto Rico, Dominican Republic, Bahamas route. When we leave St. Martin, we will now know where we are going. From prior experience, we are pretty sure that these plans, too, will change, but having a plan makes us feel better. The funk has lifted.

On Sunday night, April 9, we do the barbecue at Shirley Heights. This raucous weekly party combines yachties, locals, and hotel tourists for togetherness of the most crowded kind. When the band volume reaches the heat and light zone, we flee with Monty and Betty to listen to a sedate Oscar Peterson CD on TANDEM VINCITUR's stereo and talk about Antigua.

Anne and I find the island a bit sad. Although plantation agriculture got started rather late here, it took over the island with a vengeance. The forests were decimated and have never recovered. The land looks hard and inhospitable, the soil like it would bend a hoe point. Antiguan plantation life reputedly was as gruesome and culturally barren as in any island of the West Indies. Most owners were absentees. Their island agents or "attorneys" responded to the owners' incessant demands for profits, and their own desire to line their pockets, by brutalizing the slaves. The easiest way to skim funds while maintaining returns was to hold down costs. The largest controllable cost was food, housing, and medical care for the slaves. That grim logic, combined with the agents' taste for rum and gluttony, is said to have defined the "culture" of the Antiguan plantation.

There were exceptions, of course, but Antigua has the distinction of fomenting the first (1736) plan for a general slave rebellion in the West Indies. Given the slaves' numerical superiority, it seems odd that slave rebellions were not more frequent, and more successful. Until you look at the size and topography of most of the sugar islands. The land is all coast, the interior too small to hide a guerrilla band for long. A successful revolutionary force would have to take the whole island at once, not pick off a plantation here, then disappear into the interior, reappear somewhere else, harass, fade away—the perennially successful strategy of those who are strong numerically but weak in ordnance. Shovels and sticks beat rifles and cannon only in wars of attrition, lightning raids and retreats, not pitched battles for strategic terrain.

The St. John's revolt was the most successful ever staged on a small island in the Caribbean. The larger islands—Jamaica, Haiti, Puerto Rico—offered a more promising environment. From the earliest days of Spanish settlement, escaped slaves joined with indigenous peoples and faded into the hills. "Maroons," they were called. The people of the secret places, the refuge of slaves in flight, the dragons lurking at the edge of the planters' known world. The mythology of maroonage—the daring raids, independence, self-ownership—fueled the slave imagination. But in the small islands of the Lesser Antilles, the reality was that revolt meant failure, torture, and death.

In Antigua, the masters' obsessive fear of another conspiracy, and slave recollections of the ghastly torture and punishment of the 1736 conspirators, seem to have been the twin engines of master/slave relations thereafter. Captain Thomas Southey, who in 1827 published the encyclopedic and tedious, three-volume *Chronological History of the West Indies*—it is literally organized by year—wrote privately to a friend: "Taking it all in all, it is perhaps as disgraceful a portion of history as the whole course of time can afford; for I know not that there is anything generous, anything ennobling, anything honorable or consolatory to human nature to relieve it ." I know it is unfair and inaccurate, but somehow the very terrain of Antigua calls up Southey's words for me.

Post-emancipation Antigua was not much better. To read the oral history in *To Shoot Hard Labor: The Life and Times of Samuel Smith, an Antiguan Workingman, 1877–1982*, is to imagine America's Jim Crow South as a walk in the park for black Americans. For many years after Antigua's emancipation, land was unavailable to blacks, who were thus effectively tied to the plantations where they had been slaves. Samuel Smith was born forty-three years after "freedom" came to Antigua, yet he could say, "To be driven off the estate was the worst that could happen to you. People would suffer almost anything else—be whipped, be locked up in the estate cellar for a time." Sixty years after emancipation, the daily wage for an agricultural worker in Antigua was less than the daily cost to keep a slave on the plantation in 1834. Frankly, things don't look a lot better to us now. I am more ready to leave Antigua than I was to come.

Monday we scrub the growth off JEREMY's bottom and play on the beach. Tuesday we ready PALAEMON for sea. St. Martin is 120 miles over the horizon. We will sail overnight Wednesday to get in on Thursday morning. David Jones is predicting winds building to 35 knots by Thursday afternoon and blowing at that strength for the foreseeable future. We are not scheduled to meet our kids and grandkids until Saturday, but we had better get in early if we don't want another bashing. The wind and sea are already building as we fly out of English Harbour and romp up the west coast of Antigua. Anne turns green. We feel like sailors again.

28

MARIGOT TO SAN JUAN

PALAEMON beats into the anchorage at Marigot, St. Martin, as the rising sun bathes the town in soft amber light. David Jones was spot-on about the wind. It is still rising, and we are delighted to be in Marigot's snug anchorage. I'm not clear where all this wind is coming from. Maybe it's the "moon wind" that a boat boy in Bequia warned us about while trying to convince us to take one of his moorings. If things really get crazy, we are only a mile from the entrance to the "lagoon" at St. Martin, a major hurricane hole. True, 160 boats sank there during Lenny, but Lenny was a freak hurricane. It sat for thirty-six hours almost on top of St. Martin with winds up to 120 mph. April is not hurricane season.

By the time we get things cleared away and JEREMY BENTHAM launched, it is nearly noon. One of the three perfect times to drop into a French town. The other two are breakfast and dinner. After a cursory look for the customs officer (gone to lunch), we follow our noses to La Parisienne. La Parisienne is a bakery, café, and take-out restaurant where, were it not for all the other good restaurants in Marigot, we might eat every meal. After an overnight passage, we are always ravenous. I want one of everything. Only the absolute certainty that I will make myself dreadfully sick prevents me from placing a blanket order.

If our spirits were in the depths in Deshaies, they soar in St. Martin. As I sit at a table on the sidewalk, trying not to stuff whole croissants into my mouth, the stupidity of going to Antigua to speak English, rather than hanging out somewhere like Martinique to eat French, descends like a thunderclap. We vow to make up for our error. By the time we stumble out of La Parisienne toward the customs office, we are beaming, a *bonjour* on our lips for anyone who makes eye contact. We are not just looking forward to seeing the kids, we are looking forward to seeing what the resort is like. Perhaps we should rent a room for ourselves and be coddled for a week? Being in a place where people are serious (but not precious) about food, where one great meal is almost certain to be followed by another, induces euphoria. We are high on roasted eggplant.

Our delight, it seems to me, is traceable directly to the French government's spotty history when doing foreign land deals. Trading Canada to the

British for Guadeloupe has got to be the worst fleecing since Manhattan was acquired from its Native American inhabitants for a few chests of trinkets. Following Voltaire, the prescient French dismissed Canada as "a few acres of snow." Getting the British to take it for Guadeloupe in 1763 made the French foreign minister a national hero. And, while $18 million was a lot of dough in the early nineteenth century, Thomas Jefferson's bargain with the French for their Louisiana Territory, a hunk of real estate that doubled the size of the United States, does not suggest a French Ministry of Foreign Affairs operating on all cylinders. Then, after practically giving away most of the good stuff in the eighteenth and nineteenth centuries, the French squandered billions of francs and thousands of French lives in the twentieth while trying to hold onto indefensible territories in Indochina and North Africa.

Unlike the British, who ruthlessly cut their losses in the Caribbean by granting or forcing independence on their Caribbean colonies, the French shot themselves in the pocketbook again by treating their islands as *départements*—entitled to all the perquisites and benefits of any portion of the metropole. Because no one can remember when one of these islands last operated in the black, this commitment has meant an annual infusion of billions of francs (and now euros) into Guadeloupe, Martinique, and St. Martin. We have no idea what combination of noblesse oblige and winter vacations for French government officials maintains this profligate policy. But we silently thank the French government, almost hourly, for the privilege of experiencing French culture and cuisine on a French Caribbean island.

These historical ruminations are simultaneously churlish and overly generous. Many eighteenth-century historians treat the British as the dupes—or, more realistically, the captives—of the West Indian sugar lobby in the Canada-for-Guadeloupe deal. Guadeloupe had sugar; Canada was commercially useful largely for beaver pelts. Beaver is nice, but no one in eighteenth-century England was likely to substitute "rich as a Canadian" for the common simile "rich as a West Indian." Some in the British government, William Pitt among them, saw Guadeloupe's value, but they were hemmed in by the "West Indian sugar interest." This was more than a lobby; absentee planters had bought dozens of seats in Parliament. They wanted no part of a British Guadeloupe that could trade legally with the North American colonies and break the economic power of the Caribbee sugar planters on Barbados, Antigua, Nevis, and St. Kitts. Their monopoly on the British and North American home markets was so effective at elevating consumer prices that it was causing near-riots.

Some even argue that Britain in effect traded away the American colonies at the same time. Leaving a French presence in Canada might well have cooled France's ardor for supporting the American Revolution. Revolution has a way of spreading. And having limited its North American colonies' trade with the sugar islands in the 1763 treaty, the British government gave the West Indian sugar lobby even greater protection at the expense of the North American colonies by passing the revolution-inspiring Sugar Act of 1764. Absent these provocations, the American rebellion might possibly have been averted. The price to the British of protecting the Caribbee planters from the competition of the French sugar islands may have been the loss of all of North America south of the Canadian border.

The French case is not so straightforward either. France's *départementalisation* of its former colonies may be fiscally generous, but it's politically retrograde. The submersion of the French West Indies colonies in the general politics of the metropole tends to protect the economic interests of the *békés,* the numerically minuscule but economically dominant white French Creoles. This elite would be at grave political risk in an independent, black-dominated nation on Guadeloupe or Martinique, or perhaps both islands combined into a single political entity.

Whatever the corrupt historical interests or motives that have kept St. Martin French, we can do little but accept history's gifts and make the best of them. The marina is excellent, and only 100 yards from the kids' villa. We renew the varnish on PALAEMON in the mornings and play in the pools and the sea with Paige and Jake in the afternoons. Happily, Jay and Lisa get resort fever about as quickly as we do, so we make numerous trips into Marigot to wander through the markets and the shops and, of course, to eat.

There is an inner harbor on the lagoon in Marigot, a small three-sided affair ringed by restaurants whose tables run out onto the docks. They are all good, actually terrific, but our favorite is Tropicana. Its proprietor, Gilles Artu, is the St. Martin equivalent of Catherine in Antigua. He seems to like nothing better than guiding us through the menu, suggesting ever so tactfully what he has that is really special. Moreover, our host takes *chacun à son goût* very seriously. He is as determined to satisfy children's finicky palates as those of the most discriminating adults. When Gilles kneels beside Paige and Jake to assure them that there is plenty more butter and tomato sauce for their pasta—and, with a wink, that they are really going to like the dessert cart—they, and we, are charmed out of our sandals. After three meals at Tropicana, we are begging him to move it to Connecticut, or at least open a branch.

While Paige and Jake seldom sail with us because of "the funny green color" it turns their dad, they love to sleep aboard PALAEMON. They like the cozy confines of the cabin and are endlessly fascinated by all the nautical gear. So we have the grandkids for several evenings, while Mommy and Daddy get a chance to pay some attention to each other. For a stay in a minimum-security facility, the marina/resort compromise turns out quite well.

Perhaps St. Martin is just an island that inspires successful accommodation. I think of it as French, but, of course, nearly half is Dutch St. Maarten. This formal compromise of competing national interests by simple geographic division has worked on no other island in the West Indies. The French and English divided St. Kitts for a time, and France and Spain divided Hispaniola before Haiti and then the Dominican Republic became independent nations. But St. Kitts became British after years of friction and fighting, and the French/Spanish–Haiti/Dominican Republic division of Hispaniola has never been free of border squabbles and outright armed attack. The peaceable division of St. Martin/St. Maarten has persisted since 1648.

The secret to this success may be, first, that both sides got what they wanted—the Dutch got the salt pans and the best-protected harbor for trade, the French got most of the arable land. Second, no one else thought the island worth fighting for, save the Spanish. Spain had no interest in settlement, but only wanted to keep the Dutch away from the salt as part of an attempt to drive Dutch shipping out of the Caribbean. Once Spain gave up the impossible task of keeping the Caribbean a *mare clausum* ("closed sea"), both Dutch and French interests moved into St. Martin and decided to split the territory rather than fight about it.

The contemporary *mare liberum* ("freedom of the seas") principle of international law owes a significant historical debt to Holland's demand for access to Caribbean salt. The great seventeenth-century Dutch legal philosopher Hugo Grotius developed and justified *mare liberum* in the political context of his country's insistence that its ships be free from interference on the open seas. Our sugar canister contains the stored-up horrors of chattel slavery; the salt shaker represents one of the most important legal underpinnings of global commerce.

According to one account, the division of St. Martin/St. Maarten was accomplished by sending two walking parties—one French, one Dutch—in opposite directions from the same spot on the island's west coast. They were to walk the perimeter of the island. When they met on the east side, they drove a stake into the beach. A line from that spot to the hiker's point of origin became the international boundary. To be sure, the French violated this amicable state of affairs once, annexing the Dutch side while the Dutch were preoccupied with fighting the British. But they gave it back.

Today the border is completely open—unless you want to cross it by telephone. Although we walk or drive from the French to the Dutch side without so much as nodding our heads at an official, a telephone call is an international incident. Calls from the French side are routed through metropolitan France, and perhaps the Netherlands as well, before a phone can ring in Dutch St. Maarten, six blocks away. Because most of the boatyards, riggers, and boat supplies are on the Dutch side, we try perhaps thirty calls from the French to the Dutch side. We never get through. Not once. Globalized information transfer still has a few kinks to be straightened out.

We pick our way through the narrow channel out of Port Lonvilliers Marina a few hours ahead of the kids' departure from the resort. Our vision is blurry as we clear the breakwater while the little ones wave good-bye over and over again from the beach. But we feel a need to get moving. True, the family we just left behind on the beach will be our next firm appointment. Until they show up at our house in Connecticut in mid-July, we have no obligation to be anywhere at any particular time. Rogan and Elizabeth, our house sitters, will be leaving sometime in late June. We want to be home by July 1. Twenty-five hundred miles in ten weeks surely sounds doable. But we can't quite forget that Branford to Jost Van Dyke took fourteen weeks. After a stop in Marigot for final provisioning and clearing out, we are headed offshore again, past the Virgins to Puerto Rico.

Twenty-four hours later, our larder brimming with French breads, cheeses, and pâtés, we point PALAEMON's bow west-northwest. The wind is still up, but we are headed downwind and the seas are only 4 to 6 feet. Eight months ago, on Long Island Sound, a forecast of 4-to-6-foot seas in 20 to 25 knots of wind would have kept us in port. Tonight these conditions seem fine, even good. We fall so easily into our offshore watch routines that a trip of 200 miles seems to require less thought and planning than we used to put into a 50-mile cruise from Branford to Block Island.

St. Martin to Puerto Rico is a voyage through the heart of the freighter and cruise-liner zone. Shipping traffic is constant in the Anegada Passage between St. Martin and the Virgin Islands, around the Virgins themselves, and in and out of Puerto Rico. We often track four or five vessels at a time, several of them cruise ships bristling with thousands of lights, their combined wattage completely obscuring the red and green running lights from which we should be able to gauge the vessel's direction. But a cruise ship is not going to slip up on us. I can hardly believe it when the radar, set at a range of 12 miles, fails to pick up one of these floating playgrounds that is already so bright that it destroys my night vision. The loom of cruise ships that are well over the horizon gives the illusion of multiple moonrises, or of densely populated islands that somehow failed to make it onto the charts.

Thirty-six hours after clearing Marigot, we are docked temporarily at Puerto del Rey Marina and have taken a cab to clear customs at Fajardo. I am startled by the customs officer's "Welcome home." We buy a customs certificate that allows us to leave and reenter American waters for a year by just dialing an 800 number. Who says government cannot be efficient?

By midafternoon, we are anchored for the night behind Los Palominos, a beach- and palm-fringed cluster of small islands off Puerto Rico's east coast. The only traffic is the hotel launch, which ferries guests over from the mainland for an afternoon of sun and snorkeling. By 7 P.M., the last launch has run, the islands are quiet. Only PALAEMON and three other cruising boats tug at their anchor chains.

We struggle out of the V-berth, groggy from twelve hours of sleep, and sail Puerto Rico's northern coast to San Juan Harbor. Although we have often flown through San Juan's airport, we have never stopped to see anything beyond its confines. The only minor exception is the marina at Puerto del Rey, where, with Ted and Jan, we once launched a week's charter of the "Spanish Virgins"—the islands of Culebra, Culebrita, and Vieques, which lie between Puerto Rico and the USVI.

As the folks at Puerto del Rey warned us, the harbor at Old San Juan is not a cruiser's dream. San Juan is a major commercial harbor whose principal clients are freighters and cruise ships like the ones we have been dodging all the way from St. Martin. There are two small boat marinas, one filled to the gills with 60-foot deep-sea sportfishing boats, and an anchorage whose bottom is strewn with centuries of nautical debris. We anchor and bargain with one of the marinas for a place to tie JEREMY in order to get ashore—there is no dinghy dock at either marina. We rent part of a slip for $5 a day. I wonder who else would pay to use it. The low-tide water depth is about 6 inches.

But Old San Juan is worth seeing. El Morro, the fort that guards the entrance to San Juan Harbor, has been there since the 1500s, making the narrow, deepwater channel virtually impregnable. Here, and in Havana, the great Spanish armadas of the sixteenth and seventeenth centuries gathered to ferry the gold and silver from their mines in Mexico and Peru back to Spain. Once beyond the range of El Morro's cannon, the British, French, and Dutch navies, privateers, and plain old pirate ships lay in wait, hoping to pick off a ship or two as the fleet made its way up the Florida Straits, or along the windward route past the southern Bahamas. Even under the protection of the Spanish navy, much of Spain's New World treasure was captured. Enough Spanish ships were lost to keep treasure hunters at work into the twenty-first century. The harbor and town that gave shelter to these rich fleets was aptly called "Puerto Rico." It only later became "San Juan," transferring its original name to the whole of the island.

The Amadeus Café.

Much of Old San Juan still has the feel of a European city, a place where buildings have grown upon the foundations of their ancestors for hundreds of years. We wander the cobbled, narrow streets and lunch elegantly at the Amadeus Café, where the walls are hung with stunning paintings by Enrique Mora and his father. We compliment the art and learn from our waitress that the Galeria Mora is just around the corner. After lunch, we make our way there.

Closed.

I bang on the door anyway, and Enrique shouts from an upstairs balcony that he will be right down. He is just back from Cape Cod, his studio littered with boxes of canvases he has been working on there. We talk as he unpacks, about his work and about fishing off the cape and in Puerto Rico. He is experimenting with some new pigments that do strange things as they dry, creating variegated textures that are never quite the same. Enrique is still struggling to get them under control, but he is fascinated by the possibilities of his new "surprise art." He says the pictures literally change before his eyes—an exercise in "watching paint dry" that is the opposite of boredom.

I can see that Anne could talk technique with Enrique all afternoon. But he has a date with a tuna captain, and we need to pick up food and beer and head back to PALAEMON. We will leave tomorrow for the Bahamas, a four-day, 600-mile jaunt. We have decided to skip the Dominican Republic. Consultations with Monty and Betty, among others who have spent time there, convinced us that we would want to stay ten days to two weeks at a minimum. If we want a leisurely trip up through the Bahamas, we just don't have that sort of time. Rather than have an abortive encounter with the Dominican Republic, we add it to the lengthening list of "must-do" places and sights for our next sojourn in the Caribbean.

We are beginning to empathize with the cruisers we have met who have been sailing the Bahamas and the Caribbean full time for a decade and have never gotten south of the Virgins. But we are not entirely sympathetic. Not pressing on to San Martin to eat French food is clearly a mistake. Never getting south of Tropicana and La Parisienne is more understandable.

ANNE'S PASSAGE NOTES: HARBORS AND HISTORY

As we have made our way north, Jerry has become more and more deeply involved in the troubled history of these islands. His enthusiasm is infectious, and I am observing now with different eyes. Take harbors, for example. In an age before flight, before engine-powered vessels, sail-friendly harbors were of major strategic importance as instruments of both commercial viability and military control. Their placement and characteristics were vital. This is hardly the sort of stuff that I used to spend my time pondering. Now I find myself intrigued as we enter each new harbor, trying to imagine the attributes that might have contributed to its success or failure.

For both business and military success, a good harbor must have ample size and depth; provide all-round protection from wind and seas; encompass an easily accessible shoreline for careening vessels for repair and for loading and unloading goods; and, perhaps most critically for military purposes, offer a narrow entrance with relatively high and wide promontories on either side for placement of cannon and fortifications. Such a harbor, once well garrisoned, could be virtually unassailable. Finally, it must lie athwart the trade winds, on a route that is readily accessible from deepwater channels.

This is a long list. Not surprisingly, there are few such harbors in the Caribbean. Throughout the Windwards, Leewards, and Virgins, we find anchorages that provide wonderful protection in the prevailing easterlies but are quite open to westerly seas. The trades may be constant in their easterly direction, but hurricanes, as Lenny has so clearly shown us, are utterly capricious. Wrong-way Lenny brought pounding, ferocious seas from the west, devastating harbors that are excellent in prevailing conditions.

Most of the anchorages we have used have wide, low entrances, providing scant opportunity for fortification. Marigot, St. Lucia, was an exception, with an entrance so narrow it is difficult to find. Lord Nelson once hid a small fleet of warships in Marigot. He lashed palm fronds to the mastheads, and his fleet escaped the notice of a passing French armada. Other snug hiding places exist, but, like Marigot, are too small to be major harbors. And, almost by definition, a good hiding place will be off the most traveled routes.

Both Falmouth and English Harbours fulfill almost all the criteria, and for that reason Antigua was of critical importance to Great Britain as a military base. Nothing else in the British Caribbean compares with their advantages. Islands such as St. Kitts and Nevis offer little more than open roadsteads. How the British managed to operate big plantations there for as long as they did is a mystery to me. The harbors are not even protected roadsteads: They roll unmercifully when the winter trades are up. As we search out small sheltered anchorages for PALAEMON, and occasionally endure an open roadstead, I think more and more about a good harbor's strategic value.

But it is not until we climb the ramparts of old El Morro at San Juan, and look out to sea, that I feel the sweeping impact of what a truly

El Morro.

spectacular harbor meant in the days of European competition for West Indies treasure. From the high promontories that guard the narrow deepwater entrance, we can see for miles. From here, cannon could demolish any approaching ship well before it could lift its fire to the heights of the fort's guns. Behind us, the harbor is huge, deep, and perfectly protected. Before us lies the Atlantic, with the trades sweeping by toward the Bahama Channel, passing Hispaniola, Cuba, the southern Bahamas, and on to Florida, or into the Gulf Stream and up the U.S. east coast. A breathtaking spectacle.

Behind and below us, cosmopolitan and tradition-filled Old San Juan shines, sunlight bouncing off its brightly painted houses and rain-fresh cobbled streets. It is here, at El Morro, that the action took place. These broad promontories and cannonries made possible the lovely old buildings lying behind, and the rich civilization that inhabited them. The social value of simple blunt instruments of war.

We watch the vast Atlantic rollers crash into the shore 200 feet below. A small vessel motors out the channel, raises sail, and turns downwind, riding the bounteous trades. A tanker lumbers out under power, attended by a harbor tug, and takes a more northerly direction. To the east, a two-masted vessel adjusts sails, turning its bow from west to south-southwest to make the harbor mouth below us. Behind us, unseen from the ramparts, PALAEMON lies at anchor, fully protected, the ancient harbor continuing its centuries-old function as departure point and refuge for seagoing vessels of every size and type.

29

BAHAMAS BOUND

Four days northwest of San Juan, the Turks and Caicos define the southeastern end of the Bahama Banks. These are the "out islands," south of the Tropic of Cancer—widely scattered, sparsely settled cays with few visitors, only a few depots for water and fuel. This is not prime territory for cruisers whose principal experience is sailing or motoring the protected Bahamian banks. As one Bahamas cruising guide puts it:

> What it boils down to is this. This area lies across a direct path to and from the Caribbean. If you're going that way (or returning), then fine. Choose the best route suited to you, and do it. If you have no purpose other than poking around to see what it is like down there, maybe you should think twice about it.

Well, we are returning from the Caribbean, and the course through the Turks and Caicos is perfect for us. We have now done several thousand miles of open ocean passages. PALAEMON packs sufficient water and fuel to make the 1,000 or so miles to George-Town, in the Exumas, where supplies are available. Anchored in San Juan, we have been monitoring the weather, listening to Herb, and checking in with David Jones. The winds and seas for the next week seem remarkably benign. Could it be that we are in for some gentle offshore passagemaking?

We weigh anchor at midmorning. Our heading is west and north from San Juan, across the Mona Passage, past the Dominican Republic and Haiti, up to our landfall on the Caicos Bank. If our timing is right, we will arrive at midday, four days hence. We want maximum visibility when we first encounter the "thin-water" sailing that characterizes the Bahama banks. Winds are 12 to 18 knots off the stern quarter; the sun shines; the waves are moderate; everything on board is working and the shipping is light. This is so easy and comfortable we get bored. One of human nature's many perversities lies in the fineness of the border between bliss and boredom. Although San Juan to the Caicos Banks is geographically a straight shot, we tack back and forth across that psychological boundary many times.

Keeping a lookout for the freighters coming up through the Mona and Windward Passages adds a little edge to our watch routines, but not much. So instead I try to imagine keeping watch for the red sails of the buccaneers who patrolled these waters in the mid-seventeenth century. We are now in the playground of the pirates of West Indies legend, historical fiction, and Hollywood film extravaganza: men who got their start haunting the shores of unclaimed or sparsely settled islands, some stateless escapees from plantation indentures, some navy deserters, some refugees from lost ships. They survived by hunting feral pigs and wild cattle, and selling the smoked meat *(boucan)* and hides to passing merchantmen. Hence *boucanier*, and the English "buccaneer." As their bands grew, they diversified their enterprises, salvaging wrecks, then seizing ships. The pirates of story, song, and film had been born. Democrats in the midst of autocracy, they elected their leaders and shared equally the spoils of adventure. The captains and quartermasters received extra shares only if voted by the crews.

The buccaneers were not just democrats, they were social democrats, with a well-developed workers' compensation system. Père Labat, the radical French Dominican priest who served in the West Indies from 1694 to 1705, and whose memoirs are a source of much of the contemporary understanding of that period, recounts some of the details of the buccaneers' standard agreement:

> That if a man be wounded he has to receive one *écu* a day as long as he remains in the surgeon's hands up to sixty days, and this has to be paid or allowed for before any man receives his share. A man receives 600 *écus* for the loss of each limb, 300 *écus* for the loss of a thumb or the first finger of the right hand, or an eye, and 100 *écus* for each of the other fingers. If a man has a wooden leg or a hook for his arm and these happen to be destroyed, he receives the same amount as if they were his original limbs.

Buccaneering was often lawful piracy—that is, privateering—under letters of marque issued by British, French, and Dutch colonial governors. All were eager to harass the Spanish, and hopeful that a privateer carrying a particular colony's letter would view that territory as a haven rather than as a candidate for plunder. Providing safe harbor for buccaneers was profitable even without a prize court. Sea rovers, as the Dutch called them, had a reputation for rapidly spreading their wealth ashore. Before the settlement literally fell into the sea (in an earthquake widely interpreted as having biblical overtones), Port Royal, Jamaica, became immensely prosperous by providing easy access to any vice that a well-heeled buccaneer might fancy.

But buccaneers included true pirates as well—some by choice, others by necessity when peace broke out, eliminating lawful prizes. Many, perhaps most, moved back and forth across the legal line. When war returned and privateers were needed, colonial governors dispensed pardons as freely as privateering commissions.

For some, the plundering was spectacular. Captain Henry Morgan began life in the West Indies as an indentured servant in Barbados. He buccaneered himself into the plantocracy and the lieutenant governorship of Jamaica. Morgan became so jealous of his status as a gentleman that he sued the publishers of the English translation of Alexander Exquemelin's 1674 best-seller, *De Americaensche Zeerovers (The Buccaneers of America),* claiming reputational damage from Exquemelin's implication that Morgan had sometimes sailed without a commission. Morgan sought suppression of the book and personal damages of 10,000 pounds. He settled for an award of 200 pounds.

The only excitement that I can generate in this millennial year comes from putting over a fishing line. The Bahamian fish stories are true. I trolled for hours in the Windwards and Leewards without a strike. Here, an hour's trolling seems almost to guarantee a hook-up. But a hook-up is not the same thing as a fish in the boat. I keep hooking into things that are *big*— big enough to break lures and leaders, if not my 60-pound-test line. Sometimes I never see the fish at all. It takes out line until I have to crank down on the drag and the tackle fails. Others come to the surface, usually large dolphin, flashing brown and gold in the bright sunlight. Sometimes the fight goes on for twenty minutes or more before a hook, a swivel, a leader, or the line gives way.

I finally get one 15-to-20-pound bonito close to the boat, about 100 feet away, before losing him to the competition. A shark, perhaps 150 pounds, surges up from below. Attacker and prey rocket 10 feet into the air, crash back into the water, and are gone. The line parts so quickly I don't even feel the shark's attack. My rod, tense with life only a second ago, is an inert stick trailing a limp bit of line.

Actually, I am not too unhappy about losing all of these fish. Wrestling a dolphin or tuna into PALAEMON's cockpit, amid the stays, stanchions, and lifelines that ring the deck, would be a real struggle. And once you get one of these guys in the cockpit, he thrashes about, throwing blood everywhere and threatening to cut you off at the ankles. Butchering fish in the cockpit while underway is a major mess.

At home, we have devised a system for fastidious fishing. On Long Island Sound, we are usually trailing the dinghy and catching 2- to 10-pound blue-fish. So we simply flip the fish into the dinghy and deal with cleaning and fil-leting after we are at anchor. But JEREMY is now stowed on deck. Anyway, I am not sure I want to risk his inflation tubes by making him a storage bin for a thrashing tuna or dolphin.

Like everything else on this passage, our timing works out perfectly. We approach the Caicos Bank with the sun directly overhead. As we reach the bank, we will come rapidly out of an ocean trough nearly 1,000 feet deep, onto an underwater plateau with water depths that range from 25 feet to nothing. The "nothing" is sometimes a coral head that could punch a hole in PALAE-MON's hull.

As the depthsounder readings drop from 400 feet to 25 to 10 in the space of 500 yards, I feel more than a little queasy. I *think* I can read the water well enough to keep us out of anything shallower than 6 or 7 feet. And I *think* I can tell the difference between a coral head and a patch of turtle grass on the bottom. But I haven't had any practice at this in a while. A mistake would not be welcome. Reading the water is an art, and, as in painting, color is the key. The depths shift from the deep blue of the open ocean through turquoise, bot-tle green, then sandy green on the banks. Really sandy is not good. Nor is the dark brown or black of a coral head. On these crystalline banks, turtle grass on the bottom begins to look like coral near the top. Even the depths can be de-ceiving, the bottom so clearly visible at 30 feet that I begin to doubt the depth-sounder.

I take a vantage point up forward, standing on JEREMY's overturned hull. Anne is at the wheel. I can feel her eyes riveted on me, waiting for any signal to shift course. But we continue to keep water under the keel. As confidence grows and queasiness recedes, we begin to absorb the extraordinary beauty of the Caicos Bank. The gulls that circle PALAEMON have turquoise bellies, throats, and underwings. The white sand beneath the water seems to be radi-ating light rather than reflecting it. The undersides of the puffy fair-weather clouds are turquoise as well. In a remarkable trick of refraction, the midday sun penetrates the water vapor in the clouds, splitting the light spectrum. We are sailing under cotton-candy clouds with turquoise bottoms and pink tops.

Unlike the soaring peaks and mist-covered rain forests of the volcanic islands stretching from Trinidad to Puerto Rico, the Turks and Caicos are barren pancakes. From here up through the 700 islands of the Bahamas, the highest point of land is only about 200 feet. This is an arid archipelago, with little of the lush vegetation or the riot of tropical flowers that has enchanted us from Bermuda to Grenada.

On Caicos, the vegetation generally runs to scrub, creeping vines, and cactus. The most striking topographic feature may be the enormous salt flats that produce the contents of that Morton box in our cupboard. The Turks and Caicos are ideal salt repositories. Vast flats are inundated at high water and then easily blocked off to keep out the next modest flood tide. The sun evaporates the water, and the residue of salt is simply bulldozed into piles and scooped onto shallow-draft freighters by the buckets of mobile cranes. The flats are then flooded again, a cycle that has persisted for centuries. In the 1700s, slaves would have done the work that machines do today, at roughly the same cost in slave mortality as fieldwork on sugar plantations. Some old techniques have not changed. The flats on Salt Cay in the Turks are still flooded and dried using windmills for power.

Notwithstanding the Bahamas' historical cachet as the first land Columbus ran into on his first voyage of discovery, they were considered relatively worthless during the heyday of European competition for Caribbean possessions. Except for the salt. France and Britain nearly went to war over Turks Island salt in the 1760s, and the Bermudian economy was for years based on raking salt and trading it in North America and Europe. A salt-induced cold war between Bermuda and its sister colony, the Bahamas, lasted much of the eighteenth century. The prize was control over the salt trade in the Turks. When the British government put its foot down in favor of the Bahamas in 1803, the largely Bermudian population of the Turks simply refused to be governed by Nassau. After another half-century of squabbling, the Bahamas finally abandoned their claim and allowed the Turks and Caicos to be governed—nominally from Jamaica, in fact from the Turks and Caicos—by displaced Bermudians.

Fuzzy-headed from four days at sea and stunned by sun, sand, and cloud, we work our way north across the bank to Providenciales. With our anchor down in 7 or 8 feet of water off Provo, we contemplate clearing in. But JEREMY is stowed on the foredeck and the dinghy trip around to the customs office looks long and bumpy. Lying about, soaking up warmth and color, seems a more fitting conclusion to the sea gods' gift of a smooth offshore passage than confronting another customs officer.

In the morning, as usual, we tune in the safety and security net on the

SSB. For the first time, we put in a query of our own: Is it possible, as one of our cruising guides hints, to clear into the Bahamas at Mayaguana, only a day's sail from Provo? A "yes" could change our plans. Donald on DAISY D doesn't know. He thinks maybe so, but he's been having these senior moments lately and doesn't quite trust his memory. A nearby listener breaks in to tell us that Mayaguana does indeed have a customs office. He used it less than a week ago.

This is good news. We have already bypassed Inagua, the most southerly customs outpost in the Bahamas. We were unwilling to make landfall on an island with no all-weather harbor—in fact, virtually no harbor. Inagua's only positive feature seemed to be its customs office. From the Turks and Caicos to George-Town, Mayaguana aside, there is no convenient place to clear in. And access to legality is not a trivial consideration. Bahamian customs are reported to be a bit sticky about folks who sail in their waters without presenting their papers—fines, boat impoundment, that sort of thing. We headed for the Turks and Caicos, planning to check in and out here and then ask for a "hardship" exemption when we finally made it to George-Town. We are both lawyers; we would have a few days to think of something convincing.

We have not cleared in to the Turks and Caicos, but we are still legal, because we have been here less than twenty-four hours and have not gone ashore. With access to Bahamian legality only a day away, we can go to Mayaguana, check in, and idle our way to George-Town. We decide to move around to deep water on the other side of West Caicos and leave early in the morning, straight for Mayaguana. The Turks and Caicos go on the "next time" list. Bob and Joan had said that they could easily spend a month or six weeks here, and we still have Bob's hand-drawn charts of their "secret" anchorages. But we are hoarding time to spend on relaxed days in the Exumas. For now, we will settle for our few glorious hours on the Caicos Bank, with its turquoise gulls and pink-and-green clouds.

There are reportedly remains of a North American loyalist settlement on the lee side of West Caicos, but we see no trace of it as we sail north, looking for a dive-boat mooring to hang onto for the night. The water is remarkably deep to within 50 yards of the island. Anchoring is virtually out of the question. Even on a mooring, this open roadstead is only tenable on a night as calm as this one. West Caicos has no protected harbor. The shore is lined with jagged, pockmarked limestone for almost its entire length on the west, and shallows on the east. Stunted gray-brown vegetation struggles to keep its grip on the thin, sun-baked soil. Our mooring spot is beautiful. The gin-clear water is a deep cobalt blue, headed toward black as the sun slips over the horizon. But what were those loyalists thinking about, attempting a settlement here? This is as remote and as harsh an environment as we have ever encountered.

ANNE'S PASSAGE NOTES: MOONDANCING

It is the last night of our four-day passage from San Juan to the Turks and Caicos. My midnight watch. The night is clear and brilliant, the seas bounce but do not pound us. I see no ships. My senses tuned to PALAEMON and the sea, I see, feel, hear nothing untoward.

I watch the moon begin its rise over the pitching stern. It is full and, at the horizon, as gold as I have ever seen it. PALAEMON gambols along, her stern rail performing an intricate dance with the rising moon. We trail moon-gold phosphorescence.

I am mesmerized as PALAEMON engages in a cosmic dance with her partners, the moon and the sea. Gradually the moon turns from gold to silver and exits the dance. With a parting silvery brush of PALAEMON's stern, it continues its rise into the heavens.

I sigh and realize that I am ten minutes past my routine watch check. I leap up, banging into the dodger, and spy a ship to starboard. The practical necessity of managing the boat takes over. For the moment, the magic is gone.

Safely clear of the ship, I am quiet again in my port-side huddle in bright moonlight. My mind wanders. Much is left of our cruise, the Bahamas yet to be explored, but we are moving steadily homeward. We seem to me far different from the two people who left Cape Fear last November—not to mention the pair who left Granite Bay in late August. My mind puzzles over what is different. Certainly we manage the boat with a confidence we did not have before, our movements choreographed with each other's and with PALAEMON's. We know her sounds, her motions, her strengths. We know something about her weaknesses. We know a lot about when to be scared, and when not to be, and how to endure when the going gets tough.

I think back about my trip-long struggle with seasickness. Our first overnight passage to Cape May demonstrated beyond any reasonable doubt that this was going to be a real problem.

I had hoped that sea legs would be the answer, that the constant motion of living aboard would free me to become the seasoned sailor I aspired to be. Without sea legs, my misery would continue, and Jerry would have to shoulder more than his share of managing PALAEMON. I worried about the sleep deprivation and exhaustion that this would inevitably produce for him. One of us *had* to be OK.

As we traveled and talked to other sailors, I was surprised by the prevalence of seasickness among seasoned long-distance cruisers—often in forms that sounded worse than mine. This didn't exactly cure me, but it did help lessen the guilt. The significant role that anxiety plays was also gradually sinking in: The greater the anxiety, the worse the seasickness. This was not an easy notion to accept. Intellectually, it made great sense, but I didn't want to own up to the extent of my anxiety—not to myself, and not to Jerry. Now this was really silly—without being told, he certainly knew I was anxious.

My mental breakthrough did not come until Antigua, as I sat chatting with Andrea, the professional first mate aboard the beautiful BRAVEHEART, and a veteran of many transatlantic passages. When our conversation turned to seasickness, she said, "I thought passagemaking was just great when I was younger, and I really felt fine most of the time [she cannot be more than thirty-five now], but once I realized all the things that could go wrong, I began to worry and I began to get sick." Her seasickness is now almost as bad as mine.

So I have finally faced some simple facts: I am not going to stop being seasick, or stop worrying. But neither is a disgrace. Neither means I can't be a "sailor." These are problems to be managed, not cured.

I have given up on patches, wristbands and exotic drugs, gingersnaps and ginger ale. Instead, I have simplified meals and stowage to shorten galley time, moved clothes and toiletries to the main cabin, away from the stomach-churning rise and fall of the V-berth and the head. I shower sitting in the relative calm of the cockpit floor, nap early in each new voyage to settle my middle ear, and avoid, if at all possible, sticking my head upside down into the ice chest.

And things have gotten better. Perhaps managing, not conquering, is what it means to be an offshore sailor. I learned early that I could handle PALAEMON by myself, provided I was not intent on having her sails always set optimally and her speed constant. Within my own physical limits, I would take what the sea gave me. Handling my own exalted expectations of myself turned out to be the bigger challenge.

We have gradually, I realize, become offshore sailors. I savor the idea. Other changes are harder to pin down. My mind puzzles along as I continue my watch routine. All is wonderfully quiet.

We have slowed our pace. The sea teaches patience, a kind of serenity, but the cruising life, when fully embraced, plays a major part as well. We linger over smells, sights, and sounds that we might have missed entirely in our prior lives. We listen. And then there's Jerry, my captain, my love, my life. I thought we were close before we left. But what peace we have now, and what new depths of pleasure we have found in each other.

I realize I must wake him, a task I never like. It is calm enough that I can do it with a kiss. Today we reach the Turks and Caicos. The wind remains steady, the seas moderate, the moon casting magic everywhere. He should have a good watch.

30

BASKING IN THIN WATER

To most Americans, the Bahamas are synonymous with Nassau and Paradise Island, a world of cruise ships, casinos, offshore banking, and even drug-running. The beaches and sportfishing are legendary. Tune into ESPN on a Saturday morning if you want a dose of big-game fishing in the Bahamas. But those big-money leisure activities are not what we observe as we move up through the remote Out Islands of the southeastern Bahamas. There is virtually nothing happening here.

From pre-Columbian times to the present, most Bahamian islands have remained sparsely populated, for two excellent reasons: very little fresh water and virtually no good topsoil. Settlers tried to create plantations on the southern islands in the mid-seventeenth century by importing slave labor from Africa. And British loyalists were snockered by the British government into taking Bahamian land grants when the success of the American Revolution made their continued stay in the United States, as the Surgeon General might say, "potentially injurious to their health." Although virtually all of the attempts at slave-based Bahamian agriculture had failed by the time of the 1833 Emancipation Act, enough slaves had been imported to make their descendants the overwhelming majority of today's Bahamian population.

Like Bermuda, the Bahamas attained their greatest period of prosperity in the 1860s as a staging base for Confederate blockade-running. There was another burst of economic growth based on bootlegging to the States during Prohibition. Today's offshore bankers and drug-runners are in some sense the lineal descendants of the commercially successful Bahamians who have spent a century and a half enriching themselves by helping Americans evade American laws.

The Bahamas have now turned to tourism as their principal industry. While land-based tourists and cruise ships are the backbone of that industry, the Bahamas are really a yachtsman's paradise. Its greatest beauties and pleasures lie on or in the stunning, multihued Bahamian waters and in making landfalls on remote, powdery beaches.

We feel blessed to be sailing on the deep rather than standing on the shore in the way Robert Frost captures in these lines from "Neither Out Far nor In Deep":

> The people along the sand
> All turn and look one way.
> They turn their back on the land.
> They look at the sea all day. . . .
>
> The land may vary more;
> But wherever the truth may be—
> The water comes ashore,
> And the people look at the sea.
>
> They cannot look out far.
> They cannot look in deep.
> But when was that ever a bar
> To any watch they keep?

Of course in the Bahamas, much of the deep is really not very deep. Our approach to the small settlement and customs office at Mayaguana is protected by 2 miles of coral defining a shallow bay between the island and the sea. It takes us nearly an hour to pick our way from the gap in the fringing coral through the unmarked shallows and coral heads to a spot near the town dock. The depthsounder often shows less than 5 feet, our approximate draft. I stand on the bow, pointing out a zigzag course and occasionally running us into a coral cul-de-sac. When the anchor is finally down, Anne looks a bit pale under her tan.

There is one other boat in the anchorage, a young couple we had met briefly in Antigua. They have indeed checked in but did not find it an uplifting experience. Alex advises us that the customs officer hides in her private office and refuses to come out. Or, more precisely, her secretary responds that she is "out." It took them two tries and four hours to clear in. This shy official reportedly drives a white Toyota. If her car is behind the customs "building"— a 12-by-12 cinder-block structure that will barely conceal a bicycle—we should just wait her out.

We enter the customs cube and encounter the secretary, Mrs. Johnson, in the outer office. The door to the inner sanctum is firmly closed. We notice a collection box and make a contribution to the church building fund. Mrs. Johnson asks whether we need any bread, and we order some from her brother Roy. She gives us the customs forms and takes them directly into the rear office. In a matter of 15 minutes, we are legal and awash in Bahamian goodwill.

Did we just engage in a little low-level corruption? We needed bread, and we like to contribute to local efforts at improving the islands. We'll have to ask Susan when we get home. She's probably the world's leading authority on the economics of "corruption." Her expertise is in demand all over the globe.

Once we gain confidence negotiating shallow banks and narrow passages, the sailing is spectacular. May seems to be the perfect time to be in the Bahamas. Gentle easterlies and southeasterlies push us north—sailing sometimes in the midnight-blue waters off soundings (water too deep to "sound," or measure) and sometimes in the turquoise-and-bottle-green waters of the banks. Temperatures are in the low eighties, and, day after day, David Jones gives us happy weather news. The northers from the States have stopped pushing as far south as the southern or even the central Bahamas. We have fair skies, fair winds, and light seas. This idyll just might hold for the three weeks and 700 miles we plan to glide northwest, past the far southern Out Islands, through the exquisite Exuma Cays and the Berries, to our jumping-off point for the passage to the United States—Lucaya, Grand Bahama.

Other than shallow water and look-alike islands, our major navigational challenge is coping with the strong currents that run through the passes and around the cays. With every flow of the tide, billions of cubic feet of the Atlantic are pushed up onto the shallow Bahama Banks, only to run off again as the tide recedes. As the rising tide passes between closely separated cays, it produces currents of up to 4 knots—which will of course reverse at the next turn of the tide. The currents occasionally drive us dramatically off course, setting PALAEMON toward sandy shallows or jagged coral heads. They also force us to adopt the "Bahamian moor"—two anchors, set 180 degrees apart—to keep PALAEMON secure against the tidal current's ebb and flow. Lying to both wind and tide, the bow circles the compass. In the morning, I wake disoriented, missing the familiar sunrise over the bow that began each day in the Lesser Antilles.

The tidal flow, deep to shallow and back again, pulls bait off the banks and into the deep channels, the engine that drives the fabulous Bahamian fishery. Although I am still hooking and losing monsters, we don't really need to catch our very own fish. We seldom pull into an anchorage without having someone arrive five minutes later with a Ziploc bag of fish fillets. Through simple gift or barter ("By the way, you wouldn't happen to have a lemon aboard?"), we eat enough mahi mahi, and occasionally tuna, to grow fins. This is a perfect arrangement. I get to hook and fight fish, and we get to eat fresh fish, but I don't have to kill, dress, or clean up after them.

The strong tides launch us into "drift snorkeling." Because we often cannot swim back against the current that carries us over the fantastic Bahamian coral beds, we use JEREMY as a float. When we have had enough underwater sightseeing, we climb aboard and motor back to PALAEMON. Even the snorkeling is lazy in the Bahamas.

We edge slowly north, hopping from cay to cay. As the flora and fauna have thinned out, so have the cruising boats. The Bahamian cruising community is much less cosmopolitan than the down-island crowd. They are mostly Americans, a large proportion from Florida or other parts of the southeastern United States. Some anchorages contain a small group of cruisers, others are empty. The megayachts and ocean voyagers are gone; PALAEMON is no longer a pygmy among giants. We are the long-distance cruisers in a community where vessels' hailing ports range from Charleston to Biloxi. And we are often alone, cuddled up to a cay whose only inhabitants are lizards and gulls. The dearth of insects and tree frogs makes the nights eerily silent. We miss the clumsy boobies and the graceful tropicbirds.

The preponderance of American cruisers from nearby states is hardly surprising. Proximity has long made the Bahamas a prime destination for American vessels. In another of George Washington's powder raids, somewhat reminiscent of the Bermudian gunpowder plot, a rebel force of two ships and perhaps 200 men invaded Nassau in 1776. The governor called out the local militia, but the few who showed up at the fort decided to entertain the North Americans rather than fight them. Bahamians, like Bermudians, were often rebel sympathizers. The governor, in his nightshirt, preserved what was left of his dignity by refusing to surrender until he could go home and dress properly.

This daring raid was memorialized in a Janus-faced resolution passed by the Continental Congress. It praises the Nassau invaders for seizing much-needed powder and cannon, but then censures them for losing it on the way home to a British man-o'-war cruising off Rhode Island. The party at the fort had gone on for two weeks, and the American forces were not quite in fighting trim as they made their way back. Compromise congressional legislation that looks simultaneously toward every point of the political compass is, of course, now a highly developed literary form.

If the fledgling United States of America had had a navy or any spare troops, it should have held Nassau. Providence Island served as a major base for the British privateers who harassed and captured American merchantmen almost at will as the thirteen rebellious colonies tried desperately to keep North American–West Indian trade flowing during the Revolution. Finally, in 1782, two American vessels, combined with a large Spanish fleet from Havana, retook Nassau without firing a shot.

Having helped deliver the Bahamian capital to Spain, North Americans then recaptured it for England only a year later. A daring loyalist, Captain Andrew Deveau, had been driven out of South Carolina to take refuge in St. Augustine, Florida. Anticipating that Florida would be returned to Spain at war's end, Deveau devised a plan to take Nassau. With sixty-five men from Florida, and perhaps 150 (mostly unarmed) Bahamians recruited from Eleuthera and the Abacos, Deveau tricked a well-equipped Spanish garrison of 600 into surrendering after only token resistance. The Bahamians rowed small boats furiously from Deveau's ships to shore and back again, their "troops" sitting up on the way to shore, lying on the floorboards on the return trip. From this stunt, the Spanish estimated that Deveau had them vastly outnumbered. He also sent his demands for surrender to the Spanish garrison via two Cherokee warriors, making the Spaniards fear for their hair.

Deveau's brilliant strategy was somewhat wasted. Neither side knew at the time that the Bahamas had already been returned to Great Britain by the Treaty of Versailles. Florida had been returned to Spain. Deveau had known when to get out.

Deveau's party became the first of thousands of loyalists who would flee to the Bahamas and transform them. The British Crown gave each loyalist household forty acres, plus twenty additional acres for each African brought with them. Within five years of Deveau's raid, loyalist refugees and their slaves had more than doubled the Bahamian population, created a black majority for the first time, spread slavery throughout the islands, and reconstructed an economy based on fishing, trading, and privateering into an economy dominated by plantation agriculture. The American Revolution only remade American government; it revolutionized Bahamian society.

As we luxuriate in the Exumas, we share a number of gentle sails and lovely anchorages with Cecil and Danny Hazen and their daughter Amy, aboard DESPERADO out of Cape Coral, Florida. The Hazens are also keeping company with Les. Lester is an interesting and competent guy, but as with most of the singlehanders we have met, we have a sense of why he is alone on the boat. His leather vest (worn over bronzed, hairy skin), his massive shark-tooth necklaces, and his sweat-stained cowboy hat make him a standout in a cruising community whose basic uniform is khaki shorts and a T-shirt. And he is as pigheaded as anyone to whom I have ever given mechanical advice. Not that anyone should place any special value on my mechanical advice. Cecil and I spend two hours suggesting strategies for dealing with Lester's broken gearshift cable. He rejects them all out of hand. We finally give up and go back to our boats.

It would take a special person to spend months on a boat with Les. His wife, back in Kansas City busily divorcing him, has obviously not been "special" in quite the right way. I ask Cecil how they came to be hooked up with Les. "Just lucky, I guess," is his understated reply. The Hazens are too nice to tell Les to get lost, but no abrupt change in their plans seems too much for Lester to accommodate into his schedule. The fear that Les may decide to relocate to Cape Coral is growing aboard DESPERADO like kudzu vine.

We also spend a little time with Bruce Van Sant (of *The Gentleman's Guide to Passages South* fame) and his charming Dominican wife, Rosa. Rather than being the arrogant guy that I envisioned from reading his book, Bruce turns out to be an acute observer of the cruising life, with a deep attachment to the struggles of ordinary folks on the poorer islands of the Caribbean. He also continues to show great independence of mind. Because he ends up motoring so much—following his own advice about the "thornless" navigation of his chosen cruising grounds—Bruce has taken a straightforward and logical approach to creating the perfect cruising boat. He bought a large, comfortable motor-sailer and cut off the mast. He now doesn't have to fool with the sails (which are useless if you travel mostly before the wind comes up), and he has the easiest-riding and most seaworthy trawler in the islands.

Although Bahamian settlements often have the feel of redoubts that might be abandoned at any moment, a number of them are memorable. For reasons known only to God, the marina at Rum Cay, a desolate outpost frequented largely by dedicated big-game fishermen, has a Japanese-trained chef whose concoctions are both ingenious and delectable. The choir at the Baptist church on Staniel Cay should play Lincoln Center. And snorkeling in "Thunderball Cave," where the underwater shots were done for the James Bond flick, is literally as good as it gets.

Yet I remain ambivalent about the southern and central Bahamas. I like the wildness, the easy passages, the crystalline water. The light is amazing, hypnotic. But there is a relentless sameness to the landscape. These underpopulated, near-desert islands exude the tepid menace of a ghost town. Virtually all the cotton plantations failed, and attempts to substitute bananas or pineapples fared little better. The British government had promised the loyalist refugees that the Bahamian soil was fertile. They neglected to mention that it was only about 4 inches deep. Even a short drought destroys a year's crop as the relentless subtropical sun heats the limestone underneath the thin blanket of earth and turns the soil to hardpan or dust. So year by year, most islands were left to the lizards and the gulls, their populations migrating to Nassau or out of the islands altogether. The foundations of abandoned dwellings, the remains of docks, fragments of mills and empty cisterns stand in mute testament to failed enterprise.

My eyes are not attuned to the subtlety and nuance that surely are there, but that would require many more months of observation. Gilbert Klingel, an American naturalist and adventurer, was shipwrecked early on in his attempt to explore much of the West Indies and restricted for months to the island of Inagua. In his memoir of the same name, he writes, "We were to find it a scene of almost unbelievable beauty where color and movement, the wealth of natural existence, was woven into a fretwork of intricate and absorbing pattern." But I am not sure that I want more time to develop Klingel's practiced and appreciative eye. For he also laments, "Yet we were withal to know it as a place undefinably sad, a peculiar, pathetic, wistful place where human endeavor seemed to come to naught but emptiness and dissolution."

As our days in the Bahamas wind down, I don't feel the same regret that I felt in leaving Grenada or Bequia—the pull of a culture both comfortable and foreign, familiar but inadequately explored. Perhaps it is the Americanization of the islands that stifles interest. While courting American tourism and investment in the 1950s and 1960s, the ruling oligarchy catered to American segregationist practices that exacerbated racial tensions. Black resentment led to an American-style "black power" movement and the political defeat of the white elite—the so-called Bay Street Boys, the Nassau merchants and financiers who had called the political shots in the Bahamas for more than a century.

Bahamas laughing gull.

But the triumph of Lionel Pindling's Progressive Liberal Party was relatively short-lived, and pockmarked by the corruption against which he had campaigned. The PLP has now given way to a *laissez-faire* regime that emphasizes economic growth, meaning catering to the mostly American tourists' tastes for cruise ships, shopping, gambling, and resort vacations. The "Family Islands"—Abaco, Harbour Island, and their nearby cays—are an exception. But they are white, Anglophile outposts whose unreconstructed colonial political consciousness makes them, as the British might say, "a bit off-putting."

I am sure I am just being grumpy again, but I prefer the Bahamas' remote, lightly settled areas, even if they sometimes feel sad and desolate. So when we make the white-knuckle trip from the Exumas across the Yellow Banks, dodging coral heads, to Nassau, we anchor off relatively undeveloped Rose Island, out of sight and sound of the cruise ships and casinos. Three other boats huddle with us, refugees from the bustle and excitement, preparing to ship out to the still-remote Berries. The Berries will provide our last chance for the secluded sailing to which we have grown accustomed in the Out Islands of the southeastern Bahamas and the Exumas.

Anne's enjoyment of the lower Bahamas was impaired by an allergy that had her lips and eyes swelling and itching for most of the trip from West Caicos to the Exumas. In George-Town, a settlement of perhaps 400 people, and the winter home to perhaps twice that many cruisers, she got effective treatment in an encounter with Bahamian medicine that provides strong support for some serious reform of our health-care system.

Care is provided to Bahamian citizens by public clinics sprinkled throughout the islands. Non-Bahamians must join a clinic for a year in order to obtain treatment. This harsh burden on foreigners required that we pay the princely annual registration fee of $20. After filling out a form that took two whole minutes, we were ushered into the doctor's office. He examined Anne, discussed his diagnosis with us, and then prescribed and dispensed an antihistamine drug and a topical ointment. The cost of the doctor's visit and the medication—$16. Total time to seek and receive treatment—fifteen minutes.

Imagine, by contrast, the likely experience of a Bahamian national with a similar problem that cropped up while touring the United States. Well, it hardly bears thinking about. If this hapless soul ever got past the emergency-room wallet biopsy and received treatment, it would probably have cost two days of her vacation, all of her good humor and positive feeling about the United States, and a substantial portion of her bank account.

As we are making our way north from Nassau through the Berry Islands, Anne develops a painful urinary infection. There are virtually no settlements or services of any type in the Berries. We have a selection of antibiotics in our medicine cabinet, so I get on the VHF to see whether I can locate a vessel with a physician aboard who can advise us which might be best to use. Within a few minutes, the voice of a fellow cruiser emerges out of the ether to suggest that I call the Royal Caribbean cruise line base at Coco Cay (formerly Little Stir-rup Cay). It seems that Royal Caribbean purchased Little Stirrup, renamed it, and developed a miniresort where they can offload their ship-bound passen-gers for a day of sunning and water sports. My informant believes that the cruise ship SOVEREIGN OF THE SEAS is in port at the island and almost certainly has medical personnel on board. Thus begins the strangest doctor's visit we are ever likely to have.

The captain of SOVEREIGN OF THE SEAS is happy to help. If we will just maneuver alongside his ship, he will put his medical officer on board to check out Anne's problem. We manage this feat, sort of like a minnow at-taching itself to a whale, but our minnow has a mast that could self-destruct against the side of the ship if we get much roll. The waters remain calm. A doctor and a nurse come aboard. They take a urine sample, diagnose the ail-ment, and dispense medication. Once again, elapsed time about twenty minutes. Charges, zero.

These folks could not have been nicer or more accommodating. They offer to take Anne aboard SOVEREIGN OF THE SEAS, where they can do more sophisticated testing, if we are sufficiently concerned. Unfortunately, under their ship's rules (doubtless written by an American lawyer), they will have to keep Anne aboard until she is fully recovered and they risk no malprac-tice liability. This rule explains why they were making a house call aboard PALAEMON rather than having Anne visit the sick bay aboard SOVEREIGN OF THE SEAS.

We are not that concerned, particularly since the doc suggests that she has almost never treated a urinary-tract infection that has not responded to the medication that Anne has just been given. Within twelve hours, her symptoms have all but disappeared, and we are ready to travel again. We are also carefully reevaluating our strongly held views: (1) that the cruise-ship trade is ruining the Caribbean, and (2) that places where there are cruise ships should be avoided whenever possible.

ANNE'S PASSAGE NOTES: SETTLEMENTS

The Out Islands of the Bahamas are mostly vacant, sprinkled with settlements of 15 to 400 souls. "Town" is too grand a word for these hodgepodge clusters of habitation, crouched near rickety ferry docks in whatever open roadstead or reef-strewn shallows serves as a harbor, never far from the biweekly boat deliveries that sustain life. All food and fuel, and much of the potable water, seem to arrive this way. The thatched- and tin-roofed dwellings have no gutters leading to cisterns. Wells tap fresh water beneath the limestone, floating on the salt water that seeps through the porous rock. But we are here in the dry season. Most well water is now brackish, too salty to drink. A ferry delayed by weather, or a breakdown, is not a laughing matter.

Maybe four people per settlement have steady wages—two at a government outpost near the ferry dock, two at a Batelco (communications) office, usually the only two buildings in the settlement with air-conditioning. We can find them blindfolded, following the clatter of their generators. When the offices close, a sudden hush envelops the anchorage, a silence so deep we can almost touch it.

Other "settlers" get by somehow. Scruffy skiffs on the beach suggest fishing, but we rarely see a local boat at work. Back from the beach we find "bars," "Bar-B-Q restaurants," a "grocery store"—all attached to living quarters. We become accustomed to entering the gloom of a "restaurant" to find no one there, or the family eating lunch. Getting a meal is by appointment. Reservations are needed not to allocate space but to give the proprietor time to scare up something to serve.

Fresh goods are all snapped up within an hour of the ferry's landing. The grocery store stocks canned beans, rice, canned fruit juice, perhaps canned tomatoes, a few onions. Freshly baked "flour bread" is usually available somewhere—light white bread, slightly

Global communications.

sweet—good. A poke into two or three bars or restaurants will usually net us a couple of cold beers, a dark spot to sit away from the blinding Bahamian light.

Prowling along dusty roadways, we find a small church, a one-room school. The church is the best-maintained structure—gleaming white, its tin roof painted, resting in a well-manicured yard of sparse brown grass. Houses, one- or two-room shacks, sport abandoned engine blocks, an occasional discarded refrigerator in their barren yards. Not even a chicken pecks at the brittle ground.

Returning to PALAEMON, we look back at the small settlement we have just left. At a distance, its poverty disappears, its appearance is quaint. Not beautiful like the Caribbean communities with their colorful houses scattered up steep hillsides, their brilliant banks of flowers. But not unattractive, surrounded by cerulean blues, rose-white sand and limestone, the indigo of the sea beyond.

We wonder how Out Island Bahamians manage year in and year out. We puzzle at the sharp contrast between the desolate landscape and the people themselves: friendly, direct of eye, quick to read our needs, helpful but not pushy, remarkably well spoken. Their English is standard, not patois, their music more American than Caribbean. We look around at PALAEMON's simple luxuries. Worlds divide us.

31

CLOSING THE CIRCLE

SOVEREIGN OF THE SEAS collects her 2,000 or so frolicking passengers from the beach at Coco Cay and heads back toward Florida. We are alone off Great Stirrup Cay. The emerald-green water of the bank stretches off our stern to the south and west, the deep blue of the Northwest Providence Channel to the north and east. When we leave this anchorage, we will be headed for another world. We will stop in Port Lucaya, Grand Bahama, to restock PALAEMON before our passage back to the States. Port Lucaya, near Freeport, is technically a part of the Bahamas, but with the Florida coast only 90 miles away, its ambience is more West Palm Beach than Rum Cay.

As I check the tide table to time our passage out of the Stirrup Cays, I encounter a familiar notice in the Bahamas pages of *Reed's Nautical Almanac:* "Tide watchers wanted." Strange as it may seem, all tidal information is based on empirical observation, not astronomical theory or topographic models. Much of the information reflected in tide tables stretches back hundreds of years. Where civilization is dense and ancient, the tables are very accurate. That is not the Bahamas. Because the tides flow on and off the Bahama Banks in virtually every direction, amassing enough observations to develop good tide tables and current charts is more than usually challenging.

If Anne and I find that we are unable to readjust to land and American civilization, perhaps we can return to the Bahamas and become tide watchers. I can see our business cards now: "Anne MacClintock and Jerry Mashaw, Tide Watchers, Berry Islands, Bahamas." We could add parenthetically that by special request we are also available to watch grass grow or paint dry. As we prepare to leave, my attachment to the Bahamas is blossoming, my ambivalence receding. With Anne healthy again, the isolation of the Berries seems inviting rather than menacing.

But we must go. With an offshore passage looming, we have resumed our late-afternoon vigil at the SSB, listening to Herb Hilgenberg. He is now guiding snowbirds home to the east coast of the United States via the Bahamas or Bermuda, or on more direct passages from the Virgins to Beaufort or Norfolk or

Newport. Enough boats are heading in our general direction that we don't need to check in individually to get a weather forecast for our intended route from Lucaya to Beaufort, North Carolina. By the sound of things, when we chose the Bahamas route, we chose the fair-weather alternative. Our friends Jim and Kathleen Nelson on HIGH POCKETS are headed back to Rhode Island from St. Martin via Bermuda. Herb is guiding them around the worst of the weather, but they are going from feast to famine, motoring in dead-flat calms one day, barreling and bumping along in 30 knots of wind the next. From the coordinates they are giving Herb, they must be bypassing Bermuda and heading for home.

In some ways we envy the boats, such as RESOLUTE, that are headed east to the Azores and the Mediterranean, rather than west and north back to the States. A year or two in the Med certainly sounds enticing. The 20-to-30-day passage to get there doesn't. While the open ocean is often beautiful, our offshore experience has run basically from bruising to boring, with a few bits of ecstasy in between. We know now that offshore passagemaking is something that we can do. And I am perfectly capable of forgetting the realities of our passages from Bald Head Island to Bermuda to Jost to Grenada. I can imagine a gorgeous, fun-filled sail to the Azores and on to Gibraltar and the Med, mimicking our run from San Juan to the Turks and Caicos. But I think Anne's amnesia about offshore discomforts has been cured. If PALAEMON goes to the Med, she may go as deck cargo on a freighter rather than on her own bottom.

There are bookshelves of sailing narratives extolling the mystical oneness with ocean achieved by offshore passagemakers. People such as Bernard Moitessier, who circle the globe once and decide to just keep going, who can't bear to return to land. I still love the idea of offshore sailing. I feel certain that we will do more. But when on passage, my view remains that shorter is better than longer.

Happily, the passage from Lucaya to Beaufort is only about four days— the length of a reasonably reliable weather report. But only reasonably reliable. We are leaving the trade winds and moving back into the controlling westerlies off the U.S. east coast. Indeed, the pilot charts—those large-area black-and-white charts for each month of the year, with red arrows all over them showing average wind speed and direction—make clear that the winds in this area in May and June can come from almost anywhere.

The first twenty-four hours out of Lucaya are not auspicious. It takes nearly a day of tacking against persistent westerlies to get out to the thread of the Gulf Stream and pick up that wonderful north-flowing current. Although the winds refuse to go south of west, we manage to keep them from pushing us out of the stream. We have two days of exhilarating sailing, moving at big-boat speeds, 9 to 10 knots over the ground. Then the wind dies and the fore-cast changes. According to Herb, after twenty-four hours of calm, the wind is going to go north in earnest. We will not make Beaufort before the north wind begins to blow. It will be right on our nose and make a lumpy mess of the Gulf Stream. We alter course for the Cape Fear River and Bald Head Island, less than twenty-four hours away. By chance rather than design, we will reenter the States exactly where we left. Cruisers call it "closing the circle," or "recrossing your outbound track."

Twenty miles out, we raise the harbormaster at Bald Head Island to try to arrange for a berth. He has to laugh. We want a berth on Memorial Day week-end? He has been sold out since March.

My god, Memorial Day weekend. That rite of passage into summer that literally demands that every boater in America get out on the water to celebrate the end of weather-bound winter, and in the Northeast, the cold, damp spring. John Updike somewhere describes the New England spring poignantly but ac-curately as "an unsuccessful season." But Memorial Day? We are not prepared for this. As we enter the Cape Fear River, headed up the Intracoastal Water-way to the Wrightsville Beach anchorage from which Irene had driven us in October, we sail into culture shock.

After thirty days in the Bahamas, drifting along with cruising sailboats and a few fishermen, we are overwhelmed by the sheer level of activity both on the water and on the land. We are not sure whether we are reentering the Amer-ica we left, but do not now recognize, or whether things have changed radi-cally in our absence. At anchor in Wrightsville Beach, as the cell phone begins working again, we fire off an e-mail message to our friends and relatives with a few important questions: "Does a 'second home' now occupy every square foot of beachfront in the United States? Does every American above the age of twelve own a personal watercraft—a motorcyclelike device that zips around like a malevolent skateboard and is driven by an engine that sounds like a chainsaw? Has every person in America gained 40 pounds, or are these line-backers in size 42 bathing suits and babes bulging out of their bikinis local to North Carolina's Outer Banks?" We had never thought that returning home was going to be particularly easy, but we hadn't figured on feeling like com-plete strangers.

We are heartened to find that America is still "the land of the free." As the San Juan customs office promised, checking in involves calling an 800 num-ber and giving them our passport numbers and boat registration. Five minutes later, they call back to say we are cleared in and welcome home. For all they know, we are stuffed to the gunwales with cocaine or Haitian refugees. God bless America. I guess we just don't fit the smugglers' profile.

Culture shock or no, we are sitting smugly as well as snugly in Wrightsville Beach. We have hardly sailed the Roaring Forties or laid over for the winter in Antarctica. We have not even crossed the Atlantic. But unless we do something really stupid, or have some really bad luck between Wrightsville Beach and Connecticut, we are going to get PALAEMON—and ourselves—home in one piece. As we look back on it, the issue had sometimes been in doubt.

We have a last drink with the crews of ALGONQUIN and IWANDA. We all traveled in the usual "somewhat together" fashion from Lucaya to Wrightsville Beach. We are all headed up the waterway, as well, but at different speeds and with different destinations.

This is probably the last cruiser confab over cocktails in the cockpit that we will have for a while. Down island, where most couples are traveling alone, the anchorages are communal places. Most cruisers are eager to find old friends and meet new ones. Sailors anchored in U.S. waters are different. They are usually escaping from a harried life ashore for a one- or two-week cruise. Unless they're off with a group of local yacht-club buddies, they're looking for that secluded cove where they can feel they have broken away from their shore-bound life—where they can, for a few hours at least, imagine they are cruising in remote territory, on their own. To approach these folks and cheerily invite them for cocktails is to break into a reverie that we have often enjoyed, and upon which we are hesitant to intrude.

We anticipate a laid-back wander up through the ICW to the Chesapeake. Then it will be down the dreaded Delaware Bay, up the Jersey Shore, through Hell Gate into Long Island Sound—and home. We will putter along through the Chesapeake and try to savor the time, readjust slowly to the rhythms of American life. We have lost our defenses to the incessant demand from every information source that we immediately buy something that we can't live without or invest in something that will make us rich beyond dreams of avarice. Was America always this consumed by consumerism? Is it now? Or, are we just skimming the surface again of a culture, once as familiar as our skins, but now become strange?

So we poke and ponder up the waterway—with an unscheduled four-day stop at Bellhaven, North Carolina, when our alternator burns up. It is Saturday. The shipyard guys say they can get the alternator rebuilt on Monday. They seem confident and competent. Fifteen minutes later, we meet a fellow on the dock who spent a month here last year. When he tells us that there were enough cruisers waiting for help in the yard then to form a hostage support group, we begin to doubt the promptness of our promised alternator repair. When the next two people we meet have already been here a month *this* year, we decide to hedge our bets. I call West Marine and have them ship a new alternator. It arrives on Tuesday. I install it and check it out. It works. We collect our old alternator from where it sits untouched on a workbench and flee.

The Chesapeake is in the throes of early summer, 90-degree heat, little wind, dramatic evening thunderstorms. We creep northward along the Eastern Shore, dodging the flats, thumping through Kent's Narrows, wandering ashore in Oxford and Chestertown. Lee and Gina Reno prove that PROMISE leaves the dock by sailing over from Annapolis to spend a weekend with us in Dividing Creek. The remote, empty anchorage where we involuntarily retrieved the crabber's trotline on our way south now holds six boats in addition to PROMISE and PALAEMON. This time, we manage just to eat the crabs and leave the trotlines alone.

Along the Wye River, around Tilghman Island, fighting our way through the shallows at Knapp's Narrows, we encounter remnants of the Chesapeake skipjack fleet, the only boats in America that still dredge oysters under sail. Since 1865, oysters have been protected in Maryland by stopping the technological clock. Oystermen may only tong—that is, rake the shallower oyster beds by hand—or dredge under sail.

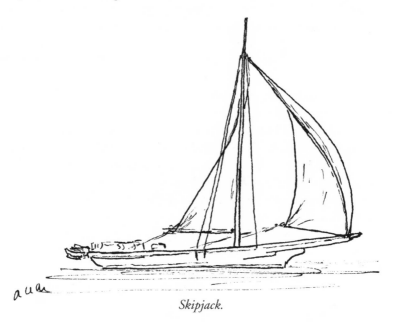

Skipjack.

The oyster-dredging bateau—"skipjack" is a name of uncertain origin—evolved into a distinctive form: broad of beam to carry tons of oysters, shallow of draft to make its way through thin water and into the safety of shallow creeks, endowed with enormous mainsails, the masts well forward to dredge downwind in light air. Each skipjack sports a stubby "yawlboat" on davits off the stern, tiny tenders that are virtually all engine. The yawlboat's job is to push a skipjack where she can't sail, help her break occasional winter ice, and provide power to dredge illegally when the wind is light and the oyster police aren't looking.

Graceful at a distance, skipjacks are workboats up close, heavily built by backyard boatwrights, cheaply rigged with blocks and galvanized iron. No yacht winches, stainless steel, or varnished wood adorn boats that have to pay their way pulling a dredge and hauling piles of muddy oysters. Like the oysters that they hunt, the number of working bateaux cycles. In the 1960s, they were falling apart at docks and on makeshift marine railways, being sold to hobbyists and donated to museums. The oyster boom of the 1970s saw oystermen buying back skipjacks from yachtsmen, rebuilding any wreck that might hold together, even prying a few out of bayside museums. In the 1980s, the mysterious MSX bacterium decimated the oyster beds again, and the skipjack fleet dwindled. Judging by the number we are seeing now, the Chesapeake oyster must be staging something of a comeback. If so, baymen will not expect the good times to last.

Like fishing crabs, oystering is a rugged, uncertain life. But there are oystermen on the Eastern Shore who will do almost anything to stay out on the bay. Hard men, too, who would debate whether to tell a son about a newly discovered oyster bed, and ram another bateau for setting up too close. And gentle men, who hope their sons will find an easier life.

No matter how slowly we move, the bay narrows, funneling us through the Chesapeake and Delaware Canal to the head of Delaware Bay. We park PALAEMON there for the night in a deserted cove hard by a massive nuclear-power plant, its giant cooling towers surrounded by water and marsh, an alien presence in the misty evening. We're up in predawn light to catch the tide down the bay. We run hard, dodging our way through shallows to make Cape May by sundown. We choose the anchorage this time. We don't feel nearly lucky enough to try getting into the South Jersey Marina twice in one lifetime.

The winds are fair toward New York, and the inlets along the Jersey Shore are navigable. So we daysail—first to Atlantic City and then to Manasquan Inlet—on our way back to Sandy Hook. The exhausting, stomach-churning overnight bashing we took on the way down is replaced by a trio of easy coastal cruises.

Sandy Hook once again provides a refuge, but this time it is not the sea offshore that fills our minds. We are quiet in the cockpit at Horseshoe Cove. The red light of the setting sun plays on the shore and on a solitary fly fisherman catching and releasing small striped bass. Tomorrow, with an early start and fair tides and winds all the way, we can scream up the coast from Sandy Hook to our Granite Bay anchorage in twelve hours. Tomorrow we will be home.

As we sail in toward shore, our senses seek out familiar sights and sounds. The summer flocks—oystercatchers and common terns, herring and black-backed gulls—line the granite ledges and screech and complain overhead. The returning osprey have rebuilt their nests on the platforms in Kelsey Island's marsh. They are circling high, their dainty, high-pitched peeps almost inaudible, pursuing their endless quest for menhaden. The Yale Sailing Club is running classes for juniors in the bay, their 420s festooned with lobster floats at the mastheads to keep neophytes from jamming the masts into the muddy bottom when capsized by an unexpected gust or an incompetent jibe.

This is a good place to call home. But we are unable to make an immediate transition to land. We anchor PALAEMON 400 yards out from our house, the same spot from which we left ten months ago. We sit in her cockpit after dinner, watching the shore turn from rosy pink to gray, listening to the willet's trill, the squark of a heron. The circle is now truly closed. Tomorrow, we will tie PALAEMON, and ourselves, to the shore.

In this familiar world, it seems odd that the earth has entered a new millennium while we have explored a different life. We know that we are not quite the same people who left here with a mixture of anxiety and anticipation, little seasoned by the salt of the sea. We have put nearly 8,000 miles under PALAEMON's keel. We have coped more or less well with what came our way. Cruising has been more physically and emotionally demanding than we had anticipated. The sea has taught us lessons both hard and gentle. The "Isles of the Caribbees" have filled us with wonder and joy, and despair.

When we left, I thought I would learn something about myself on this trip—something important, perhaps profound. Perhaps I have. But the important lesson is not about the world of adventure, about competence or courage or fear. It is instead that my deepest joy remains the same: to share a partnership of love and respect and need, a partnership only made more visible and intense by the savor of the sea. My joy goes ashore with me.

BIBLIOGRAPHY

CHESAPEAKE AND DELAWARE BAY

Carr, Lois. *Robert Cole's World: Agriculture and Society in Early Maryland.* Chapel Hill: University of North Carolina Press, 1991.

Chappell, Helen. *The Chesapeake Book of the Dead: Tombstones, Epitaphs, Histories, Reflections, and Oddments of the Region.* Baltimore: Johns Hopkins University Press, 1999.

Collings, Francis. *The Discovery of the Chesapeake Bay: An Account of the Explorations of Captain John Smith in the year 1608.* St. Michaels, MD: Chesapeake Bay Maritime Museum, 1988.

Ellis, Carolyn. *Fisher Folk: Two Communities on Chesapeake Bay.* Lexington, KY: University Press of Kentucky, 1986.

Forester, C. S. *The Age of Fighting Sail: The Story of the Naval War of 1812.* Garden City, NY: Doubleday, 1956.

Gillmer, Thomas C. *Pride of Baltimore: The Story of the Baltimore Clippers, 1800–1990.* Camden, ME: International Marine, 1992.

McManemin, John A. *Privateers of the War of 1812.* Spring Lake, NJ: Ho-Ho-Kus Publications, 1992.

Morgan, Philip. *Slave Counterpoint: Black Culture in the Eighteenth-Century Chesapeake and Low Country.* Chapel Hill: University of North Carolina Press, 1998.

Price, Jacob. *Capital and Credit in British Overseas Trade: The View From the Chesapeake, 1700–1776.* Cambridge: Harvard University Press, 1980.

Shomette, Donald. *Ghost Fleet of Mallows Bay and Other Tales of the Lost Chesapeake.* Centreville, MD: Tidewater Publishers, 1996.

Shomette, Donald. *Pirates on the Chesapeake: Being a True History of Pirates, Picaroons, and Raiders on Chesapeake Bay, 1610–1807.* Centreville, MD: Tidewater Publishers, 1985.

Snediker, Quentin and Ann Jensen. *Chesapeake Bay Schooners.* Centreville, MD: Tidewater Publishers, 1992.

Svenson, Peter. *Green Shingles: At the Edge of the Chesapeake Bay.* New York: Faber and Faber, 1999.

Vojtech, Pat. *Chesapeake Bay Skipjacks.* Centreville, MD: Tidewater Publishers, 1993.

Warner, William W. *Beautiful Swimmers: Watermen, Crabs, and the Chesapeake Bay.* Boston and Toronto: Little, Brown, 1976.

Whitehorne, Joseph. *The Battle for Baltimore: The War of 1814.* Baltimore: Nautical and Aviation Publishing Co. of America, 1997.

BERMUDA

Ahiakpor, James. *The Economic Consequences of Political Independence: The Case of Bermuda.* Vancouver: Fraser Institute, 1990.

Berlitz, Charles, *Without a Trace.* Garden City, NY: Doubleday, 1977.

Clark, Phipps. *A Proposal for a Comprehensive Program Toward Racial Integration and Economic Equity: Interim Report.* Hamilton, Bermuda: Clark, Phipps, Clark and Harris, Inc., 1978.

Hendrick, Basil. *Anthropological Investigations in the Caribbean: Select Papers.* Museum of Anthropology, Greeley, CO: University of Northern Colorado, 1984.

Hollis, Hallett. *Rosabelle: Life in Bermuda in the Nineteenth Century.* Pembroke, Bermuda: Juniper Hill Press, 1995.

Kennedy, Jean. *Bermuda's Sailors of Fortune.* Hamilton, Bermuda: Baxter's Ltd., 1963.

Kennedy, Jean. *350 Years of Bermuda's Parliament.* Hamilton, Bermuda: Baxter's Ltd., 1975.

Kerr, Wilfred. *Bermuda and the American Revolution: 1760–1783.* Princeton, NJ: Princeton University Press, 1936.

Manning, Frank. *Bermudian Politics in Transition: Race, Voting, and Public Opinion.* Hamilton, Bermuda: Island Press, 1978.

McCallan, E. A. *Life on Old St. David's, Bermuda.* Hamilton, Bermuda: Bermuda Historical Monuments Trust, 1948.

Wilkinson, Henry C. *The Adventurers of Bermuda: A History of the Island From Its Discovery Until the Dissolution of the Somers Island Company in 1684.* London and New York: Oxford University Press, 1958.

Wilkinson, Henry C. *Bermuda in the Old Empire.* London: Oxford University Press, 1950.

Zuill, W. S. *The Story of Bermuda and Her People,* 3rd ed. London and Basingstoke: Macmillan, 1999.

VIRGIN ISLANDS

Bank of Commerce. *The Virgin Islands: A Description of the Commercial Value of the Danish West Indies.* New York, NY: National Bank of Commerce, 1917.

Booy, Theodore H. N. de. *The Virgin Islands, Our New Possessions and the British Islands.* Westport, CT: Negro University Press, 1970.

Bough, James and Roy Macridis, eds. *Virgin Islands, America's Caribbean Outpost: The Evolution of Self-Government.* Wakefield, MA: W. F. Williams Publishing, 1970.

Boyer, William W. *America's Virgin Islands: A History of Human Rights and Wrongs.* Durham, NC: Carolina Academic Press, 1983.

Creque, Darwin. *The U.S. Virgins and the Eastern Caribbean.* Philadelphia, PA: Whitmore Publishing, 1968.

Dookhan, Isaac. *A History of the Virgin Islands of the United States.* Kingston, Jamaica: Canoe Press, 1994.

Eadie, Hazel. *Lagooned in the Virgin Islands.* London: G. Routledge and Sons, 1931.

Gladwin, Ellis. *Living in the Changing Caribbean.* New York: Macmillan, 1970.

Hill, Valdemar. *Rise to Recognition: An Account of Virgin Islands From Slavery to Self-government.*

Lawaetz, Eva. *The Danish Heritage of the U.S. Virgin Islands.* St. Croix, VI: St. Croix Friends of Denmark Society, 1977.

Lewis, Gordon K. *The Virgin Islands: a Caribbean Lilliput.* Evanston, IL: Northwestern University Press, 1972.

Lewisohn, Florence. *St. Croix Under Seven Flags.* Hollywood, FL: The Dukane Press, 1970.

Morton, Henry. *St. Croix, St. Thomas, St. John: Danish West Indian Sketchbook and Diary.* Dansk Vestindisk Selskab: St. Croix Landmark Society, 1975.

Nissan, Johan. *Reminiscences of the 46 Years' Residence in St. Thomas.* Nazareth, PA, 1838.

O'Neill, Edward. *Rape of the American Virgins.* New York: Praeger, 1972.

Ottley, Earle. *Trials and Triumphs: The Long Road to a Middle Class Society in the U.S. Virgin Islands.* Charlotte Amalie, St. Thomas, USVI: E.B. Ottley, 1982.

Pederson, Erik. *The Attempted Sale of the Danish West Indies to the United States of America, 1865–1870.* Frankfurt: Haag and Herchen, 1997.

Suckling, George. *An Historical Account of the Virgin Islands, in the West Indies From their being settled by the English near a century past, to their obtaining a legislature of their own in the year 1773; and the lawless state in which His Majesty's subjects in those islands have remained since that time, to the Present.* London: Printed for B. White, 1780.

U.S. Federal Maritime Commission, Office of Economic Analysis. *Virgin Islands Trade Study: An Economic Analysis.* Washington, DC: U.S. Government Printing Office, 1979.

Weinstein, Edwin. *Cultural Aspects of Delusion: a Psychiatric Study of the Virgin Islands.* Glencoe, IL: Free Press of Glencoe, 1962.

Westergaard, Waldemar. *The Danish West Indies Under Company Rules (1671–1754), and Supplementary Chapter (1755–1917).* New York: Macmillan, 1917.

Zabriskie, Luther. *The Virgin Islands of the United States of America: Historical and Descriptive, Commercial and Industrial Facts, Figures, and Resources.* New York and London: G. P. Putnam's Sons, 1918.

ST. VINCENT AND THE GRENADINES

Adams, Edgar. *Linking the Golden Anchor with the Silver Chain: A Historical and Socio-Economic Perspective on Shipping in St. Vincent and the Grenadines.* St. Vincent and the Grenadines: privately printed, 1996.

Adams, Edgar. *Mock Hangings: A Cultural Tradition in St. Vincent and the Grenadines.* Kingstown, St. Vincent and the Grenadines: privately printed, 1999.

Background Notes: St. Vincent and the Grenadines. U.S. Department of State, Bureau of Western Hemisphere Affairs, 2000.

Bullen, Ripley P. *Archaeological Investigations on St. Vincent and the Grenadines.* 1972. *West Indies.* Orlando, FL: Bryant Foundation,

Cox, Edward L. *Rekindling the Ancestral Memory: King Ja Ja of Opobo in St. Vincent and Barbados, 1888–1891.* Cave Hill and Bridgetown, Barbados: University of the West Indies Press, 1998.

Gullick, C. J. M. R. *Myths of a Minority: The Changing Traditions of the Vincentian Caribs.* Assen, Netherlands: Van Gorcum

Jinkins, Dana, et al. *St. Vincent and the Grenadines: Bequia, Mustique, Canouan, Mayreau, Tobago Cays, Palm, Union, PSV: A Plural Country,* 4th ed. New York, NY: W. W. Norton, 1985.

Knecht, Peter A. *St. Vincent and the Grenadines.* Washington, DC: U.S. Government Printing Office, 2000.

Mitchell, Pat. *Bequia, Sweet, Sweet.* London and Basingstoke: Macmillan, 1994.

Potter, Robert B. *St. Vincent and the Grenadines.* Santa Barbara, CA: Clio Press, 1992.

Rubenstein, Hymie. *Coping With Poverty: Adaptive Strategies in a Caribbean Village.* Boulder, CO: Westview Press, 1987.

Ward, Natalie F. R. *Blows, Mon, Blows: A History of Bequia Sailing.* Woods Hole, MA: Gecko Productions, 1995.

GENERAL CARIBBEAN

Albury, Paul. *The Story of the Bahamas.* London and Basingstoke: Macmillan, 1975.

Aspinall, Algernon. *West Indian Tales of Old.* London: Duckworth, 1912.

Augier, F. R., et al. *The Making of the West Indies.* London: Longmans, Green, 1960.

Balink, Albert, *My Paradise Is Hell: The Story of the Caribbean.* New York: Vista Publishing Corporation, 1948.

Brathwaite, Edward. *Caribbean Man in Space and Time: A Bibliographical and Conceptual Approach.* Kingston, Jamaica: Savacou Publications, 1974.

Bridenbaugh, Carl and Roberta. *No Peace Beyond the Line: The English in the Caribbean, 1624–1690.* New York: Oxford University Press, 1972.

Brizan, George. *Grenada: Island of Conflict.* London and Basingstoke: Macmillan, 1998.

Cobley, Alan, ed. *Crossroads of Europe: The Europe-Caribbean Connection 1492–1992.* Cave Hill and Bridgetown, Barbados: University of the West Indies Press, 1994.

Cobley, Alan Gregor, and Alvin Thompson, eds. *The African Caribbean Connection.* Cave Hill and Bridgetown, Barbados: University of the West Indies, 1990.

Conrad, James and John Perivolaris, eds. *The Cultures of the Hispanic Caribbean.* London and Oxford: Macmillan, 2000.

Craton, Michael and Saunders, Gail. *Islanders in the Stream: A History of the Bahamian People,* Volumes I and II. Athens, GA and London: The University of Georgia Press, 1992 and 1999.

Craton, Michael, et al., eds. *Slavery, Abolition and Emancipation: Black Slaves and the British Empire.* London: Longman, 1976.

Craton, Michael. *Testing the Chains: Resistance to Slavery in the British West Indies.* Ithaca, NY and London: Cornell University Press, 1982.

Davis, David Brion. *The Problem of Slavery in the Age of Revolution 1770–1823.* Ithaca, NY and London: Cornell University Press, 1975.

Dodge, Steve. *Abaco: The History of an Out Island and its Cays.* Decatur, IL: White Sound Press, 1983.

Dookhan, Isaac. *A History of the British Virgin Islands, 1672 to 1970.* England: Caribbean Universities Press, 1975.

Duffy, Michael. *Soldiers, Sugar and Sea Power: The British Expeditions to the West Indies and the War Against Revolutionary France.* Oxford: Clarendon Press, 1987.

Dunn, Richard S. *Sugar and Slaves.* Williamsburg, VA: University of North Carolina Press, 1972.

Fuson, Robert H. *The Log of Christopher Columbus.* Camden, ME: International Marine, 1987.

Gaspar, David B. *Bondmen and Rebels: A Study of Master-Slave Relations in Antigua.* Baltimore and London: The Johns Hopkins University Press, 1985.

Gaspar, David, and David Geggus. *A Turbulent Time: The French Revolution and the Greater Caribbean.* Bloomington and Indianapolis, IN: Indiana University Press, 1997.

Gonzalez, Nancie L. *Sojourners of the Caribbean: Ethnogenesis and Ethnohistory of the Garifuna.* Urbana, IL: University of Illinois Press, 1988.

Goslinga, Cornelis. *The Dutch in the Caribbean.* Gainesville, FL: University of Florida Press, 1971.

Hart, Francis Russell. *Admirals of the Caribbean.* Boston and New York: Houghton Mifflin, 1922.

Jimenez de Wagenheim, Olga. *Puerto Rico: An Interpretive History from Pre-Columbian Times to 1900.* Princeton, NJ: Markus Wiener Publishers, 1998.

Johnson, Harold and Karl Watson, eds. *The White Minority in the Caribbean.* Kingston, Jamaica: Ian Randle Publishers, 1998.

Kadish, Doris Y.ed. *Slavery in the Caribbean Francophone World.* Athens, GA and London: University of Georgia Press, 2000.

Klingel, Gilbert C. *Inagua: Which Is the Name of a Very Lonely and Nearly Forgotten Island.* New York, NY: Lyons Press, 1997.

Knight, Franklin W. *The Caribbean: Genesis of a Fragmented Nationalism,* 2nd ed. New York. NY: Oxford University Press, 1990.

Kurlansky, Mark. *A Continent of Islands: Searching for the Caribbean Destiny.* Reading,MA: Addison Wesley, 1992.

Laurence, K. O. *Immigration into the West Indies in the 19th Century.* Barbados: Caribbean Universities Press, 1971.

McDaniel, Lorna. *The Big Drum Ritual of Carriacou: Praisesongs in Rememory of Flight.* Gainesville, FL: University of Florida Press, 1998.

Morales Carrion, Arturo. *Puerto Rico and the Non-Hispanic Caribbean: A Study in the Decline of Spanish Exclusivism.* Rio Piedras, PR: University of Puerto Rico Press, 1952.

Murray, D. J. *The West Indies and the Development of Colonial Government, 1801–1834.* London: Oxford University Press, 1965.

Nettels, Curtis P. *The Emergence of a National Economy, 1775–1815.* New York, NY: Holt, Rinehart & Winston, 1962.

Newton, Arthur P. *The European Nations in the West Indies, 1493–1688.* New York: Barnes and Noble, 1933.

Nicholas, Tracy and Bill Sparrow. *Rastafari: A Way of Life.* Garden City, N.Y.: Anchor Books, 1979.

Ogot, Bethwell A. *Africa and the Caribbean.* Kisumu, Kenya: Anyange Press, 1997.

Pares, Richard. *Yankees and Creoles.* London: Longmans Green, 1956.

Ragatz, Lowell J. *The Fall of the Planter Class in the British Caribbean, 1763–1833.* New York and London: The Century Co., 1928.

Robertson, E. Arnot. *The Spanish Town Papers.* New York: Macmillan, 1959.

Rodway, James. *The West Indies and the Spanish Main.* New York, NY: Putnam, 1896.

Rogozinski, Jan. *A Brief History of the Caribbean: From the Arawak and the Carib to the Present.* New York, NY: Penguin, 1992.

Rouse, Irving. *The Tainos: Rise and Decline of the People Who Greeted Columbus.* New Haven, CT and London: Yale University Press, 1992.

Smelser, Marshall. *The Campaign for the Sugar Islands.* Chapel Hill, NC: University of North Carolina Press, 1955.

Smith, Keithlyn B., and Fernando C. Smith. *To Shoot Hard Labour: The Life and Times of Samuel Smith, an Antiguan Workingman, 1877–1982.* Scarborough, Ont: Edan's Publishers, 1986.

Smith, M. G. *Kinship and Community in Carriacou.* New Haven, CT and London: Yale University Press.

Southey, Captain Thomas. *Chronological History of the West Indies,* 3 vols. London: Longman,1827.

The "Spectator's" Essays Relating to the West Indies. Demerara, Ireland: The Argosy Press, 1885.

Toth, Charles W., ed. *The American Revolution and the West Indies.* Port Washington, NY and London: Kennikat Press, 1975.

Toth, Charles. *Anglo-American Diplomacy and the British West Indies, 1783–1789.* The Americas XXXI, 1975.

Treves, Sir Frederick. *The Cradle of the Deep: An Account of a Voyage to the West Indies.* New York: E.P. Dutton, 1911.

Tyler, S. Lyman, *Two Worlds: The Indian Encounter with the European 1492–1509.* Salt Lake City: University of Utah Press, 1988.

Van Tyne, Claude H. *The Causes of the War of Independence.* Cambridge: The Riverside Press, 1922.

VerSterg, Clarence L. *Robert Morris, Revolutionary Financier.* Philadelphia: University of Pennsylvania Press, 1954.

Waugh, Alec. *A Family of Islands.* New York, NY: Doubleday, 1964.

Williams, Eric. *From Columbus to Castro: The History of the Caribbean, 1492–1969.* New York, NY: Vintage Books, 1984.

Woodbury, George. *The Great Days of Piracy in the West Indies.* New York, NY: W.W. Norton, 1951.

INDEX

Abacos, 249–52
abandon-ship bag, 13
Abu Kari II, 202
Admiralty Bay, 199–211
Ackerman, Bruce, 2, 197, 198, 205–6
Ackerman, Susan, 2, 197, 198, 205–6
ALGONQUIN, 259
allergies, 252
alternator, 259–60
Amadeus Café, 232
American Revolution, 101, 125, 126, 228, 245, 249
Amerindians, 158, 159, 160
anchors, 70, 105–9, 247
Anegada Banks, 111
Anegada Passage, 230
Angelou, Maya, 200
ANN MARIE, 22
Annaberg, 135, 136
Annapolis, Maryland, 33–41
antibiotics, 17, 253
Antigua, 125, 158, 185, 212, 220–27
   charter-yacht show, 98–99
Arawaks, 139, 159–62, 166
Artu, Gilles, 228
asinegoes, 135
Atlantic City, New Jersey, 16, 20, 261
Autohelm 7000 autopilot, 20–21, 74, 113–16
Aztecs, 159

Bahamas, 38, 39, 40, 62, 66, 72, 117, 159, 161, 236–42, 245–55
   See also specific location
"Bahamian moor," 247
Bald Head Island, 69, 74, 81, 82, 84, 258
Baltimore Clippers, 25–26, 43
Barbados, 125, 160, 161, 185, 227, 238
barometer, 82
Batelco, 254
Bay Street Boys, 251
Beaufort, North Carolina, 38, 49, 60, 62, 80, 219, 257
BEAUJOLAIS, 43–44
Bellhaven, North Carolina, 259–60
Bequia, 146, 156, 180, 192, 197–211, 215, 216, 219
Bermuda, 68, 70, 83–85, 89–91, 92–104, 105–10, 127, 240, 245
"Bermuda 87," 219
Bermuda Harbour Radio (BHR), 89–90, 98
Bermuda Triangle, 70–77
Berry Islands, 247, 252, 253

"Big Drum Dance," 189–90
Bight, 142
Billy Bones, 142
blackbirds, 209
Blows, Mon, Blows (Ward), 204–5
bluefish, 239
boat boys, 192–96, 200, 206–7, 208
Boat U.S., 42, 43
boatbuilding, 186, 205
Body in Pain, The (Scarry), 153
bonito, 238
bootlegging, 245
Boyle, Thomas, 43
BRAVEHEART, 95, 98, 223, 243
Brazil, 161
Breakwater Harbor, 31
British Navigation Acts, 220
British Virgin Islands, 5, 39, 66, 68, 70, 84–85, 125–29, 164
   See also specific location
Brizan, George, 166–68, 178
broaches, 12
Bruce and Johnson's Marina, 151
buccaneers, 237–38
Buccaneers of America, The (Exquemelin), 238
Buffet, Jimmy, 30, 112
buoys, 90, 117
Buzzards Bay, 46

Cadmus, or a Treatise on the Elements of
   Language (Thornton), 126
Caicos, 38, 40, 236–42, 252
Caliste, Canute, 187–89
Callwood, Foxy, 111, 187
Callwood, Lessa, 111
Canada, 80, 226–27
Cape Fear, 63–64, 66, 68, 69, 258
Cape Hatteras, 38, 62
Cape Henlopen, 29, 31
Cape Lookout, 38, 62, 63
Cape May, 11, 16, 24, 25–30, 261
Cape Verde Islands, 202
Caribbean, 7, 39, 156–63
   See also specific location
Caribs, 132, 158, 160, 166, 201
Carriacou, 146, 180, 181–90, 202, 215, 216
Carter Creek, 49
Catherine's, 223
Cay Electronics, 152
cell phone, 78, 188, 258
Charleston, South Carolina, 66–68
CHARLIE CHAN, 23

Charlotte Amalie, 127, 133–34
charterers, 127–29, 198
CHASSEUR, 43
Chesapeake and Delaware Canal, 29, 31, 261
Chesapeake Bay, 29, 33–41, 49, 55–57, 259, 260
"chicken neckers," 36
Chronological History of the West Indies (Southey), 225
City Island, New York, 10
Civil War, 59, 66–67, 92–93, 158, 245
Clean, Sweet Wind (Pyle), 202
"closing the circle," 258
Coast Guard Island, 11
Coburn, George, 60–61, 169–70
Coburn, Teresa, 60–61
Coco Cay, 253, 256
Cod: A Biography of the Fish That Changed the World (Kurlansky), 34–35
Columbus, Christopher, 68, 132, 138, 157, 158, 202, 215, 240
Comte de Cerillac, 166
Conroy, Pat, 62
Continent of Islands (Kurlansky), 7
coolant system, 222
coral, 101, 239, 246, 252
Coral Bay, 141–42
Corrotoman, 50
crabbing, 33–36, 42, 56, 57
crew, 77, 121
cruisers, 128–29, 248, 250
Cruz Bay, 142
Cuba, 60, 83, 112, 157, 161, 162, 165, 166
Culebra, 231
Culebrita, 231
customs
  American, 258–59
  Bermuda, 90–91, 98
  Carriacou, 183
  Deshaies, Guadeloupe, 217–18
  Fajardo, Puerto Rico, 231
  Grenada, 172
  Inagua, 241
  Jost Van Dyke, 112, 119–22
  Mayaguana, 241, 246–47
  USVI/BVI, 142

DAISY D, 170, 241
Davis, Marcie, 86
de Gaulle, Charles, 218
Delaware Bay, 29–30, 31–32, 259, 261
DELIVERANCE, 92
Deltaville, Virginia, 54–55
Deshaies, Guadeloupe, 217–18
DESPERADO, 249–50
Deveau, Andrew, 249
Diamond, Jared, 158–60

Dividing Creek, 260
dolphins, 238–39
Dominica, 192–93, 201
Dominican Republic, 38, 40, 60, 62, 158, 229, 232–33
Don't Stop the Carnival (Wouk), 175
Drake, Francis, 132
Dred Scott decision, 41
drugrunners, 245
"Dry Belly Ache," 183
Du Parquet, Governor, 166
Dutch Guiana, 160

East River, 10, 11
eels, 35, 139, 140
egrets, 15
El Morro, 231–32, 234–35
Eleuthera, 249
engine, 23, 84, 220, 221–23, 259–60
English Harbour, Antigua, 220, 234
Exquemelin, Alexander, 238
Exumas, 40, 236, 241, 247, 249, 252

Fagel, Robert, 48
Fajardo, Puerto Rico, 231
Falmouth Harbour, Antigua, 220, 234
"Family Islands," 252
Fedon, Julian, 168
Fells Point, 43
fiberglass, 65
filter, fuel, 84
first aid, 17
fishing, 238–39, 245, 247–48
  See also overfishing; seining
flies, 31–32
FOLKLORIC, 208
Fonseca, Isaac, 150
Fort Lauderdale, Florida, 38, 40, 60, 62, 80, 219
Fort Sumter, 66–67
Fox, Bob, 44
Foxy's Tamarind Bar, 111, 119, 123, 124, 128, 129
Frangipani Hotel, 208
"freedom of the seas," 229
Freeport, 219, 256
French Revolution, 93–94, 168, 215
French West Indies Company, 166
Friendship Bay, 199
Frost, Robert, 246
Frying Pan Shoals, 64
fuel tank, 84, 150–51, 220, 223

Gardelin, Governor, 136
Garifuna, 202
Gateway National Recreation Area, 13
Gentleman's Guide to Passages South, The (Van Sant), 40, 250

George-Town, 236, 241, 252
Georges Bank, 35
Gibbs Hill Light, 90
Goldberg, Jack, 17
Goodrich, Bridges, 93–94
Gorda Sound, 5, 6, 156
Gouyave, Grenada, 177
GPS, 3–4, 10, 74, 151–52
Granite Bay, 262
Great Bahama Bank, 102
Great Harbour, Jost Van Dyke. *See* Jost Van Dyke
Great Stirrup Cay, 256
Greater Antilles, 126
Greeley, Horace, 82
Greenberg, Jack, 96
Greenwich, England, 129
Grenada, 92, 146, 164–70, 171–80, 182, 191–92, 216
Grenada: Island of Conflict (Brizan), 166–68
Grenadines, 2, 146, 180, 191–96, 197–98
Grotius, Hugo, 229
Guadeloupe, 212, 217–18, 227
Gulf Stream, 38, 39, 63, 69, 80, 81, 219, 257–58
Guns, Germs and Steel (Diamond), 158–60

Haiti, 60, 93, 158, 167, 168, 215, 224, 229
Hamilton, Bermuda, 103
Hampton, Virginia, 58–60
Handschumacher, Bob, 39–41, 66
Handschumacher, Joan, 39–41
harbors, 233–35
Harbour Island, 252
Harris, Wilson, 133, 173
Havana, Cuba, 231, 249
Hazell, Eldon, 204–5
Hazen, Amy, 249–50
Hazen, Cecil, 249–50
Hazen, Danny, 249–50
Hell Gate, 10, 259
HENZ II, 223
HERMAN MELVILLE, 83–84, 95, 96, 103, 108, 117, 146, 158, 217
Hermit's Island, 53
herons, 54
Herzog, Janet, 223
Herzog, Paul, 223
HIGH POCKETS, 257
Hilgenberg, Herb, 80–84, 98, 103, 109, 112, 113, 256–57, 258
Hillsborough, Carriacou, 182, 216
Hispaniola, 40, 60, 61, 83, 157, 161, 162, 166, 229
History, Fable and Myth in the Caribbean and the Guianas (Harris), 133
hogs, 61–62

holidays, 99
Hope Bay, 199, 205–6
Horse Whisperer, The, 15
Horseshoe Cove, 9, 262
Hurricane Bob, 46
Hurricane Dennis, 15–16, 25–32, 61, 63
Hurricane Floyd, 45–48, 61, 63
Hurricane Irene, 63, 65, 66
Hurricane Lenny, 92, 103, 181, 183, 216, 226, 233
Hurricane Mitch, 83
hypothermia, 106

Igbos, 187–88
Iceland, 35
ICW (Intracoastal Waterway), 38, 40, 58–64, 219, 259
immigration. *See* customs
IMPROBABLE, 98
Inagua, 241, 251
Indian Creek, 55
injuries, 118–19, 197–98
INSPIRATION, 165
insurance, 60
Internet, 78, 98, 141
Intracoastal Waterway (ICW), 38, 40, 58–64, 219, 259
INVINCIBLE, 97
Isla de Aves, 164
IWANDA, 259

Jamaica, 125, 126, 166, 185, 224, 238
"Jamaica Cure," 35
Jefferson, Thomas, 227
JEREMY BENTHAM, 1, 25, 60
JEREMY BENTHAM II, 60, 108, 138, 151, 172–73, 188, 193, 226
jerry jugs, 128
Johnson, Mrs., 246–47
Johnson, Samuel, 4
Jones, David, 164, 170, 225, 226, 236, 247
Jones, Elaine, 96
Jones, Gwen, 96
Jost Van Dyke, 70, 84, 103, 111, 117–22, 123–31, 142, 167

Kelsey Island, 2, 262
Kemp, Thomas, 43
Kent's Narrows, 260
KESTREL, 60, 61
Kilmarnock, Virginia, 127
Kincaid, Jamaica, 200
Kinship and Community in Carriacou (Smith), 185–86
Klingel, Gilbert, 251
Knapp's Narrows, 260
Kurlansky, Mark, 7, 34–35

La Parisienne, 226
Labat, Père, 237
Ladd, Larry, 165
Ladd, Shirley, 165
LADY HAMMOND, 94
Lake Huron, 139–40
language, West Indian, 195–96
latitude, 129–30
LATITUDE, 127
laughing gulls, 251
L'Esterre, Carriacou, 186, 187
Les Cheneaux Islands, 139–40
Leeward Islands, 92, 125, 126, 130, 132, 146, 191
Lesser Antilles, 126, 164, 166, 191, 195, 225
Leverick Bay, 156
life raft, 2, 13
Lighthouse Marine, 200
limbo, 173
Little Stirrup Cay, 253
Locklies Marina, 53–54
Long Island Sound, 1–4, 8, 10, 230, 239, 259
longitude, 129–30
Lookout Bight, 182
Los Palominos, 231
Louisiana Territory, 227
Lucaya, Grand Bahama, 166, 247, 257

Maclean, Mr., 184–85
mahi mahi, 248
"Maids, The" (Caliste), 189, 190
mainsheet, 152
maintenance, 65, 68, 69, 146–55, 220, 221–23
Mamaroneck, New York, 10
Manasquan Inlet, 261
Marigot, St. Lucia, 217, 228, 234
markets, 206, 208–11, 223
Marmor, Ted, 197, 198, 205–6
Marmor, Jan, 197, 198, 205–6
maroons, 224–25
Martinique, 180, 212, 216–17, 227
MARY ANNE, 14
Mashantucket Pequot Tribe, 10–11
Masonboro Inlet, 63
Mayaguana, 241, 246
MAYFLOWER, 103
Mayle, Peter, 74
Mayreau, 192, 197
Mears Marina, 37–41
medical care, 253
MENACE, THE, 208
Mexico, 157, 159, 231
Mid-Atlantic Waterway Guide, 16, 26, 63
MISS ANN, 50

Moitessier, Bernard, 257
Molly Malone's, 144
Mona Channel, 158
Mona Passage, 236, 237
MOONLIGHTING, 114, 117, 118, 219
Mora, Enrique, 232
Morgan, Henry, 238
Moriale, Ernest "Dutch," 53
mosquitoes, 32, 220
Mount Hartman Bay, 171–80
Mount Pelee, 216–17
Mustique, 198, 199
My Paradise Is Hell, 127
Mystic River, 46

NAACP, 52, 96
Napoleonic Wars, 125
Nassau, Bahamas, 245, 248–49
Nation, Betty, 222, 224
Nation, Monty, 222, 224
National Oceanic and Atmospheric Administration (NOAA), 25, 78
"Neither Out Far nor In Deep" (Frost), 246
Nelson, Horatio, 19–20, 220–21, 234
Nelson, Jim, 257
Nelson, Kathleen, 257
Nevis, 125, 185, 220, 227, 234
New London, Connecticut, 10–11
New York Harbor, 9, 10
nighttime, 72–75
NOAA (National Oceanic and Atmospheric Administration), 25, 78
Norfolk, Virginia, 38, 60
Norman Island, 142
Northwest Providence Channel, 256
nutmeg, 175–77

Oately, Bernie, 91, 99
Odyssey, 48
Ollivierre, Athneal, 204
Organization of Concerned Virgin Islanders, 134
osprey, 262
Out Islands, 236, 245, 247, 252, 254–55
Outerbridge, Jean, 103–4
Outerbridge, Pete, 103–4
overfishing, 34, 101, 204
oystercatchers, 262
oysters, 260–61

Padanaram, Massachusetts, 46
PALAEMON, 1–2
  draw, 26
  interior, 3
  sea-ready, 12–13
  waterline, 65

Panama Canal, 165
Paradise Island, 245
Pares, Richard, 14
Parke, Governor, 125
Parks, Rosa, 43
patois, 195–96
pelicans, 58
"Pen Them Up" (Hazell), 204
Penobscot Bay, 34
Peru, 157, 231
Peter Island, 164
Peterson, Oscar, 224
Petite Martinique, 182, 184
picaroons, 36
Pindling, Lionel, 252
pirates, 237–38
Pitt, William, 227
pollution, 34, 101, 187
Pompa, Melodye, 170
porpoises, 24, 58
Port Elizabeth, 208
Port Lucaya, 256
Port Lonvilliers Marina, 230
Port Royal, Jamaica, 238
Powell, Henry, 160
prescriptions, 16
Prickly Pear Island, 156
privateers, 43, 125–26, 133, 249
Progressive Liberal Party, 252
Prohibition, 245
PROMISE, 36, 260
propane tanks, 68
Providence Island, 249
Providenciales, 240, 241
Puerto Rico, 40, 60, 62, 124, 132, 134, 158,
    166, 224, 230–32
Pyle, Douglas, 202

racial integration, 51–53, 67
radar, 21–23, 231
radio
  Bermuda Harbor (BHR), 89–90, 98
  SSB, 79, 80, 85–88, 98
  VHF, 78, 85–88
radiospeak, 85–88
Rappahannock River, 34, 49, 50, 54, 55–56
Raytheon Electronics, 151
Reagan, Ronald, 165, 169
Red Hook, St. Thomas, 127, 142
Redford, Robert, 15
Reed's Nautical Almanac, 24, 31, 256
Reedville, Virginia, 58
Reedy Point, 32
refrigeration systems, 44
Reinwald, Bobby, 17

remora, 139
Reno, Gina, 36–37, 260
Reno, Lee, 36–37, 260
RESOLUTE, 219, 257
Revolutionary War, 100–101
Reynolds, Heather, 200, 201
rigging, 21, 220, 221
Roadtown, Tortola, 126, 150, 151–52
Roátan, 201
Robertson, Elizabeth, 126
Rockefellers, 138, 142
Rogers, Woodes, 98
Rose, Terry, 63, 64, 65, 66
Rose Island, 252
Royal Caribbean, 253
Rum Cay, 250, 256

Saba Bank, 164
St. Augustine, Florida, 249
St. Croix, 132, 133, 158, 164
St. George's Harbour, 83–84, 89–91, 92–104,
    105–10, 170–80, 200
St. John, 117, 133, 135–37, 141
St. John's, 223, 224–25
St. Kitts, 125, 137, 166, 185, 220, 227, 229, 234
St. Lucia, 180, 192, 201, 212, 234
St. Maarten, 229–30
St. Martin, 50, 92, 144, 146, 212, 226–31
St. Michaels, Maryland, 42–43
St.-Pierre, Martinique, 216–17
St. Thomas, 62, 66, 117, 126, 132–45
St. Vincent, 166, 180, 192, 198, 201, 202,
    207, 212, 215
Salt Cay, 240
Salt Whistle Bay, 192–93
San Juan, Puerto Rico, 231–35, 258
Sandy Hook, New Jersey, 9–18, 261–62
SAUCY JACK, 68
Scarry, Elaine, 153
schooners, 43, 202
sea cucumbers, 140
Sea Harbor Resort, 173
seacocks, 68–69
seagulls, 239, 241, 251, 262
seasickness, 19–20, 242–43
SECOND MILLENNIUM, 170
Secret Harbor, 171, 174
seining, 181–82
Seven Years' War, 125
sharks, 238
Shirley, Governor, 126, 220
Shirley Heights, 224
Silver Banks, 111
Skinny Legs, 141–42, 144
skipjacks, 260–61

slavery, 102, 133, 135–37, 158–63, 167–68, 184–85, 201, 221, 224–25, 245
Smallwood, Mrs., 123–24
Smith, John, 33, 59
Smith, M. G., 185–86, 189
Smith, Samuel, 225
snorkeling, 129, 138–40, 143, 248
Solomons Island, 46
Somers, George, 92
South Jersey Marina, 26–30, 261
SOUTHBOUND II, 80, 81
Southey, Thomas, 225
SOVEREIGN OF THE SEAS, 253, 256
Spain, 132, 157, 159, 229, 249
Spanish Town, Jamaica, 126
Spanish Town Papers, The (Robertson), 126
"Spanish Virgins," 231
spinnaker, 31
Stamford, Connecticut, 10
Staniel Cay, 250
Statue of Liberty, 11, 16
steering, hand, 114–15
Stirrup Cays, 256
sunset, 199, 206

Tainos, 159–62, 166
TANDEM VINCITUR, 222, 224
Taney, Roger B., 41
Tangier Island, 55
terns, 32, 262
THOR, 117
Thornton, William, 125–26
"Thorny Path, The," 39
"Thunderball Cave," 250
tide tables, 256
Tides Lodge, 49–50, 57
Tilghman Island, 260
To Shoot Hard Labor: The Life and Times of Samuel Smith, an Antiguan Workingman, 1877-1982, 225
Tobago Cays, 192–96, 206
Tortola, 117, 126, 127, 137, 142, 150
towing, 42
trade winds, 38–39, 40, 68, 103, 130, 164
Treaty of Paris, 167
Treaty of Versailles, 167, 249
Treaty of Vervins, 157
Trinidad, 4, 146, 191
Tropicana, 228
Trump, Donald, 20
tuna, 238–39, 248
Turks, 38, 40, 102, 236–42
turtles, 138–39

Umbrellas, 2
Union, 192, 207–8
Updike, John, 258
Urbanna, Virginia, 50–53
U.S. Coast Guard, 79, 98, 127

vaccinations, 17
Van Sant, Bruce, 40, 72, 250
Van Sant, Rosa, 250
Veblen, Thorsten, 37
Venezuela, 124, 156, 164, 191
Verrazano Narrows, 9, 16
Vieques, 231
Virgin Islands (U.S.), 38–39, 40, 132–45, 230

Wallace, William, Jr., 202
War of 1812, 67–68
Ward, Nathalie F. R., 204
Washington, George, 41, 100, 248
watch system, 17–18, 75–77, 129, 130
water pumps, 148–50
Waterside Marina, 60
Waterway Guide. See Mid-Atlantic Waterway Guide
weather information, 25, 29, 78–84
"West India Cure," 35
West Indies, 7, 127, 157–58, 221
    problems of, 215–16
    trade, 14–15
    See also specific location
West Marine, 260
West Marine 1500 Rally, 39–40, 59, 83
whaleboats, 202–5
Whitestone Bridge, 10
Wickhams Cay Rigging, 150
WILDWOOD, 39
Wilmington, North Carolina, 63, 65–66, 68
Wind in the Willows (Grahame), 49
windlass, 107, 118–19
Windward, Carriacou, 186–87
Windward Islands, 130, 132, 146, 180, 191–92
Windward Passage, 83, 103, 237
World War II, 13, 99
Wouk, Herman, 175
Wrightsville Beach, 63, 182, 258, 259
Wye River, 260

Yale Sailing Club, 262
yawlboats, 261
Yellow Banks, 252
yellow fever, 161–62

ZORRA, 117